TROUBLED SKIES
OVER QUAKER HILL

A SEARCH FOR THE TRUTH

TROUBLED SKIES OVER QUAKER HILL

A SEARCH FOR THE TRUTH

LESSIE AULETTI

atmosphere press

Prelude

When I was eight years old my family left our farm west of Bremerton and moved into the city. Daddy sat us down one Sunday morning in early June, the week before school let out for the year, and told us of the coming change. "You might want to say goodbye to your friends", he counseled, "as we probably won't be back up here on the Hill." Danny's face turned white and he asked if something were wrong— something he could help with. For a moment I thought I saw tears in Mama's eyes, but Daddy shook his head and told Danny that everything would be okay. The move would be a new beginning for our family after the turmoil of the last few years. I had my doubts but kept the opinion to myself. Robbie started to cry. He had never known anything but the farm. Danny and I had lived in the city during WWII, but Robbie was too young to remember that.

Danny and I were not Daddy's biological children. He and Mama married when I was fourteen months old. Danny remembered living with OurFather as we referred to our biological male parent, but I was only three months old when he left Mama, Danny, and me and married his girlfriend. Robbie was born to Mama and Daddy when I was 2-1/2 years old and Danny was five. Daddy considered us 'his kids', all equal in his eyes. For some reason Mama's mother (OurGrandmother to Danny and me, not to be confused with Daddy's mama Gramma Vanac or OurFather's mama Gramma B) was not fond of our family and preferred Mama's older sister our Aunt Noreen, our uncle and her two boys.

We each had our own jobs in the family—Daddy supported us with wages earned in the Bremerton Shipyard, Mama cooked and cleaned and took care of our many needs. Daniel, the eldest child, stood brave and tall, protecting Robin (Robbie to us), the youngest and second son, and me from what he perceived as a danger, all the while pretending that he didn't care. I, Leah, always in the middle and the only daughter, was responsible for maintaining the peace. I had become my mother's confidant—the keeper of her secrets, those things she couldn't share with anyone else, and personally responsible for holding up the sky above us. Now that sky was crashing in around me. Now we were leaving the farm and everything that stood for stability in my life and the path ahead was dark. To make matters worse, the United States had entered into another military conflict on the other side of the world in a country called Korea.

*I sit alone and think to myself that my sweet Quaker friend Anne Marsh is no longer part of my daily life. I dream of her at night, and long to sit before her fireplace in the cabin atop Quaker Hill and watch her capable hands sew squares for her granddaughter's wedding quilt. I miss her calm eyes and smiling face and the feel of her arms around my shoulders. She is **my** confidant, as much as I can share with anyone. I can cry with Annie, cry from my heart, and I cannot do that with* *anyone else in my world.*

I miss the farm and my animal friends, especially my cats, and the hens that lay eggs for my breakfast. I miss the cows and the smell of milk fresh from the udder. The city smells of car exhaust and people's chimneys and furnaces fueled with oil or coal delivered by trucks that lumber up the city streets and chase us from the sidewalks. I practice listening with my heart, the skill Annie helps me see in myself.

Before we left for the city, I asked her: "How do you know if you got one of those listening hearts?"

"Thee doesn't 'get' one, girl," she answered with simplicity, "thee is born with one. Some think a listening heart is a burden. Others know its blessing. God has given each recipient a choice in the matter—thee can choose to learn how to use it, or thee can choose to ignore it. Think on this thing, Leah—what might God want thee to do with thy heart? We will talk more of this another time."

But time has run out. There will never be another afternoon for Annie and me. Annie and the farm are gone, and my heart is heavy. I hear Annie saying:

"Forgive them, Leah, for they know not what they do".

CHAPTER I
In Which We Experience the Beginning of the End

At first, I missed the farm almost as much as I missed Annie. I had become a child of forest and field, especially in those last few months when I learned to appreciate solitude and couldn't imagine replacing meadow grass and green trees with tidy fenced-in lawns and pavement. All summer while the city steamed and grass turned brown, I daydreamed of our little creek and the cool, dark woods that shaded me from the harsh world.

Although our new house on Seventh Street in Bremerton is an old, two-story clapboard ex-boarding house with bedrooms enough for all of us, the fenced back yard seems cramped and confining after the spacious acreage of the farm. Daddy is close enough to the shipyard to walk to work and Mama takes in ironing to make up the difference for all those eggs and chickens, rabbits and piglets, and buckets of milk no longer readily available. She and I make occasional forays to the "Pony Market" down in Charlestown for pot roasts and ground meat she either slow cooks with vegetables or makes into meatloaf. For years, it remains our little secret as the market in question sells horse meat—slightly sweet and far leaner than beef, at less than half the cost. Daddy's eyebrows raise the first time Mama serves one of those pot roasts, but the boys never seem to notice the difference.

"Our Boys in the Military" were still returning from WWII taking jobs promised by the Government as younger men left for Korea and Daddy was nervous. He had been offered a position heading up the machine shop at the Hanford Nuclear plant in south-central Washington and established in 1943 as part of the Manhattan Project. Hanford was home to the B Reactor, the first full scale plutonium production reactor in the world. Plutonium manufactured at the site was used in the first nuclear bomb, tested at the Trinity site and in Fat Man, the atomic bomb that was detonated over Nagasaki, Japan.

Unfortunately, Daddy couldn't get the necessary clearances because of his family in Eastern Europe. I suppose he was hurt by this, because he had held a top-secret clearance all during World War II, at times working almost round the clock on intricate precision parts to guide the huge Naval guns, and on bomb sites for the planes that took off and landed on the small decks of aircraft carriers at sea. Now the changing times prevented him from caring for his family as he used to—not that we had ever been rich people—but it hurt him to see Mama ironing shirts and trousers, sheets and doilies for other families.

The long summer between our move and the start of school stretched before us. Danny quickly made new friends and was out the door early each day, but I hadn't that luxury. Mama needed my help more and more with household chores and keeping an eye on Robbie while she ironed.

I keep these thoughts to myself as I hear the sputtering sound the iron makes as it smooths out the newly sprinkled pillowcases Mama is ironing for Mrs. Johnson or Mrs. Jones or whomever today's laundry belongs. The steam rising from her heavy iron has a particular scent of bluing and starch. As the pillowcase dries under Mama's deft hand it becomes crisp and smooth. She props the iron up on its heavy metal base, careful to place the cord out of the way, and folds the pillowcase in thirds, lengthwise, then smooths it carefully and folds it in thirds crosswise. She places it on the stack of pillowcases already ironed and reaches for another.

"Can I help you, Mama?" *I ask. She has taught me how to iron and I do most of our own things, except Daddy's white shirts.*

"No, Cookie," *she sighs as she picks a new case from the stack in the basket.* "Not the ones I get paid for—but thanks for asking."

Sometimes she lets me sprinkle and roll them. I use the sprinkling bottle filled with fresh warm water from the tap and cover every item as evenly as possible, then fold and roll each into a neat bundle that is stacked in the basket. The object, says Mama, is to dampen, then roll so that the water can distribute itself evenly throughout the garment. That makes the wrinkles come out easier. She tries to be finished before Daddy comes home, but sometimes the basket is just too full. If he catches her still at the board, his face gets a funny, sad, angry look that makes me feel bad inside. My thoughts, my observations—I keep these hidden from Mama and Daddy and the outside world. These are the things I will share with Annie when I can see her. I save them up. Someday, I dream to myself, I will see her again on Quaker hill.

Mama and Daddy stopped talking to each other that summer. I don't mean they never said a word, but everything seemed superficial. Even Danny noticed that the content was missing from our lives. We drifted on from day to day like robots, busily going about our daily chores, then retiring to our rooms at night to recharge the batteries. Mama looked sad and Daddy looked angry—angrier than I had ever seen him—without ever saying what he was angry about. In fact, they stopped quarreling all together, and that was scarier than any of their fights had ever been!

To make matters worse, my health that had improved so much after the sulfa pills came into my life post WW II, took a nosedive. I, along with the boys, caught red measles and rubella, back to back. We had no sooner recovered than I developed scarlet fever. To keep Danny and Robbie from my contagion my parents quarantined me in the upstairs bedroom overlooking the porch roof partially obscured by the huge elm tree in the front yard. At first, I was so sick that I couldn't raise my head from the pillow.

My head aches fiercely and Mama keeps a damp cloth in the refrigerator to place across my eyes in an attempt to relieve some of the pain. A fine, bright red rash covers my entire body, including the soles of my feet and my palms. The skin inside my mouth turns red as well. Heat rises in waves from my body and Mama sponges me off periodically, changing my wet night clothes and drenched sheets. Sometimes weird stories flit through my head, like dreams but I am awake. Mama says I am delirious, whatever that means, but giving them a name does not make me feel less afraid.

The doctor comes nearly every day in the late afternoon, bringing his brown leather bag that bangs on his leg as he climbs the stairs to my purgatory. I can hear him and Mama as they talk outside my bedroom door. "Be sure to keep the room absolutely dark," he tells Mama. "She could go blind from this. No light at all until the fever is completely normal and her headache is gone." Mama murmurs too softly for me to catch her words. Then the doctor replies; "It's worse because of the measles. Her chances of losing eyesight are much greater with the double damage." Mama whispers something else, then the doctor says, "Here, wipe your eyes. We don't want her to worry." I do not talk of these things with my mama or my daddy. They mustn't know that I am afraid.

The door opened a crack and they quietly slipped in. Dr. Haller put his bag down on the bedside table as Mama removed the lamp. He sat on the edge of the bed, fumbled in his bag for a moment, then slipped a thermometer tasting of acrid alcohol under my tongue.

"Hold that tight for a minute, honey. I need to know how hot you are." He winked at me.

I sigh and rest my head back on the pillow. The thermometer pokes the underside of my tongue and I shift it to one side, careful not to let it fall from my mouth. He feels my forehead with his cool, smooth hand, then fumbles in his bag and produces a stethoscope. Mama helps me to sit upright, plumping the pillows to brace my back. Dr. Haller slips the metal stethoscope under my pajama top and listens to my heart and chest carefully. The cold metal makes me shiver. I cough dutifully, even though doing so makes my throat hurt and my eyes ache miserably.

"I'm sure I have something in here that will help you feel better." I heard him rummage around in his bag again, eventually producing a glass vial filled with white pills. Mama delivered a glass of water and the doctor slipped two of the tablets into my mouth as he removed the thermometer.

Aspirin, I think to myself as the tablets melt slightly on my dry tongue. I can taste their sourness as my mother supports my back and places the water glass to my lips. I take a sip large enough to wash down the pills sticking to my tongue. I do not even gag, thanks to Annie who taught me how to swallow pills. Mama lays me back down onto the sticky sheets. She asks the doctor what my temperature is as he shakes the thermometer and replaces it in a metal case. Way too high, he answers her. Hopefully, the aspirin will take it down. Give her lots of fluids and remember—no lights. He winks at me again and rises from my bedside. Get some sleep, Cookie, he says as he and Mama leave the room. I can hear the bag slap, slap, slapping against his leg as he and Mama descend the stairs in silence.

Time passes and what little light that creeps into my bedroom fades to black. I hear Danny downstairs, practicing his piano lesson. Today is lesson day, I think to myself, and I have missed it. I gulp so hard that my throat hurts and tears, hotter even than my forehead, creep down the outside corner of my eyes and trickle into my ears. I cry silently for the lesson I have missed, and for all the future lessons I will miss if I go blind.

Shortly after we moved OurGrandmother stopped the pretense of paying for Danny's piano lessons, finally admitting that OurFather had financed them. He now wished for Mama and Daddy to pick up the payments as he was in the process of moving back to Washington. Danny hated taking piano and did so under duress. I loved learning how to make music jump from the ivory and black keys on the beautiful upright grand piano OurGrandmother let us use. It would have been simple for her to teach us herself, but for the coldness existing between her and Mama and Daddy. Daddy said that she preferred Mama's older sister and her children and made it pretty evident that he didn't approve. Mama tried to keep the peace but OurGrandmother's visits always seemed to end with Daddy and her 'having words' and OurGrandmother stomping off in a huff. Mama would sigh and say it didn't matter that her mother favored Auntie Nor and our cousins.

OurGrandmother's choice of Danny was ironic under the present circumstances, I thought to myself bitterly. Perhaps she had chosen wisely. She was a nurse and possibly had some prescient hint of the future Scarlet Fever might bring me. Why waste piano lessons on a blind granddaughter? Nonetheless, I had attended each lesson and avidly absorbed every scrap of knowledge imparted to the impatient Daniel by his teacher, then hurried home to practice. There was no more piano playing by me that summer. I eventually learned that Grammy B (OurFather's mama) paid for Danny's continued lessons.

After two weeks of confinement to my bed in darkness—days without books or visits from my brothers who I could hear playing in the streets with the neighborhood kids, often until dark—Mama brought me a radio. Dr. Haller said it was still far too dangerous for my eyes to expose them to even the filtered light of my bedroom window. The radio saved my sanity. I listened to "Pepper Young's Family", and they became my own. I followed the tribulations of "Ma Perkins" and "The

Second Mrs. Trent". At night after Danny and Robbie went to bed, I brought the radio under my covers and tuned in to shows like "The Whistler" and "Inner Sanctum". Mama would duck her head inside my room, wiggle her finger at me in admonition, then go off to her bed alone. Daddy waited downstairs, ostensibly reading the paper and checking on doors and windows. I began to wonder if he was waiting until Mama was asleep before he reluctantly mounted the stairs and retired for the night. He usually came and sat on the edge of my bed for a few moments, giving me a kiss and a hug, all the while studiously ignoring the obvious bulge of the radio hidden beneath my covers.

"Don't stay awake too late," he'd whisper, "and don't let Mama catch you." Then he would pat my head and wink at me. God, how I loved both of these people, and how I wished I could repair the widening rift between them.

Gradually the doctor and Mama allowed me more time in the light. *These days are the longest of my short life, as I feel perfectly well except for the unbearable itching as I shed skin all over my body—wherever the rash has developed. Danny nicknames me Snake Girl and Robbie refuses to come anywhere near me as Danny has him convinced that the shedding skin is contagious. I return to my room and dream of Annie and Quaker hill.*

The summer wound to an end as my body slowly returned to normal. By the time Dr. Haller pronounced me well enough to venture outside, there was just enough time for Mama to make me a new dress for school.

CHAPTER 2
In Which I Learn the Sound of Silence

I started the third grade at Washington Elementary School, ten short blocks from our house on Seventh Street, with a new teacher named Mrs. Apland. One of our very first assignments was learning to write letters. Mrs. Apland encouraged all her students to write to a grandparent.

I wrote to Annie—the first of many letters over the years, mostly never mailed and, therefore, unanswered. That first letter, in which I poured out the pathos of my summer, I gave to Mama to mail. My classmates received answers to their missives with varying degrees of regularity. Every day I ran home as fast as my still wobbly legs would carry me up the hill, eagerly anticipating a reply from Annie. Each day I was disappointed and finally, after a month, I gave up hope. Mrs. Apland suggested I write to someone else, so I acquiesced and sent a letter to my Grammy B. Her swift reply completed the assignment and I finally pushed the letter to Annie out of my mind. Mama said, and I knew it was true, that we had left without saying goodbye. I supposed that Annie was angry with me. No wonder she had not answered my letter.

During September and October, my vision began to blur—

slowly, at first, but by the time the holidays came around I could no longer cover it up. On the Monday following Thanksgiving, the school nurse called me into her office and asked me to read the eye chart. I failed, miserably. She sent a note home to Mama and before the week was out, I found myself in yet another doctor's office. The summer of illness was now exacting a toll on my eyesight, a progressive nearsightedness that threatened to leave me blind if it did not stabilize. Mama looked stunned, like a rabbit trapped by dogs in a dead-end ally. A later author called it 'going tharn', and the minute I read the term I thought of Mama and the way her eyes had looked that day as the word 'blind' bounced back and forth between the walls of the small examining room.

The situation forced Mama and Daddy to talk, something they had ceased doing beyond the polite hellos and good-byes proper etiquette dictated. Danny and I sat on the steps after lights were out for the night and listened to their stilted conversation. They sat at the kitchen table, the single bulb illuminating Mama's stricken face. Danny couldn't see Daddy's expression, but he whispered their conversation loudly in my ear.

"Gaw, Danny! I can hear for myself," I hissed. "I'm goin' blind, ya know, not deaf!"

Danny gave me a withering look. "Yeah, I know. You always have something goin' that makes you the center of attention, don'tcha?" Danny's caustic remark cut me deep. I didn't ask to be sick—all I wanted was to be a regular kid like he was.

In the kitchen, our parents were discussing how they could afford this new threat to their daughter's well-being. Even with my poor vision, I could see Danny glaring at me as Mama offered to clean houses in addition to her ironing. My stomach lurched at the thought of my mama scrubbing out other people's toilets so that I could have glasses. I rose and started down the stairs when Danny grabbed my wrist and pulled me back down beside him.

"Look, Leah, they don't need to know we listen. Don't you think they have enough problems without us knowin' everything?" This was a very astute observation from my older brother who usually thought only of himself. "I don't want Mama to clean other people's houses any more'n you do."

In the kitchen Daddy was saying that they should borrow the money from OurGrandmother. Mama started to cry and put her face in her hands. My heart ached for Mama. I silently pleaded with my daddy to take her in his arms and heal the hurt between them. Danny and I leaned forward as if encouraging the act. Daddy sat stiff and straight. Danny could see him reach across the table towards Mama. Then he stopped as if he thought better of it and withdrew the hand. Danny exhaled forcefully and Daddy looked up from Mama's grief, his head swiveling around towards the two of us hidden in the shadow of the stairwell. He rose, walked around the table to Mama, and patted her on the back—like a little baby, Danny observed in disgust, and said they would think of something. I began to shiver, snuggled next to my big brother as if I had swallowed a block of ice. Danny put his arms around me and helped me upstairs to my bedroom.

"Daddy's right, Leah. We'll think of something—all of us—and don't you dare go blind! How could I be mean to a blind kid, especially if she's my little sister!" With that comforting thought, he pushed me through my bedroom door and darted into his just before Mama came upstairs to bed.

I heard Mama shuffle past me to the bathroom, then, a few minutes later my door opened and she stuck her head in. I could see her fuzzy outline backlit against the dimly lit hall. She stood there for a long moment, then the door closed and she was gone.

Fall turned to winter, a miserable, drizzly winter filled with soggy leaves and puddles full of drowned worms and wind blowing spurts of rain through any small openings in our winter jackets. Danny and I slogged in our red rubber boots to and from school and I learned to deal with fogged, water-spattered glasses. My prescription changed three times between Christmas and Easter vacation, each new set of lenses creating a crisis. Mama and Daddy hardly spoke; they sat on opposite sides of the living room monitoring our homework or listening to the radio, the silence between thick as syrup.

At night in my room, I practice being blind, walking around with my eyes closed, and trying to memorize furniture placement. I try to imagine my world growing fuzzier and fuzzier until it dims altogether into one continuous blur, all detail irretrievably lost. Danny and Robbie are no help as they now play a game called Blind Man's Dog in which Danny stumbles around blindfolded, led by a rope attached to Robbie. Robbie crawls about like some manic cocker spaniel, barking and yipping with Danny in tow, bashing into furniture until Mama banishes them both to the basement. I grow quiet, filling my hours with all the books I can take from the library. Mama worries that too much reading will further weaken my eyes; Daddy's attitude is that I should be allowed to read as much as

I like, as it is entirely probable that my sight will fail altogether, and at least I will have had the pleasure of my books.

One particularly rainy Saturday afternoon when Danny was at the movies with his buddies and Daddy was working overtime I tried to talk with Mama. Robbie colored in his Hopalong Cassidy coloring book and I sat at the kitchen table quietly sprinkling the clothes from a new basket of laundry while Mama ironed some other little girl's white pinafore.

I can't let Mama know, but sometimes I recognize on kids at school the clothes that Mama irons for money. It makes me feel funny—ashamed, I guess—that because of me, my mama has to take in laundry. Mama says it is honest work and she does not mind, that what is important is her family and having things like new shoes and glasses. Daddy works as much overtime as he can, she explains patiently, but there is still not enough money to compensate for the things we grew on the farm. Someday I will understand, she counsels. But I want to understand now. I burst to ask her why she and Daddy do not talk to each other anymore. I ache to spill my fear of going blind, but each time my mouth opens, my brain clamps it shut again. Mama has too much on her plate to listen to my little girl problems.

After the sprinkling, Mama excused me and I went upstairs to my room.

I lay on my bed remembering the last time I talked to Annie. I had so much to tell her, so much to ask, and I had missed my chance. I understood why she hadn't answered my letter. Mama had explained it and she had every reason to be angry with me.

Even so, deep inside, I knew Mama's explanation lacked the ring of truth. I knew that Annie would listen—if not with her ears, then with her heart. I took a pencil and a piece of notebook paper from the folder on the little table I used for a desk and, plumping myself back on the bed, I wrote another letter to her. Even though I would never mail it, and therefore would never receive an answer, my spirits lightened as the words spilled like gushing waters out of my heart onto the paper. Gradually daylight slipped away and I fell asleep in peace.

The last week of school brought changes to our lives that would affect us for a long time to come. Daddy received a layoff notice from the Shipyard the month before and had searched diligently for a job. He finally found a position with a new company starting up in Tacoma and was already commuting back and forth. We were to follow as soon as school recessed for the year. On Friday Mama took me for my monthly appointment with the eye doctor who delivered good news, pronouncing my eyesight stable for the moment. This prompted Daddy and Mama to treat us all to a hamburger at the Triple X Drive-in to celebrate.

"Order what you like, kids." Daddy smiled from the front seat and winked at Mama. "And French fries all around!" The carhop stood outside Daddy's rolled down window with her pad and pencil ready to take our requests. I ordered a plain burger and a chocolate shake. Daddy said we should all have shakes and Mama laughed. It sounded good to hear that laugh. She hadn't laughed like that in a long time. Mama reached her hand to Daddy and he took it, raising it to his face and kissing her fingers. "A new start, my bride", he whispered just loud enough for me to hear. Mama smiled and my heart smiled, too.

After the carhop brought our food on its metal tray that fit onto the car window, we ate and laughed and tossed fries at one another. Daddy told us about our new house on Procter Street in Tacoma. Mama collected our wrappers and Robbie's partially eaten burger. We returned to the house renewed, at least for one night.

In the morning Danny, Robbie, and I diligently followed Mama's orders, the boys packing up their toys and clothing in boxes, while I helped ready the kitchen for our coming move. The air smelled fresh and clean and the sun shone brightly this warm Saturday, the first weekend in June. Mama hummed to herself as she wrapped plates and crockery in newspaper and packed them neatly into cardboard boxes.

"Will you sort the stuff in that junk drawer, Leah?" Mama pointed to the cabinet where family clutter had collected over the near year we had lived here. I pulled out the drawer until it stuck. No amount of yanking dislodged whatever impeded its forward progress. Patiently I began pulling out the odds and ends jammed together. Pens and pencils, old bills, articles cut out of the newspaper soon littered the kitchen counter. With the drawer emptied, I reached inside, feeling blindly for whatever held it captive. My fingers encountered what seemed to be a wad of paper. With one final tug, the drawer gave up its secret, spitting out a badly mangled envelope.

Time slows down as I reach for the object that has jammed the drawer. My eyes see a small envelope, unsealed and apparently never mailed. The stamp affixed to the now crumpled upper right hand corner is not canceled. I take it in my hand, this unobtrusive envelope, and raise it towards my mother, a questioning look in my silent eyes. Her eyes are huge and dark, eyebrows raised in perfect half circles float above them. Her mouth opens in slow motion—oh, no, it says—oh, Leah, I am so sorry—but my ears do not hear. My eyes see the name in the address block, neatly printed in my own, still maturing hand. It is Annie's name. Mrs. Anne Marsh, Route 1 Box 2379— My eyes see but my heart refuses to acknowledge my mother's moving mouth as a scream rises in my throat and dies there—a silent scream that ends forever what was left of my childhood illusions. I lay it on the table, this crumpled letter to Annie, and smooth it with my hand. Mama rounds the table and places her hands on my trembling shoulders but I do not let her touch me—not the place inside that has sealed tight. She can only hold my body close and whisper again and again "Oh, Leah, I am so sorry." Finally, I take the letter and leave. My ears hear her last plea as I round the hallway and start up the stairs to my half-packed bedroom; "Let me explain, honey— please let me explain."

CHAPTER 3

In Which We Travel to California and Rescue Our Auntie

Our new house in Tacoma was on Procter Street, only two blocks from a row of busy stores and shops. One of them sold radios and other electronic appliances, including a wonderful new device called Television. All the neighborhood kids crowded around Brackman Electrics big display window to watch Howdy Doody and Buffalo Bob every afternoon, even though we couldn't hear what they were saying. Danny was big enough to bully his way to the front and occasionally pushed Robbie in front of him so he could see the wonders of a new age—talking pictures on a tiny glass screen. When the days were too hot to stand out on the baking concrete, the three of us took refuge on the large covered front porch of our two story rental to play Monopoly and Rummy and War and Crazy Eights.

Eventually, Danny and I discovered the gulch, a dark and tangled jungle of broken trees, blackberry canes, Creeping Jenny, and trash that covered the banks of a small creek running through a deep crack in our neighborhood. I could climb down beneath the Twenty-eighth Street Bridge, taking care not to trip and fall, then pick my way carefully along the creek for a mile or more before debris forced me up the bank again.

All the neighborhood boys played War in the gulch, using crudely carved pieces of wood as rifles. Much to my regret, I was again the sole girl, and of necessity had to be either one of the boys or be their target. Neither choice appealed to me. I soon found a hidey-hole and lookout up under the cement foundations of the bridge, tucked close against the hill. Here I kept to myself and wrote long letters to Annie—letters that lay in my private paper box unmailed.

From my vantage point under the bridge, I watch my brothers in the young male ebb and flow of games, where acquaintances become lifelong buddies, yesterday's enemies are today's best friends, and pack dominance is established. I wish I had someone—anyone, with whom to share my observations. Mama's problems keep her preoccupied. I listen, providing an escape valve that allows her to 'blow off steam', as she calls it, but hesitate to take up her time with childish chatter. Besides, if she knows I spend my days spying on the boys from under the bridge she might keep me home! Those letters to Annie give my emotions an outlet in a summer that stretches far too long. At night I dream of her, sipping tea and nodding as I pour out the details of my guilty heart. She puts down her cup and holds my shaking hands from across the simple wooden table with its brightly checkered cloth, smiling and soothing the ache that never seems to ease—an ache that sits like a brick on my chest and sometimes makes it difficult to breathe.

It was on one of those semi-silent long summer evenings

when Mama received a frantic phone call from Auntie Mary Anne. Danny and I were sitting at the kitchen table playing a board game when the phone rang.

"She needs help." Mama turned to Daddy with that worried look she reserved for especially trying problems. "Apparently Philip's having another affair with a woman he works with. How ironic that Mary Anne thinks I, of all people, can help her out!" Mama's voice had an edge to it that made Daddy wince. "She wants me to come and collect her and the kids and bring them home to Washington."

Daddy sighed deeply and pulled on his pipe. It produced only a dry, sucking sound so he removed it from his mouth and began the process of cleaning and repacking the bowl with tobacco, something he often did when he was thinking. "I suppose you better go down and see what you can do—but I would hope that your mother and sister can contribute a little gas and eating money. No, no—don't get that look on your face. We'll do what we have to do regardless. Family is family, after all. It's just that I can't get away from work right now with the new job and all. Tell her we'll work something out and get back to her."

Mama picked up the telephone and asked for the long-distance operator.

Danny and I pretended not to notice the adult conversation, although my brother pretended so hard that he actually missed a turn and inadvertently allowed me to advance my position without protest. This happened so rarely that my glee got the better of me and he quickly recalculated and put my marker back where it had been.

"Good try, Leah—but not good enough!" he chortled as he

threw the dice. I knew better than to protest. If I objected to Mama, she would make Danny rescind his action. The win would be Pyrrhic, however, as Danny would make my life miserable in retaliation.

Danny was going into seventh grade in September and he lorded over me this change of school and social position. However, for the first time, we would be attending separate schools and I would no longer be Danny's little sister and forever in his shadow. For a few years, at least, I would have the privilege of being Robbie's big sister—someone to be looked up to. This was my secret delight, as Danny hadn't thought of the change from my point of view.

Mama replaced the telephone on the receiver and turned her attention to us. "Up the stairs with the two of you," she called and motioned with her hand towards the stairs. "And put that game away before you go."

We set about placing cards, markers, and dice into their respective slots in the box, taking our time about it, as well. Mama ignored this obvious ploy to extend our stay within ear reach of the ongoing conversation regarding our auntie and her domestic problems. She waited us out, arms crossed over her chest, tapping the toe of her right foot on the hardwood floor.

When it became obvious that Mama had no intentions of renewing her conversation with Daddy until we were upstairs in bed, we finished the cleanup and said our goodnights. As we rounded the corner into the long hallway at the top of the stairs Danny nodded to me and motioned towards the little walk-in closet Robbie used for a bedroom. It had a screened opening that allowed hot air to circulate from the living room below into the upper part of the house—handy for allowing airflow, but also handy for listening in on living room conversations. We hunkered down around the air vent as quietly as possible, careful to neither awaken the sleeping Robbie nor attract the attention of our parents who were engaged in a heated discussion of Auntie Mary Anne's marital problems. At least, for the moment, they had forgotten their own!

They talked for another hour, finally retiring for the night. As Daddy left the living room, he raised his head towards the corner where Danny's bedroom air vent penetrated the ceiling. "And time for you two eaves-droppers to hop into bed, as well." He saluted with his pipe and ambled slowly out of our field of view.

The next morning at breakfast Daddy winked at me over our cereal bowls. "Help your mom around the house this morning—you and Danny and she are going on a trip."

"Where to?" inquired Danny.

"To California—Mama and I decided that she should drive down and bring Aunt Mary Anne and your cousins up here for a while."

"What about Robbie," I asked as I reached for toast and jam. "Isn't he coming with us?

"No, he'll go to stay with your grandmother in Bremerton. Your Aunt Noreen is going along to help Mama drive, so Robbie will be with your cousins."

Aunt Noreen arrived just before bedtime, bags in hand, and we set out at daybreak the following morning in our newly acquired 1939 Pontiac. Daddy had traded in our Model-A Elizabeth plus, according to Mama, the family fortune, for this shiny, maroon beauty. Mama had to admit she adored driving it and was looking forward to taking the trip to California. She was a little hesitant in its capacity to carry back three adults and four children plus clothing and incidentals for everyone, but Daddy convinced her to pack light and to have Aunt Mary Anne do the same. Aunt Noreen would help Mama do the driving, and with the two sisters together, both Daddy and our uncle felt we would all be safe. Besides, Auntie Nor and OurGrandmother would help pay for food and gasoline. On the surface, the trip appeared well-planned, and an adventure for the sisters.

"I'm not exactly sure that Mary Anne knows how to pack lightly, Hal, especially with two kids," Mama commented with some skepticism. "Noreen had enough trouble putting every-thing in one small bag, but we'll try." So, with kisses and hugs all around, plus more than a few tears from Robbie who was devastated at being left behind, we were off.

The journey down was pleasant enough, swift and full of singing along with Mama and Auntie Nor teaching us three part harmony. I would go to the ends of the earth on a trip with my mama—probably with my Aunt Noreen, as well. It was the long ride home that became what was later labeled by Mama as The Mercy Trip from Hell!

We arrived in Watsonville, a small farming community, in the blazing afternoon heat of late July. Auntie Mary Anne met us at the door in tears. Amanda Sue stood behind her holding little Philip by the hand, an odd little grin on her face. As Mama and Auntie Noreen comforted their older sister, Amanda Sue confronted me.

"You know, I haven't forgotten your hospitality from last

summer. My mama says I should make you feel at home, just like you did," she paused for effect; "but I don't have any cowboy boots for you to try on." Even though the day was oven-hot, a shiver ran down my spine. It didn't look like our return jaunt would be nearly as pleasant as the drive down.

We were in Watsonville exactly forty-eight hours before we hit the road home. In those short hours Amanda Sue taught me a few life lessons that I have never forgotten. First and foremost, among them was my introduction to the infamous Black Widow Spider. Having lived on a farm for several of my formative years I was not unfamiliar with the typical barnyard spiders, bees, wasps, and yellow jackets, along with the occasional rat or mouse. I was neither attracted to them nor repelled; rather, I left them a wide berth and expected the same in return. However, none could compare with the vicious and brutal Black Widow that, according to my cousin, tracked down and poisoned small children, dragging their stunned and paralyzed bodies back to her den, there to be sucked dry by all the spiderlings.

We had been assigned the chore of retrieving suitcases from the dark and forbidding detached garage when Amanda Sue began her tale of death and dinner as seen from the spider's viewpoint. She had just reached the part about blonde-headed children being especially attractive when we arrived at the black hole that opened into the garage. She entered first and had gone a mere three or four steps when she rocketed back out the door screeching at the top of her lungs.

"It's coming for you, Cookie—The Black Widow's coming for you, and she's the biggest one I ever saw!"

Amanda Sue shot by, leaving me frozen just inside the garage. In the blackness I could see nothing, my poor eyes unable to quickly adjust to the dim interior. In my mind's eye, however, I could see the spider, body the size of a basketball, lurching towards me at blinding speed. I could hear the rustle of limbs and imagined rows of boxes being moved out of place as the unknown scrabbled towards me in the black. When I could bear no more my feet found traction and I hurtled backward from the garage, stumbling in the process, and landing with a thump on my fanny.

Amanda Sue laughed with glee, pointing at my undignified sprawl on the cement. "I was just teasing you," she gloated. "Come on, I'll show you." She strode past me into the darkness, but no amount of coaxing or name calling could force me into that garage. Eventually, she emerged with the suitcases—contempt skulking behind her eyes whenever she looked at me.

Amanda Sue didn't save all her nastiness for me. She had plenty to spread around, her favorite target being her younger brother Little Phil. She would coax him into her red Radio Flyer wagon on the pretext of a ride around the block. Auntie Mary Anne would point with pride at how generous and loving little Amanda Sue was towards her brother. Amanda Sue would prance about in her ruffled pinafore and patent leather strap shoes, then drag her brother around the corner and run the wagon off the steep flood control curb, dumping little Phillip into the street.

"I'm gonna tell on you," I whispered in her ear the second or third time I saw her pull this dirty trick.

"Go ahead," she whispered back, little spittle wads

bouncing off my ear. "Nobody'll believe you!"

And indeed, they did not. Mama thought I was trying to get attention and snatched me up smartly by my arm, dragging me around the corner of the house and giving me a 'good talking to' that would have pleased OurGrandmother. Danny knew the truth but kept his own counsel.

The second afternoon of our stay Amanda Sue took me for a walk down to the little main street, ostensibly to show off her town. In actuality, she trotted straight to the diner where Uncle Phillip's girlfriend waited tables. "There she is," muttered Amanda Sue as she pointed out a rather pleasant looking short woman with blonde hair. She was a little dumpy, and not much of a beauty, but her smile was sweet. As a matter of fact, she looked a great deal like Auntie Mary Anne, except for the hair color.

"Don't you tell your mom that I took you here!" She threatened me with her big, blue eyes. "I'm not supposed to know about her. She's a homewrecker, you know. My mama cries at night over her and I will **NEVER** forgive Phillip for doing this."

"Phillip," I exclaimed. "Don't you call him daddy? He's your father!"

"Not anymore," spat out Amanda Sue. "Not anymore."

I secretly liked my Uncle Phillip, but then, he hadn't done anything bad to me.

Early the next morning we all piled into the car. Nowadays, we would be arrested for having that many people in one car, but then, nobody seemed to care, as long as the doors stayed closed. The three sisters sat in front with little Phillip sharing the laps of those not driving. Amanda Sue, Danny, and I shared the back seat with boxes and shopping bags covering the floorboards except for one small spot over the 'hump' where the transmission bulged up. It was on this hump that Amanda Sue decreed I should stand since "she's the smallest and the shortest, Auntie Mayleen, so she should stand there. Besides, she can look out the front window, ya know!"

Mama wasn't too keen on this arrangement, especially since I suffered from chronic carsickness if not seated either in the front seat or next to a window where I could look out. Her neck, as were those of her sisters, was in direct line of fire if my stomach gave out.

"Okay, we'll try it for a while—but you three need to trade off."

Amanda and Danny gave each other a knowing look, and I resigned myself to standing up all the way home—and I did.

Auntie Mary Anne, Amanda Sue, and Little Phillip stayed a week with us in Tacoma after our return from California. Mary Anne needed a little down time before she went to Bremerton to stay with Our Grandmother and Auntie Noreen and her family. Amanda Sue bunked with me, sharing not only my bed but everything I owned. I would never again fail to share with her (willing or not) but I knew that the sharing was not reciprocated.

Daddy remarked at dinner the evening after Auntie Nor arrived and whisked aunt and cousins off to Bremerton that although it was nice to have family visit, it was even nicer when they left. He winked at Mama and reached for her hand. "I know things have been difficult around here in the last few months, Mayleen," he said as his eyes found hers, "but I promise you, it's going to get better, soon. Today the boss put me in charge of the machine shop and things are looking up."

I look at Danny across the table from me and see the smile on his face. It matches mine. My heart smiles, too, as Mama takes Daddy's hand and gives it a squeeze. Tonight I will go to bed happy, I think to myself.

CHAPTER 4

In Which Broken Vows
are Further Shattered

Amanda Sue had a doll. Oh, what a small, inoffensive sentence. Amanda Sue had a doll—a doll that I secretly coveted, probably as much as Amanda Sue had coveted my tan cowboy boots with the red rosette insets. The doll had belonged to her long-dead sister Shirley Anne, who had passed away suddenly from leukemia, ten years or more before either Amanda Sue or I were born. According to Mama Shirley Anne was beautiful both inside and out, with a sunny smile, a winning personality, and beautiful naturally curly golden locks that hung to her shoulders. With her sky blue eyes and peaches and cream complexion, she was the apple of her daddy and mommy's eye. I suppose that Shirley Anne was a tall act to follow and that Amanda Sue might carry a burden of her own that had shaped her personality. However good her long dead sister was in actuality, in death she had become a saint. Nothing Amanda Sue did could possibly compare. Therein lay the bones of her yoke.

But Amanda Sue had the doll. It had a hard, composite baby doll body, fully jointed, with real curly blonde hair that you could comb and style.

Her eyes opened and closed when she changed positions and she had a little pouty rosebud mouth with pink lips. Amanda Sue carried her around in a little leatherette suitcase filled with specially made clothing including a fur coat, little patent leather shoes, and real silk stockings.

No one touched that doll except Amanda, who treated the doll with contempt. "I should have had a doll of my own," she complained bitterly, "but Mama and Daddy said I should be content with my sister's hand me downs." I secretly laughed to myself, as I was always being saddled with hand me downs—even those Amanda Sue herself had outgrown!

The afternoon she threw the doll down the stairs in a fit of rage was the last straw for me. I retrieved it from where it lay huddled against the front door with its arm wrenched from the socket and, instead of returning it to Amanda Sue, hid it in Mama's lamp table behind a stack of books. Amanda didn't think to retrieve the doll until much later, only to find that the doll was nowhere to be found. Although she accused me of stealing it, I stood my ground under Mama's lashing tongue. The mystery of the doll's disappearance died down after a couple of days, although Amanda Sue kept her eyes on my every move.

In time, we all forgot about the doll and she lay in her lamp table tomb that went into storage at Daddy's sister's farm when we moved several months later.

Aunt Mary Anne smoked cigarettes like Auntie Nor. Unlike her relatively flush younger sister, however, she rolled her own, often borrowing Daddy's pipe tobacco. She had a neat little machine into which she laid cut to size paper in a special trough, filled it with tobacco, moistened the paper's edge, then turned the crank handle. Paper and tobacco disappeared inside the box and out the other side came a finished cigarette. Danny coveted the box and one afternoon Amanda Sue purloined it from her mother's suitcase and brought it out to the back stoop. She had also filched a pack of papers. Danny had been tasked with snatching a little of Daddy's tobacco from his humidor, but Mama had almost caught him red-handed. He retreated in haste without the prize.

On the front lawn grew a strange little plant the neighborhood kids referred to as 'rabbit tobacco'. It had green wiry leaves around a central stiff grayish stem topped with a cluster of white flowers in spring which turned to seed pods by July. When these seeds were perfectly dry, one could pull them off the stem producing a brown, crumbly stuff that looked remarkably like short cut cigarette or pipe tobacco. It had a rather herby aroma. We would chew on the stems, being careful not to let a 'friend' pull the stem from our lips, leaving us with a mouthful of brown flakes.

Danny sent me down to collect as much of this 'rabbit tobacco' as possible. When I returned with a double handful, he motioned for me to drop the stuff on a piece of newspaper, then he and Amanda Sue set up the cigarette machine. Amanda did a pretty good job of reproducing cigarettes. She cranked out five or six without a hitch, then let Danny have a try. His lacked the finesse of Amanda Sue's but were still serviceable. On a dare, he put one to his lips and lit up with a kitchen match snitched from Mama's stash near the fireplace. He took a deep drag and, turning a lovely shade of puce, nearly coughing his head off.

"That's wicked stuff," he sputtered as he withdrew the 'smoke' from his lips and eyeballed it admiringly. "I fully intend to surprise the boys with a few of these. That should divide the wimps from the rest of us!"

Amanda Sue grabbed for hers before Danny could make off with all of them.

"What're you gonna do with yours," Danny inquired.

"I have a special plan," she snickered. "Don't you worry yourself about that, Danny-O."

"Hey, Leah! You wanna take a drag?"

I wanted to fit in with my big brother, but something in his eyes made me decide against taking a puff of this roll of rabbit tobacco. It didn't smell at all like Daddy's Prince Albert.

"I don't think so, Danny—and you better not give that stuff to Robbie, or Mom'll find out about it." He gave me his patented big brother disgusted sneer and turned back to conniving with Amanda Sue. I wandered off leaving them to their machinations, putting the cigarette machine and the rabbit tobacco completely out of my mind.

The little cousins had found a piece of cardboard and were using it to slide down the side slope of the nearly dead brown August lawn. They let me have a turn and we spent most of the afternoon passing the cardboard back and forth until it wore out and the brown grass was replaced by stubble and dirt.

At supper, Amanda Sue, and Danny kept passing looks back and forth. Every time their eyes drifted to Aunt Mary Anne they could hardly contain their giggles. It didn't cross my mind that they would play a prank on a grownup or I might have spilled the beans then and there.

"What's up with you and Amanda," Daddy inquired of his eldest son. "You look like the cat that ate the canary."

"Oh, nothing, Daddy," Danny replied. "We just had fun this afternoon, that's all." Amanda Sue's eyes would have given her away if any of the grownups had noticed, but Mama brought in dessert and by the time everyone had their cake slice, she had those enormous baby blues under control. The only eyes I ever saw capable of competing with my cousin Amanda Sue's belonged to Elizabeth Taylor.

Late that night, long after we were all in bed, I heard someone out on the front stoop. My bedroom window overlooked the front porch, so I crept as quietly as possible as not to wake Amanda who was sharing my bed and pulled back the curtain to take a peek. Auntie Mary Anne sat there, chin in her hand and her elbow balanced on her knee. She looked so lonely, so alone in the warm, summer night, that I crept out of my room and down the stairs to join her.

"Oh, hi Cookie," she acknowledged me as I sat quietly down beside her. "I was just looking for some stars, but there's too much light in the city to see them."

"I miss the stars, too," I murmured. "We could always see them from the farm." She put her arm around my shoulder and pulled me close. She smelled of tobacco and Mitcham's deodorant and clean clothing, and the musty aroma of good mash whiskey. I thought that what she needed most was someone to listen to her with their heart. I knew that I was far too young for her to confide in; I could only hope that Mama had listened well.

"Tomorrow we are leaving for Bremerton to stay with your grandmother. I'll bet you won't be missing your cousin

Amanda, will you? I know she can be a real pain, but I'm sure she loves you."

I wasn't so sure about Amanda Sue, but I nodded, anyway. Auntie Mary Anne's voice had a husky quality that always made me think she was holding back the tears. "I'll miss you," I said quietly, and I meant it, but Amanda Sue could go as far away as the moon, for all I cared, and I wouldn't miss her, at all.

She reached into her shirt pocket where she kept her cigarettes and fished out a neatly rolled cylinder. "Oh, I didn't realize I had any ready-mades left. What a nice surprise!" As she lifted the cigarette towards her lips, I grasped with sudden clarity Amanda Sue and Danny's little joke.

"Oh, Auntie," I said quickly as I reached for the cigarette, "I don't think you want to smoke that!"

She gave me an odd look, then examined the cigarette more closely. "Well, I'll be! That sure isn't what I thought it was. I wondered where my machine and makings went to this afternoon. Did you know about this, Cookie? Is that why you came down here?"

"No, no!" I exclaimed. "I just wanted to sit with you— really! But Amanda and Danny had something going with those phony cigarettes, and I wouldn't want anything to happen to you."

She pondered the smoke for a quiet minute, then turned to me.

"Well, I'll make sure they pay for this," she laughed her husky, Aunt Mary Anne laugh, deep in her throat and kind of croupy. "Don't say anything. Before we leave tomorrow those brats will find that little games can backfire!"

We sat together quietly for another few moments before she motioned me back to bed. I heard her out there on the steps for a long time, though, and for a little while, I was sure she was crying.

The next morning during breakfast when she knew both of the cigarette barons were watching, she poured herself a cup of coffee and sat down at the table. After a few sips, she reached dramatically into her breast pocket and pulled out a cigarette.

"What a nice surprise," she exclaimed as if amazed at her change of fortune. "I found this last night while I sat on the front steps and thought I'd save it for my morning coffee time." Danny and Amanda Sue leaned forward in unison as she brought the tube to her lips and flicked her silver Zippo lighter. As she placed the cigarette's tip into the flame, they almost fell onto the table.

Auntie Mary Anne took a mighty drag on the cigarette, then suddenly her eyes bulged out and her hand went to her throat. She choked, held her breath, and dropped from her chair straight to the floor where she thrashed about for a moment before going stiff as a board. Everyone in the kitchen watched in stunned silence, especially Amanda Sue, and Danny. Mama screamed softly and Daddy leapt from his chair, dropping to his knees and shaking Mary Anne, calling her name. When he received no response, Danny began to fidget in his seat. Amanda Sue looked as if someone had smacked her hard. Her pouty little rosebud lips began to quiver, and a single tear made its way down her peaches and cream cheek.

"Is my mama okay, Uncle Hal?"

"I don't know what's the matter with her, Amanda Sue.

Oh, look at this cigarette. My God—this isn't tobacco! Mayleen, call the ambulance—she's been poisoned!"

Danny turned quite pale and slipped quietly from his seat at the table. Mama grabbed him by the arm as he tried to tiptoe unnoticed from the kitchen. Amanda Sue's face became bright red as she ran around the table to where her mother lay on the kitchen floor.

"Mommy, mommy—don't die," she cried. "Danny just wanted to play a trick on you!"

At this sudden betrayal, Danny jerked himself around and shouted that the idea had been Amanda Sue's as well.

As suddenly as she had fallen, Aunt Mary Anne sat up. Her eyes met mine and she winked. "It's just a darned good thing I took a close look at that cigarette last night on the front steps, you two little brats. Who knows what might have happened if I had actually smoked the thing."

Mama swung Danny around, ready to smack him hard on the fanny, but Aunt Mary Anne stopped her mid-swing. "Don't spank him, Mayleen. From the look on his face, he's been punished enough." She turned to Amanda Sue, who at least had the decency to look chagrined. "And as for you, my fine daughter, if you ever again do such a thing to anyone, *you will regret it forever.*"

Amanda Sue looked as if she believed every word her mother had to say.

Danny didn't come away totally unscathed. After Daddy left with our aunt and her offspring, carrying them off across the Narrows to Bremerton and life with OurGrandmother, Mama put him in charge of scrubbing and waxing the hardwood floors. He glared at me as if he knew that someone had ratted him out, but he never had proof. Aunty Mary Anne was as good as her word and never told a soul about our late-night discovery.

After the relatives left Mama and Daddy politely avoided each other during the extended summer evenings. They quarreled at night when they thought we were asleep. Danny and I shared a room again, upstairs and directly over our parents' room. Our heat register was not connected to the furnace nestled in the basement; instead, it drew hot air directly from the bedroom below. Danny and I lay on our stomachs peering through the register during these fights, listening to every word and keeping an eye, limited as our view was, on Mama. Not that we saw Daddy get physical with her, but he was always loud and sometimes wild enough to scare us.

"If he ever hits Mama, I'll kill him," Danny whispered fiercely one night when Daddy punched the door with his fist. Danny lay on his stomach, leaning on his elbows, fists clenched. "He'd better not touch her!"

I sat cross-legged, a blanket pulled tightly about my shoulders to ward off the late evening chill. "I don't think he'd hurt Mama—do you, really?"

Danny had been privy to OurFather and Mama's quarrels before my birth and had witnessed first-hand his physical anger. Smashed coffee cups and threatened fists to her face had made a lasting impression on his young mind. I too had witnessed OurFather threaten Gemma and more than once he had come close to hitting me, stopping only when he realized Mama would have him arrested if she ever found a mark.

He rolled on his side to face me. "I wouldn't have believed

it before, but something's changed. Who is this woman they keep fighting about? Is Daddy seeing someone else? I know you know something, Leah. You're holdin' out on me and I wanna know why!"

"I can't tell, Danny. I made a promise and I won't break it. You have to ask Mama—better yet, ask Daddy who the lady is— if you dare!" I didn't think Danny would ask Mama, and he'd never approach Daddy with his questions.

Daddy usually stomped out of the bedroom and slammed the door behind him, leaving our mama crying into her hands, and returned only after she fell asleep in misery. My heart broke for her but saying anything risked a change of bedroom which would cut us off from further information. Finally, Danny grew disgusted with Daddy and began adding to our mother's troubles with his smart mouth. I had put so much hope into Daddy's upgraded position at work and his promise to Mama that things would be better that tears slowly leaked from my eyes and I had to wipe them on my shirt sleeve before Danny saw.

"Where did all this hostility come from, Danny?" Mama asked in exasperation one morning when he'd actually been rude to Daddy and escaped a serious whacking only because Daddy was late leaving for work. At least Daddy's new job distanced him from his woman friend in Bremerton—a condition of Mama's staying in the marriage. This did nothing to improve his mood and he took to working extra hours in an attempt to stay away from home. Mama doubted this explanation for his absence as his paycheck didn't seem to reflect extended workdays, and she accused him of keeping in touch with his other lady love.

"I'm tired, Mama. Daddy yells at us all the time and I wish you was home at night, 'stead a workin' at that darned college. I'm big enough to get a paper route like my friends, but I always gotta be here takin' care of Robbie and *her*!" He jerked his thumb in my direction.

I held my tongue. Danny usually saw his friends in the evenings while Mama worked three-to-eleven at the college canteen and I waited impatiently for Daddy to get home from the machine shop (or wherever). I didn't want to take Daddy's plate from the table until I was certain he'd eaten somewhere else. In my mind I saw him at a restaurant with his girlfriend, laughing and eating and drinking his VO and water (tall, please) while Mama sold gum to college students and cleaned coffee cups from round coffee house tables. Often, he came home long after we had finished dinner and I had settled Robbie into bed. He swore me to secrecy. but kept out of Danny's way. The two had an unspoken agreement—Danny didn't squeal on Daddy, and Daddy let him go where he pleased, as long as he was in bed when Mama got home.

"I'm sorry, Danny. Things will get better, I promise you." Our mother tried hard to sound positive. "Please be patient, and don't irritate Daddy."

Danny would grumble assent, then extract some reward from her, such as movie money or relief from chores. I longed to tell my mother the truth. Daddy was a liar and Danny was a hypocrite. I was caught in a double bind, and the truth of my situation added to that brick on my chest. In those un-mailed letters to Annie, I told it all.

I was actually relieved when school started—Fourth Grade, new school, new people. From mid-September on rain lashed the city, drenching us on our daily walks to and from school. Robbie started First Grade there and now tagged behind Danny, imitating his every move. Tacoma schools were so crowded that classes K-3 had double sessions, each meeting for half a day. At lunchtime, I collected Robbie from his classroom, delivered him home to a babysitter, then hurried back in time for afternoon class, often eating my sandwich along the way.

For the first time, I failed to make new friends. I took pleasure in my classwork, maintaining a high academic standard, but spent recesses reading alone, my back leaned up against the old brick building. Our lives seemed so temporary—unstable at best, chaotic at worst—that I hadn't the energy to cultivate friends I sensed soon would be left behind. My eyes, although not on a nosedive to blindness anymore, slowly declined, leaving the threat of future darkness forever lingering in the back of my mind.

Mama still worked at the local college, now bussing pots and pans and running the huge commercial dishwashers in the dining room from noon until eight o'clock at night. Danny and I had even more chores. Worse, Mama's new shift cut into his after-dinner plans, dumping him into an ever blackening mood, lightened only when he thought up some new method of tormenting Robbie or me. I cooked dinner and babysat Robbie during the week, then helped Mama with housework on the weekends.

Daddy disappeared from our lives during Thanksgiving vacation after one last terrible fight two months short of two years to the day since I walked into my parents' room looking for nail polish and overheard the telephone call. Mama and I had many long talks about 'the situation,' as we called Daddy's departure. The family, Daddy's brothers and sisters and Mama's sisters, and all the grandparents, kept pushing her to take Daddy back, but Mama didn't believe him when he promised to give up his women friends. I felt she should do whatever made her happy.

Danny waffled between pride at being the man of the family and a 'breadwinner' (Mama had allowed him his precious paper route) and wanting Daddy home. He missed camping and fishing and men things, he said. Robbie just missed his Daddy.

I missed Daddy too, but I didn't miss the fights, and I didn't miss the looks from Daddy when he thought no one was watching—the looks aimed at me and filled with accusations. Mama seemed happier, now. She was beginning to smile again and had gained a little weight. I developed a wait and see attitude toward any change in Daddy's behavior. What I wanted was to see Daddy's heart and to hear him say he loved my mama. I needed him to ask Mama to forgive him his trespasses as it says in the Bible, and I needed him to take me in his arms as he had so long ago on the farm and brush his late evening whiskery face on my cheek and call me his little Cookie. But he couldn't. He had betrayed us once, and I didn't trust him; I was no longer quick to forgive.

CHAPTER 5
In Which I Learn About Chinese Gongs

While Mama and Daddy were caught in the Dance of their Marriage's Death, as Danny called it, OurFather made a pronouncement that caught both Danny and me by surprise. He had remarried, without so much as introducing us to his lady love.

Although OurFather's new wife was named Nina, pronounced **NINE**-a (like the number), he proclaimed that Danny and I should call her "Mother". Danny got that I-won't line between his eyebrows, something that Robbie and I took great care to acknowledge with respect as it usually meant that Danny was determined. OurFather answered him back in kind—making it perfectly apparent to me that the 'I-won't' line (and the unyielding force behind it) was hereditary. I smiled widely at **NINE**-a, showing my jack-o-lantern mouth of missing and variously re-growing teeth, secretly vowing to myself that the day I gave this woman the courtesy of calling her Mother was the day that OurFather dropped my now dead body next to another trash can in some far away alley. Consequently, Danny mumbled at the woman for years, and I avoided any instance in which grammar or situation demanded an actual name until I was well into my twenties.

NINE-a was from a longstanding local Kitsap County family, after whom the county had named a road, and this impressed me greatly! She was tall and slender, taller than OurFather, with reddish-blonde hair. Her hands were beautifully groomed—each fingertip enhanced by an exceedingly long and polished nail. These fingernails mesmerized me, as I had bitten mine to the quick for as long as I could remember, often making my fingers bleed in the process.

Daddy and Mama daubed evil-tasting liquids upon each mangled finger nightly, to no avail. Daddy threatened dire consequences if I persisted in nibbling at what was left of my nails, even holding a trip to the woodshed over my head. I tried to keep them out of my mouth, but at times of stress, or when I was occupied in thought, they crept there unbidden. Although I could not stop myself, I was determined someday to have long, bright red talons like my current stepmother.

OurFather had another pronouncement, one that solidified my opinion of him. Biology notwithstanding, it takes more than sperm and egg to make a parent, and he had done nothing, aside from his incidental deposit, to qualify him as such in my eyes.

He stands there, so much taller than I am, and as much as I would like to disavow myself of heritage, I see my brother and myself written on his face, as he is written upon ours. He opens his mouth. I try to block the sound but cannot. His lips move and I can read them. He is forbidding Danny and me to call daddy the man who feeds us, who tucks us in at night—the man to whom I will always flee with skinned knees and injured pride—the man who holds me in the night when bad dreams *awaken me. The man who sheltered me in his arms and brought me home from the hospital where I was born. I get that same I-won't line between **my** eyebrows and I stare back hard at OurFather. And in my heart, I acknowledge the forever difference between a father and a daddy, and if I can figure out a way to erase the father, I surely will. I look at my mangled fingertips and decide I do not want long, red nails.*

OurFather and his bride bought a piece of land on a hill overlooking the Navy Yard in Bremerton and settled in to build a house. The street was named for a huge Madrona tree that stood, proud and sheltering, dead center of the lot **NINE**-a had selected for her own. Within a few weeks, the tree lay on the ground, chopped into fireplace-sized sections destined for burning. I wondered what the street would be called now that the Madrona was gone, but OurFather just gave me a withering look and curled his upper lip.

While the new house took shape OurFather and **NINE**-a resided in a little first building that would be converted to a detached garage/shop when construction on their home was complete. Danny and I visited them on alternate weekends once a month. OurFather required Mama to provide all transportation but forbade her to drive to the property. When the weather was nice, I struggled up the hill dragging my possessions behind me in Grampa B's old duffle. When the weather was nasty, Mama would drop us off at Gramma B's house, six blocks away.

Gramma B was OurFather's mother—chubby and grey-haired and the oldest of twelve siblings. Several of her brothers and sisters lived in Bremerton or its surrounds. *She loves my mama and calls her 'Little Mayleen' for as long as she lives. She is married to Grampa B, who met her when she came as a widow from South Dakota with her three teenage boys.* Along with Daddy's chubby mama, she provided Danny and me with a second loving grandmother, although the family dynamic prevented us from spending nearly enough time with her.

I loved visiting with Gramma and Grampa B and came once a year for a whole week. Grampa B talked and laughed with me in his shop out back by the alley and let me eat all the raw vegetables I wanted out of his garden. Gramma taught me to bake old family favorites from South Dakota and skipped with me down the alley. Sometimes she jumped rope with me in the basement where I slept in a little twin bed under the high-up window. On the cold cement floor was a white bearskin with the head attached, teeth bared, eyes wide open. Grampa shot it when he was in the Alaska Territory and had it made into a rug. *I lay on the bearskin and pet its hard, cold head and think about faraway lands closed tight in snow and ice and dream and pretend that I will not have to make the six-block walk to OurFather's house when I wake.*

In time, the house on Madrona Street was finished. It had two bedrooms and a bathroom distributed down the hall to a door that led into the laundry/furnace room and the side yard. The kitchen opened from the breezeway and overlooked the dining room through which one had to pass to the step down into the (sunken and very fashionable) living room holding two huge recliner chairs, a small sofa, and the huge rock wall that contained the fireplace. A stack of wood from the proud, old Madrona tree sat on the hearth that extended the entire length of the wall—a compact little house, nicely appointed, but a bit cramped, with no thought to a boisterous son or quiet, solitary daughter.

On the dining room wall, directly behind and hovering over the chair in which OurFather ordered me to sit for my meals, hung a huge old Cuckoo clock. OurFather brought it home from Germany, restoring it to its original guilt-edged glory. The clock was from someplace called the Black Forest.

I think it sounds like the woods where Hansel and Gretel encountered the witch and I do not like the thought of sitting beneath something that comes from such an evil-sounding place. OurFather tells me not to be stupid.

The clock is operated by two weights dropping at a controlled rate, drawing a long brass chain through its mechanism in metered increments. Gears move the ivory hands on the clock face and signal the emergence of the cuckoo, a bird that at the top of each hour leaps out from behind a door to tell the world what time of day it is.

The bird is yellow and has real feathers. I think that it looks just like a little stuffed canary, trapped forever inside the clock, condemned to drone the time into eternity.

This clock is one of OurFather's most prized possessions, he tells Danny and me, and forbids either of us to touch it. In fact, he warns us, the child who dares to place a finger on this precious item will be punished most forcefully.

He squatted down on his hunkers and drew us to him, fixing his gaze on me.

His eyes mesmerize me—I feel like that little bird in the clock befixed by the gaze of a hungry snake. From OurFather's mouth comes the most terrifying threat I have ever heard. He says:

"**Leah Anne**—if you **ever** touch that clock, I will personally beat you until you ring like a Chinese gong. Danny, the same goes for you."

He has used my full name—the one that Mama uses when she requires my complete attention, or when I have committed some unpardonable offense, or when Daddy says that we are taking a walk to the woodshed. He has threatened a terrible punishment—and I have no knowledge of Chinese gongs! But I do have an idea about beatings, and this frightens me even more than my lack of knowledge about gongs.

Danny says "okay", without a backward glance at the object of discussion. He sits across from it and can watch with glee as I rise from my chair some night and accidentally trespass into its space. He can laugh as I am hauled by OurFather like some puppy who has peed on the carpet out into (I presume) the yard where my humiliation may be witnessed by the entire neighborhood, and there reduces me to blubbering jelly with whatever implement is used to ring Chinese gongs. I shall probably die from humiliation if I do not succumb to the beating.

I began dreading the weekends at OurFather's house more than I ever had. Before our little talk about the Cuckoo clock, I had resigned myself to the visits, even trying to make friends with **NINE**-a, although her use of those dagger-fingernails began to repulse me. She liked green olives, the kind with the little red centers, that came stacked in a narrow glass jar. Instead of decanting them with a fork or a little wooden pick like my mama did, **NINE**-a would position her right index finger over the bottle opening and JAB! Quick as a heron extracting a fish from the water her finger-beak appeared with an olive skewered on its crimson tip. Delicately she would lift the prize to her mouth, opened wide in exaggerated anticipation, and pop it in, extracting the olive and retrieving her finger, nail intact, in one fluid motion. The whole operation made me shudder.

Those fingernails were more important than anything—or anyone—else, including OurFather, a fact that did not pass unnoticed by him. On more than one occasion she refused to cook dinner when one of her precious nails had broken. OurFather's angry outbursts could be heard outside in the breezeway where I preferred to remain until tempers (and crockery) stopped flying. OurFather got back from **NINE**-a as good as he gave.

Mama and Daddy had the occasional disagreement and the even less occasional war of the words, but Danny and I had never seen one of them throw something at the other. Daddy might fling a few choice words about with abandon and Mama slam the silverware down on the table, but that was the extent of it. They would mutter to themselves, Daddy retiring to either barn or shop (or, more recently, some bar for a drink) and Mama making a phone call to Auntie Nor, but in the end, they kissed and made up. Even at their current hostilities, Daddy had not touched our mother. Danny and I firmly believed they would eventually make up and things would return to normal, whatever that was with grownups.

I stand in the breezeway between the garage/shop and the kitchen door, waiting for OurFather and his new bride to settle the differences between them, bouncing an old tennis ball on the cement and counting how many times I can repeat before it gets away from me and rolls out onto the wet driveway. I dash quickly into the rain before the ball can gain momentum and roll down Madrona to the cross street below. Danny has told me about OurFather's temper and that OurFather hit our mama with the back of his hand before he ran away with Gemma. Mama makes excuses for OurFather when I talk to her about what I see on these weekend visits. She says that he is an unhappy person. Annie says I should listen with my heart.

I am unhappy standing in the wind and rain under the overhead shelter of a metal roof bouncing, bouncing my little tennis ball on the cement and the side of the garage while grownups destroy their kitchen crockery in a fit of temper. And I know in my heart of hearts that if I raise my voice or throw a cup I will be beaten until I ring like a Chinese gong, whether or not I have touched OurFather's cuckoo clock, a sin far worse, in my mind, than the specter of a broken fingernail.

Finally, the squabble stopped, and **NINE**-a opened the door and snatched me back inside. OurFather squatted down and looked me straight in the eyes. "What happens here, stays here," he whispered as little strings of spittle hang at the corners of his mouth and his eyes squinch down, mean and full of unspoken threats. *I look at the clock on the dining room wall and nod my head.*

The double bed in the room assigned to either Danny or me had an old chenille bedspread with rows of little round red and blue cotton balls that made it uncomfortable to sit or lie down for any length of time. A bedside table with a small lamp atop it sat to the right of the heavy wooden headboard. The lamp's parchment shade directed all the light straight down on the tabletop and was impossible to move so that one could read in bed. Under the window sat an old-fashioned chest of drawers with most of the knobs missing. My little duffle bag sat on the only chair, forlorn and unpacked, as if waiting for the instant I seize it and hurry to meet Mama. OurFather believes that 6 pm is an appropriate time for his daughter to be in bed for the night—lights out, no radio, no books.

If I need to use the bathroom, I tiptoe down the hall and cringe at the sound of flushing. **NINE**-*a sometimes springs from her bed and escorts me back to my solitary room, admonishing me to 'just hold it, Cookie!' I am terrified that my wonky bladder will betray me. I hate the nights alone in that back bedroom accompanied only by my imagination and the sounds of nighttime outside the window. Mama says I can stand anything for two nights. On Sunday she comes to take me home and I lug my bag down to the bottom of the hill where she waits.*

CHAPTER 6
In Which the Gong Rings

In summer, the courts required Danny and me to spend one week each with OurFather, in spite of his defiance of those same courts to pay child support. Mamma and Daddy preferred not to fight with OurFather, who had re-established himself in Bremerton and the Shipyard there. Grammy pleaded with him to pay for all his children, not just the secret son, our adopted brother in Nevada. Since **NINE**-a had no knowledge of James, and OurFather intended to keep her out of the loop at all costs, Danny and I had also had a special warning concerning him. According to OurFather, he did not exist. Danny was willing to go along with this subterfuge, but I rebelled at essentially killing off another sibling, just to conceal his reality from OurFather's new wife. Grammy kept her lips sealed and counseled me to do the same. Apparently, OurFather had neglected to inform **NINE**-a about Gemma; she remained unaware that OurFather had been twice married before her.

I complied with Grammy's advice and kept my mouth shut.

In the early summer of my tenth year, I arrived for my

obligatory week late on a Friday afternoon, a week that actually encompassed two weekends. Mama dropped me off at the bottom of the hill and waited as I lugged up my bag. Overhead a few stray clouds shielded me from the sun. When I reached the top of Madrona Street, I turned and waved. Mama waved back, put the car in gear, and pulled away. Ahead I could see OurFather nailing pickets onto the framework of a new fence extending from the side yard, around the front lawn, ending just beyond the four mailboxes set in a row along the road.

I plunked my duffle down on the gravel and squatted beside OurFather, silently watching as he placed a new picket. I often helped Daddy with repairs and building projects, serving as a second set of hands to fetch tools and hold items in place while he worked on them. We had a good relationship, although he might have preferred one of my brothers at his side as he bent over the engine of our fairly new Ford Tudor. I was, however, exceptionally good at setting the gap in the spark plugs.

"Hand me a nail, Cookie." OurFather motioned toward the box sitting next to my feet. I reached down, removed a few, and extended them, heads out. He selected three, put two between his lips, and placed the third at the ready for his hammer. I squatted beside him and steadied the picket while he pounded the nails, four per picket—two at the top support board, two at the bottom. We continued in this manner to where the rails made the right-hand turn at the long run to the mailboxes. OurFather rose, gave me a hand up, and directed me to take my duffle into the house.

On Saturday morning, we finished attaching pickets to the

remaining skeleton with barely a word spoken. Daddy always talked when we worked, explaining what he was doing and taking time to demonstrate why it was done in a particular manner. OurFather barely acknowledged my presence. However, after he had examined the full length of fence line, he spoke. "If you paint it, Cookie, I will pay you. Now, you have to do a good job and be quick about it, but it's worth five dollars to me. What do you say?"

I sighed. OurFather was good at offering money to Danny and me for doing work around his house, but he rarely came through. In the end, he always found some small defect that rescinded the 'contract'. It was of no use to point this out. Although Danny always believed this time was different, I knew I would paint every inch of that fence and not receive a dime.

I spent all day on Sunday and most of Monday painting in the hot sun, and I believe to this day it was the only coat of paint ever applied to that fence, but in the end, OurFather failed to pay. I cannot remember just why he refused the five dollars, but I never forgot the lesson he taught me. Blood may be thicker than water, but you can't trust it to pay a debt. I would gladly work for my daddy without a cent of pay because he loved me, in spite of our lack of genetic relationship.

During the day **NINE**-a went through the things in my duffle bag, shaking her head and tut-tutting under her breath as she examined the clothes so lovingly washed and maintained by Mama. So what if my pajamas were home made by Grammy—each stitch and seam was sewed with love. My parents provided warm clothes, good food and a roof over our heads. We managed without the fluff. At night, I heard **NINE**-a talking with OurFather, the two of them scheming to lure either Danny or me to live with them.

In the evenings OurFather read aloud from the newspaper and **NINE**-a played with her stupid green parakeet, Chris. Chris's cage hung at the window next to the breakfast nook. **NINE**-a freed him every morning, letting him fly at will about the house until she confined him at bedtime. He was a nasty little bird, taken to landing on my head and leaving after relieving himself. I resented that bird—he flew free while I was forbidden to listen to the radio or read a book in the privacy of the 'guest' room. OurFather required my entire attention. As he said, he had little enough time to find out what kind of person I was becoming.

I sit on the brick hearth beside the fireplace in OurFather's living room, as quiet as the stack of wood beside me, and swing my legs in time to OurFather's monotonous voice trolling out the news stories from the front page of the Bremerton Sun. My bare heels thump, thump on the bricks as I try to keep my eyes open and concentrate on his reading. He will ask questions and I will try to answer them.

***NINE**-a's stupid bird flies back and forth between the living room and the kitchen, through the dining room. From where I sit, I see him light on the cuckoo clock and let loose his white, sticky poo onto the chain that OurFather pulls down each night before he goes to bed. All day long weights drop slowly, giving momentum to the cogs that operate the mechanism controlling the poor little bird trapped inside. I think about the nasty green bird on the outside, and his poo on the chains, and OurFather's hands pulling down the chain. I smile, and OurFather asks "What is so funny, Leah?"*

Every night during newspaper time **NINE**-a sat on her chair, her long crimson nails flashing back and forth, as she crocheted some thick mustard colored yarn into squares. Her yarn basket sat beside her filled with already finished squares. *She has tried to teach me to crochet, but I have 'clumsy hands', unlike her niece Barbara who is younger than I am. Barbara has red hair and freckles and looks like **NINE**-a. Her picture sits in the place of honor on the table next to **NINE**-a's chair. Danny's picture sits on the mantle over the fireplace. There is no picture of me.*

Now OurFather looks at me, peeking out over the top edge of the newspaper, and asks me a question. It is about the war in Korea. He asks if I know where Korea is and I answer him that it is by China. He grunts and goes back to reading aloud. I open my mouth to ask him a question. I hear my voice ask when I will get the five dollars for painting the fence. I cannot believe I have done such a thing! I cringe as I hear the newspaper slap hard on the floor and OurFather gets out of his chair and snatches me off the hearth, the bricks scraping the backs of my legs. "Time for you to go to bed, Leah," he snarls, but he does not hit me.

I bolted for the three little stairs that rise from the sunken living room. carefully skirting the edge of the dining room wall, staying as far from the cuckoo clock as I can get, then scooted down the hall to my room. It was only seven-thirty, the air still full of sunlight and birds and the sound of the kids down the hill at the last house before Madrona Street ends, playing kick the can. Too early even for OurFather to send me to bed in the summertime. I got into my pajamas—the ones made by Grammy—and slipped between the damp chartreuse sheets that smelled faintly of mildew, pulled the pillow over my head, and let the tears slip silently from my eyes. *Only four more days, I think to myself, until Mama comes to the bottom of the hill and I can drag my duffle back down the road to our bottle green Ford.*

Saturday morning dawned with the wispy overcast that so often covers the sky in early summer. Two days left. At least it wasn't drizzling, as so often it did in late June.

As usual, **NINE**-a let her parakeet out of its cage to fly free in the house. I watched it once again perch on her finger and peck food from her tongue as we ate our breakfast at the nook in the kitchen. My stomach turned as I watched, but I ate my Sugar Crisp, OurFather's favorite cereal, and drank my grapefruit juice (especially sour after the cereal). As I cleared the breakfast things the stupid bird landed on my head. *I do not want to think of what it is doing in my hair.*

I flipped my head to the side and the bird flew into the dining room. From the corner of my eye, I saw it land on OurFather's precious clock. Suddenly the clock tipped and the bird slid off and fled into the living room. I watched horrified as the clock began a slow-motion slip to the side then dropped from its peg on the wall and thudded to the floor, narrowly missing the chair I sit in every night at dinner. The door where the little bird lives flew open, expelling a set of yellow feathers dangling at the end of a spring. What was left of the little bird flipped back and forth on its coil of wire as I stared, wide-eyed, at the tangle of chain and weights and broken wooden pieces, scattered along the wall.

I fell to my knees, then rolled into a little ball in the entry between the kitchen and the dining room as what was left of the clock emitted a strangled clanging sound. The floor rocked under my small body and I realized we were experiencing an earthquake.

The back door opened and OurFather bolted through. "Is everything okay in here?" He looked at me, huddled on the floor. "What's the matter, Cookie?" I closed my eyes and pointed towards the dining room wall. The floor trembled with an aftershock and the chains from the fallen clock rattled on the floor.

*OurFather rushes past where I lie in a ball, his eyes glued to the spot on the dining room wall where the precious cuckoo clock should hang. He makes a croaking noise deep in his throat. I wait, trembling, for his hand to yank me from the floor and carry me to wherever he will beat me. I quake with my own fear—a quake far stronger than Mother Nature has produced this morning. Today I will finally know how it feels to ring like a Chinese gong. On this day, I will probably die, and my mama and my daddy will cry at my funeral, and Danny and Robbie will fight over who gets my stuff. Someone is standing over me. Someone reaches down and pulls me up by the arm. It is **NINE**-a.*

"For God's sake, Leah—what are you doing down on the floor? Get up right now!"

I hear my voice saying that the clock is broken. The clock is lying on the floor in many pieces and the little yellow bird will never again pop out of its open door above my head at the dinner table and count the hours. OurFather will now beat me until I ring like a Chinese gong. **NINE**-a laughed—long and hard until she coughed.

She looked into my eyes and called me an idiot and a fool.

She says that OurFather was joking—he was teasing me. But I remember the look in his cold, hard eyes and the tone of his voice, and how he called me **LEAH ANNE**. And I know that deep in his heart, he was not joking. He torments me and he likes to see my fear. I realized with sudden clarity that teasing is not funny. It is mean and cruel and grownups should know better.

Something changed in me that day. As I glared up at my stepmother, I remembered the look on my teacher's face as she tormented me over some stupid arithmetic mistake and how she, too, pulled me up by the arm and laughed at me. I put a seal over my heart—a wall as tall and wide as the universe—and I took back my power, whatever power a little kid has. I regretted the teasing I had dealt out to Robbie the summer of Hatchet Annie and vowed never to hurt someone as I was hurt by OurFather and **NINE**-a. The beating I had anticipated with the demise of the clock would have hurt far less than the great hole torn in my innocence. I suppose I had thought that sometime, in some far-off future, OurFather would look at me with pride and tell me that he had made a mistake the day he left me sitting and crying in that Callow Avenue alley beside the dumpsters. Now I knew the day would never come.

The time of testing was over, and the door in my heart labeled *OurFather* slammed shut with a bang.

CHAPTER 7
In Which I Learn about Pianos

While we were still living at the farm, OurGrandmother came to visit with an ulterior motive, according to Daddy. She needed a home for her piano, and as we now had enough room to allot a spot in our living room (preferably on an inside wall) she was willing to allow us the privilege of using it. The usage came with strings attached, albeit those strings pleased Mama in one regard and not in the other.

OurGrandmother had been in touch with OurFather in California and he had agreed to pay for one set of music lessons for 'the children' (obviously, Danny and me, as Robbie was not his child). According to her, she was to be the sole arbiter as to which child had the honor of using her precious ivory keys to learn the art of piano music.

The second condition was that Mama should have the piano thoroughly cleaned, tuned, and repaired at her and Daddy's expense.

Both Mama and Daddy agreed that the piano, a magnificent although badly damaged cabinet grand, should come to live with us, but were somewhat hesitant in agreeing to pay for all necessary repairs. As Mama pointed out, the piano had for some long years been stored in a garage, nibbled at by mice and badly used by her older brother's children, in whose garage it had resided.

In the end, OurGrandmother agreed to half the cost, and the magnificent old lady, as I came to call the piano, came to live in our house.

This particular piano had a history. It had come to OurGrandmother on her fourth birthday, she being somewhat of a prodigy at the instrument. The piano was superlative—her harp, (I always thought of the piano in the feminine) tilted sideways to fit in the upright cabinet, was grand piano size, her outside was an ebony finish over rosewood, with ivories and ebonies of the best quality. When properly tuned, she sang—a tribute to her many years of mellowing the wood and strings and felts that composed her music apparatus. She had magnificent, pressed copper panels replete with vines and cherubs adorning her upper front, the music stand, and two large panels below the keys where the pedals snuggled at the bottom. If I sat on the stool my feet just touched the bottom panels and I loved to caress the surfaces with my toes. My fingers wandered gently over the broken and scratched ivories as mellow tones vibrated up my arms and thrilled my soul. I knew I had been born to play that piano.

OurGrandmother had played at Carnegie Hall when she was twelve years old, and this piano had sat upon that prestigious stage for that performance. In later years, having married and born four children, she was obliged to care for them after a rather nasty divorce. She used this piano to play at movie theaters across the country from Michigan to Washington State, where she met and married my grandfather and bore him two children, Mama and Auntie Nor.

During the Great Depression, OurGrandmother, now divorced from my Grandpa Stevens, lived with various relatives from California up the coast to Bremerton. For several years, the piano was stored in a Bremerton garage where Mama's young niece and nephew trod up and down the keyboard with their shoes and the mice had made nests inside. When the hired truck delivered her into our custody, Daddy and his friends trundled her in on a huge dolly. She was missing one of her four tiny wheels so Daddy propped a cube of wood under her leg to replace (temporarily) the missing item, positioning her with great care against the inside living room wall shared with Mama and Daddy's bedroom.

We were all present as Daddy removed the padded cushions revealing her scarred and battered body. Mama gasped at the hammer marks on the keyboard cover, remarking to Daddy that such abuse was criminal. Daddy muttered a few Czech words under his breath and took a deep pull on his pipe, blue smoke escaping his mouth and curling up the sides of his face. Closer inspection revealed many of the ivories had had their tips broken off, obviously by that same hammer. Mama began to cry. Daddy took her in his arms and murmured that the damage could be repaired, and if it took more than her mother was willing to help with, we would make do.

OurGrandmother had Auntie Nor drive her out to the farm on Sunday to inspect the piano. "Well, have you found someone to restore it to service," she demanded after a cursory inspection and a running of the keys revealed it to be badly out of tune and several strings short of a full harp.

"I have located a tuner," Mama replied. "One of the doctors at The Clinic recommended him, so he should be able to do a decent job. I don't know what to do about the appearance, though."

"Let that be, Mayleen, and get the thing in service. When that is accomplished, I will decide who is to receive the lessons," and she motioned for Auntie Nor that she was ready to leave.

"Mama, don't you want to stay for a cup of tea, at least? You haven't been out here for a month. The children would love to have you visit a bit, and Hal can take you to town when you are ready if sis needs to get home to her family." Mama took her mother's arm and tried to seat her in the armchair next to her. OurGrandmother snatched herself away, holding her large purse to her bosom as if for protection, and turned to leave. "Some other time, Mayleen," she murmured with distaste, "I have seen quite enough of your ragamuffins for the moment."

Mama's face crumpled up and I thought she was going to cry. Daddy puffed furiously on his pipe, gripping the stem so tightly between his teeth I thought it might break.

Robbie's mouth flew open and he pulled at my leg until I leaned down to him. "What's a ragged muffin," he whispered. "Is it like a pickaninny?" Danny hissed at him and demanded to know where he had heard that word. "*She* says it," he pouted, pointing at OurGrandmother. "Well don't *you* say, it, or Mama'll give you a fair old whacking," Danny replied. Robbie stuck his thumb in his mouth and commenced sucking. Danny turned away in disgust and left for our shared bedroom before he blurted out something Mama would think required punishment.

I had no illusions about my mother's female parent and her disregard for our family. Nonetheless, I stood spellbound by that fabulous piano now adorning our living room, praying that OurGrandmother would choose me for the privileged lessons.

Within a few weeks, the tuner appeared. He repaired the harp, replaced a few felts and broken hammers, and did his best to restore her to full voice. "Sorry I can't do anything for the outside, ma'am," he remarked to Mama. "That pressed copper is really special. And from her tone, I can tell this is a special instrument."

Mama sat on the stool Daddy had retrieved from the dump and refinished in black. The seat was on a long screw that allowed one to raise or lower it appropriately for the height of the player. She adjusted it and opened a piece of music. With a blissful sigh, she reached her small hands out to the keys and brought forth melody. I watched her hands dip and rise and fly over the restored keys, mesmerized by her ability to pull such beauty from ivory and ebony.

Mama paused in the playing and turned to me, twirling around on the stool. "Come have a try, Cookie. I wish I could play as well as your grandmother can, but she didn't teach me much. Let's see how you like it." She pulled me up on her lap and showed me how to place my hands on the keys. The ivories felt cool and smooth beneath my fingertips. I gingerly pushed down with the little finger of my right hand and was rewarded by a gentle tone. Mama gently laid her hands over mine and pressed our fingers down, playing a simple tune. Mary Had a Little Lamb twinkled into the room.

"Oh, Mama," I whispered in awe. "Do you think *she* will

pick me for the lessons?" Mama patted my shoulder and lifted me from her lap. "If you would like to learn, I'll put in a good word for you."

Over the next few weeks OurGrandmother 'evaluated' Danny and me, according to Auntie Nor, while determining which of us deserved the privilege of lessons. Mama mentioned that in the best of all worlds OurGrandmother could give the lessons herself, therefore including both of us. She declined the opportunity, pointing out that her responsibilities lay with tending to Auntie Nor's children. Daddy shook his head and muttered to Mama that she should have known better than to expect reason from her mother. Danny wanted nothing to do with piano lessons. He grumbled under his breath every time the subject came up, "For your sake, Leah, I hope she picks you. At least you *want* to learn."

At one of her evaluations, as she sat sipping a hot cup of tea made, as she pointed out to Mama, "properly, in the way of polite society" with two cubes of sugar and hot milk, her eyes became cloudy as she gazed at me. I smiled at her, hoping to gain favor in them. In a low, disembodied voice, she spoke directly to me, her words sending an icy finger down each side of my spine. "You don't need lessons, little girl who is not a child. The music is inside you already. Someday you will let it loose."

"What did you say, Mama?" Auntie Nor looked up from her cup of tea.

"I didn't say anything," snapped OurGrandmother.

My aunt's eyes met mine, a puzzled rise to her eyebrows, as I sat silently contemplating the cup of cocoa clasped between my hands. I had heard her tell my auntie before that

I was not a child. I had seen her eyes do that funny clouding over thing before when she would speak oddly with a different cadence to her words—words that seemed to foretell future events. These episodes, unreported by me, had happened on a few occasions when Robbie and I were alone with her. Her demeanor frightened Robbie who would hide his head in my chest and tremble. Her words made me lie awake at night and think on things to come.

In the end, the lessons went to Danny. She admitted that OurFather in California was actually paying the freight, so to speak, and *his* vote was the one that counted. Daniel was the son, he was older, and therefore, more likely to benefit from the lessons.

I was crushed; Danny was outraged, and Mama just shook her head. "I suppose he paid for her half of the piano tuning, too," we heard her tell Daddy that night. Daddy replied that he thought OurFather was trying to buy his way back into our lives.

Danny commenced with his piano instruction, reporting under duress to Ted Brown Music on Thursday afternoons, all the while protesting to Mama that he was missing football practice. Mama arranged for me to sit in on the lessons, observing but not actually laying hands on the instrument, a brown studio piano with little character. Every week Danny tried his best to dodge out, but Mama was firm. Her children would take this opportunity and make the most of it.

I listen quietly, taking in every aspect of Danny's lessons, putting them to use at the piano whenever Mama lets me have time. Danny's practicing comes first, of course, as his progress is closely monitored by OurGrandmother, who reports (se-

cretly, she thinks) to OurFather in California. Auntie Nor keeps Mama apprised of this duplicity, risking OurGrandmother's wrath if she is caught out. Apparently, he was pleased, as the lessons continued, and I sucked in every bit of it.

When my time to practice came, I rolled the piano seat as high as it would go on the sturdy screw, climbed up, and carefully opened Danny's copy of John Thompson's Piano Course for Beginning Students. Then, as I applied each lesson to the piano, my stocking feet caressed the copper panels, keeping the cherubs and vines brightly polished. Although I practiced every day, Danny was the one who performed at the recital.

I sit next to Daddy and Mama and watch with pride as my big brother plays his recital piece even though in my mind, I am the one sitting at the shiny black grand piano in the recital room, my fingers darting back and forth across the keyboard. The audience is mesmerized by my talent, and Mama and Daddy beam in their seats. I rise from the piano bench, music in hand, and make a curtsy to the audience who applaud my performance. Daddy whistles and stamps his feet and Mama leans to him and whispers into his ear "oh, Hal, don't embarrass her!" The teacher presents me with a plaque of accomplishment.

But it is Danny who stands when his name is announced. It is Danny who plays his piece, perfectly, but without much enthusiasm. He smiles at Mama and Daddy when he receives his framed certificate, then scurries over to his seat and plops down with relief. I scowl at him. It should have been me. He puts his arm around me and whispers that he has plans for the rest of the lessons. If he has his way, the next recital will be mine. Even though those plans never materialized, and Danny received lessons for four more years, I loved that my big brother had tried his best for me.

In the end, OurGrandmother's piano sits in my living room. Danny can't play a note, but I do, every day, even though my eyes grow dim and my fingers don't fly nearly as swiftly or as accurately across the keys. Mozart and Chopin and Debussy fill the room on sunny afternoons. Sometimes, when I am alone in the house, OurGrandmother enters my body and plays through me. On those days, the music is glorious, and I can hear her whisper in my ear that she was right about me—my soul is old and I was never a child in this lifetime, but I had opened myself to the music, and it came forth. *Once I thought I heard her say that she was sorry, but perhaps I was just imagining it.*

CHAPTER 8
In Which I Learn the Truth
about Affairs of the Heart

Mama could no longer afford the rent on our large Tacoma house with what she made at the college, so she packed us up and moved us into a small, two-bedroom duplex in Park View—back in Bremerton and closer to her family. All the spare furniture, including the lamp table where Amanda Sue's now long forgotten doll sat hidden by an old pillow, was taken by Daddy and stored in Aunt Barbara's barn in Federal Way, including Mama's (and my) beloved piano. Robbie and I settled into classes at Park View Elementary school as if we had never left. Danny rode the bus to the Junior High School in town, glad to be reunited with all his friends from grade school, although he failed to tell them that we no longer lived on the farm.

Christmas came and went, and the New Year blew in cold, windy, and spitting snow. Mama found a job keeping books and answering the phone at the local fuel company, arranging deliveries of coal and oil to families all over the area. To augment her income, she worked Friday and Saturday nights at a local bottle club where she checked coats and hats and umbrellas for tips. Mama had obtained her job at the bottle club through an old high school friend, Lee.

When we lived on the farm, Mama and Daddy often socialized with Lee and his family. They had horses boarded out in the area and came on the weekends to ride. Lee and his wife Joyce had three children, two sons aged the same as Danny and Robbie, and a daughter, Penny, who was just a year or so older than me. He also had a cabin on one of the local lakes where we often joined them during the long summer days. I'm not sure if Daddy knew that Mama and Lee had been more than just friends when they were younger, but it was obvious that Lee still thought of Mama as desirable. Mama laughed off his puppyish advances and Daddy didn't seem to take them seriously.

Over the Fourth of July celebration the summer before we left the farm, both families spent a couple of days at Mason Lake at Lee's family cabin. Penny and I played with our dolls in the remains of a dilapidated outbuilding adjacent to the cabin. The boys fished and splashed around in the muddy-bottomed lake, their laughter peppering the warm summer air far into the evening. After dinner, Daddy and Lee built a fire and we all sat around roasting marshmallows and making S'mores until it got dark enough for the community fireworks to start. The boys ran around like maniacs, their sparklers spraying the velvety sky with bright stars. Firecrackers rattled grownup nerves and rockets decorated the sky with brilliant displays of color and splendor.

As the celebration wound to an end, one of the lakeside groups started lighting off Roman candles. A few older boys ran around aiming the missiles in reckless abandon, narrowly missing each other and once accidentally setting some lakeside brush on fire. Daddy and Lee tried to run them off, away from us children, but not before a stray spark landed directly in my left eye. Fortunately, the little gunpowder particle was nearly spent before it hit me, or the damage to my eye would have been more severe. Even so, by morning it had swelled shut and was extremely painful. Daddy had to return to his job in the shipyard and the rest of us were planning to stay until the weekend when Daddy would retrieve us. Lee offered to take Mama and me into Shelton to find a doctor to tend to my eye. His wife stayed behind, keeping track of Penny and our brothers. Danny had apparently heard of Lee long before I was aware of him, as he whispered to me when we were in bed one night that OurFather accused Mama of 'having a fling' with Lee. This happened shortly before I was born during one of their arguments over his roving ways. After he left with Gemma, he told everyone in town that Mama had named me Leah because Lee was really my father.

"Don't worry about it," Danny consoled me when I began crying, "OurFather named you after our great-grandma, Leah Anne who lived in South Dakota. Mama wanted to name you Holly 'cuz you was born at Christmas, but you got stuck with Leah, instead. He was just tryin' to make Mama feel bad about throwin' him out!"

I sit alone in the back seat, a bag of ice held tight to my eye. I cannot help but notice, however, that Lee keeps looking over at Mama and smiling. Mama smiles back, and quietly slips her hand across the seat and pats his. I think to myself that these two people have a history, and quite probably still have feelings for each other. I hope that Daddy has not seen that look in Mama's eyes when hers meet Lee's. She and Daddy are supposed to have that look for each other.

In the end, my eye mended, except for a little scar that didn't bother me too much. We moved off the farm and into town and except for once when we ran into Lee and Penny at the pony market, they seemed to have lost touch with each other. Now he was back in Mama's life, and I didn't know what to think! I supposed that Mama needed a friend; after all, Daddy had one, but that didn't seem right to me. I vowed to talk to Danny about it if the subject ever came up.

"Are you ashamed of where we are living?" Mama inquired of Danny one afternoon when she overheard him telling Robbie and me not to give our address to any of his old friends. He shrugged and smiled sheepishly at Mama.

"Do you think I want my friends to know we live in a dump like this?"

Mama sighed deeply.

"You have a roof over your head, young man, and food on the table. I would think you'd thank the good Lord for that." I thought I detected the brightness of a tear at the corner of her eye as she turned back to chopping vegetables for stew, but maybe it was the onions.

Danny stomped off in an ugly mood. I made a mental note not to cross his path any time soon.

The place was old, but far from a dump. Actually, Mama had made it quite homey with our own curtains and rugs and furniture. It was small, forcing Danny and Robbie to share a bedroom. I bunked with Mama and sometimes on the nights she did not work, we talked like two little kids far into the wee hours. We may have lacked a few of the niceties, like a telephone, but none of the necessities. She worked two jobs to make sure we had them and kept the house and our clothing clean and patched as well. Most of all, we had our mother's unconditional love. Oh, Danny and I helped—he, reluctantly, but how much can a couple of little kids really do?

Daddy was another matter. Now that Mama had taken a stand and moved us away from his neglect, he was incensed, actually recruiting OurGrandmother to his side. She rode the city bus up to Park View on our second Sunday back to plead his case with Mama who ordered Danny, Robbie, and me into the boys' small bedroom while they talked. She closed the door firmly behind her, but Danny carefully re-opened it a crack so that we could hear their conversation. Mama had 'that look' on her face and we had seen sparks fly between Mama and OurGrandmother before. With heads touching, we crowded as close as possible to the door. OurGrandmother was speaking in her no-nonsense you'd-better-listen-up tone of voice.

"Well, all I can say is that you have certainly dealt with the matter of Cookie in an unsatisfactory manner."

"What does she mean by that?" I queried Danny. He just shook his head.

Mama mumbled something barely out of our hearing and OurGrandmother continued.

"You and Hal allow her to bury what happened when you should be forcing her to face up to the truth. She's just going to keep having nightmares until she remembers and it's your fault. If you wish, I'll have a talk with her, myself."

Mama obviously answered that in the negative as OurGrandmother harrumphed. I had been on the receiving end of that particular sound on several occasions.

OurGrandmother was a nurse and she preferred to deal with the real world, as she called it. No fancy imaginings for her. I tried her patience in that regard.

Mama continued the conversation quietly. I strained to hear if she was talking about me but caught only the rise and fall of her soft voice. After a few minutes, Danny began fidgeting and muttering under his breath, but before he could act on his impatience the voices raised in volume.

"These children need their father," Our Grandmother admonished. "Why should he support them if he can't even see them?"

"Nobody prevented his visiting all the time we were alone in Tacoma," Mama retorted. "I sure didn't see any support, either. That's why I moved them here, where I can at least pay our way."

Grandmother snorted. "You call this providing—commodities oatmeal and butter and eggs? I tell you it is embarrassing to know that my grandchildren are practically living on welfare!" She paused for a moment.

Danny and I looked at each other in amazement. It was one thing for Danny to intimate that our living conditions were beneath his standards, but this was the first hint we had of how badly off we were.

"Daddy should be helping Mama out," Danny hissed into my ear. He was so annoyed that little drops of spittle dampened the side of my head.

"I been cuttin' him slack on a lotta the stuff he's been doin' lately 'cuz I thought he was at least helpin' Mama pay the bills." His voice rose to within a heartbeat of being heard by Mama and OurGrandmother in the living room. Without thinking, I clamped my hand across his mouth and he snatched it away, giving me one of his patented one-eyebrow glares. He had a way of beetling his eyebrows together so that they met in the middle—a look that meant he was extremely annoyed. Today I knew he meant it for Daddy.

From the living room, OurGrandmother's voice rose in scarcely controlled anger. "You are the one who threw him out."

Mama took a deep breath. "Need I remind you, Mother— he is seeing another woman!"

"It has been my experience," retorted OurGrandmother, "that a man who is getting all of his needs met at home has no need to stray. Remember, Mayleen—once may be the man's fault, but twice is another story."

"That does it," Danny snorted. I wasn't quite sure what OurGrandmother meant, but apparently, Danny did. He hurled himself through the door like an enraged bull.

"You can just quit being mean to my mother." Danny stood, hands on hips, straddle legged, between OurGrandmother and Mama, quite obviously ready to defend her to the death. "Daddy is the one who caused the trouble, and he's the only one that can fix it. And keep out a Leah's business, too!"

That last part caught me by surprise—I had no idea what business he was talking about, but I appreciated his defense.

"Well!" OurGrandmother huffed through clenched teeth. "It is obvious that you lack any sort of good manners at all, Daniel! And to think I have wasted piano lessons on you."

"I didn't ask for 'em, did I? You shoulda given 'em to Leah. She loves the piano and now it's prob'ly too late, 'cuz a her eyes."

Danny's outburst caught Mama completely off guard, but she recovered quickly.

"That'll be enough out of you, young man! Apologize to your grandmother."

"And if I don't?" snarled a defiant Danny. "You gonna have Daddy give me a spanking? I'm the man of the family around here, and I guess it's up to me to defend you and my sister. Nobody else is gonna do it!"

"If your mother were acting in the proper manner, no one would need to defend her," retorted OurGrandmother. She rose from her chair and drew herself to full height.

OurGrandmother was an awesome sight when she was angry. She was several inches taller than Mama and outweighed her by close to a hundred pounds. She stood straight as an arrow, encased by an old-fashioned string tied corset. Other kids had grandmothers you could cuddle with—OurGrandmother presented more armor than a tank and she used her girth as a weapon. She seemed perpetually annoyed except when she dealt with our aunt's offspring. Family rumor held that she favored Aunt Noreen because Mama still spoke with our grandfather who, whether finally tiring of OurGrandmother's off-putting ways or her hundred hook corset had found himself someone else. Apparently, she failed to take to heart her own advice about wandering husbands, blaming him entirely for their divorce.

Mama found her voice on this Sunday afternoon.

"Leave him out of this, Mother. I'll deal with him later. I think it's time for you to go home."

"If that is how you feel, I will be on my way. Don't ask for help, my dear. You won't be receiving it until you come to your senses." She eyed my mother up and down, her glance settling on Mama's flat tummy, then she retrieved her large pocketbook and coat and strode slowly out the front door. It slammed behind her as if adding an exclamation point to her exit.

"Well! That was a truly unpleasant visit. Trust my mother always to be on hand to help in a crisis!" Mama sounded sarcastic as she viewed the still quivering front door. "Now, on to another unpleasant piece of business." She turned to Danny. "Just what did you imagine you could accomplish by confronting your grandmother that way?"

Danny shuffled his feet.

"Well—speak up, young man!"

Danny appeared to regain his earlier courage.

"I couldn't let her keep talkin' to you like that, Mama. Whatever Daddy's done, it's his fault. And what was all that stuff about Leah and her nightmares?"

"Don't try to sidestep the issue. You were rude and out of line," Mama paused as if catching her breath, "and I love you for sticking up for your sister and for me—just don't ever do that again, promise?"

Danny said he would try.

Mama continued; "Whatever the problems are between your daddy and me, they have nothing to do with you and Robbie and Leah. We just have to work these things out between the two of us. Your daddy loves you, you know that. Now, let's try and make the rest of today a little more pleasant."

I wasn't so sure that Daddy loved us—if he did, how could he love another woman?

CHAPTER 9
In Which I Learn the Folly of Crime

Now that we were living back in Bremerton, my aunt Mary Anne occasionally brought Amanda Sue and little Philip to visit us. They were living in a small apartment court next to Auntie Nor's house on Cambrian Avenue in Bremerton within a few doors of OurGrandmother's unit. It was not the most comfortable place for them to live, but it was cheap and close to family.

On this particular occasion, Auntie Mary Anne dropped off Amanda Sue to stay the day with me and provide me with a little cousinly company, taking Little Philip with her. I wasn't very happy with the thought of spending the afternoon with Amanda. After our episode with the cowboy boots and my horrible ride home from California, we didn't speak much. It was apparent that we did not like each other, and that was not going to change in the near future unless something drastic transpired.

Amanda Sue minced through the front door announcing her entrance with a swirl. "Well, Cookie, I intend to initiate you into my new club today!" She grinned evilly and chuckled deep in her throat. "Only three of my friends belong to the club. You will be in good company — *if* you qualify, that is."

Mama raised her eyebrows and stared in Amanda Sue's direction, making a questioning harrumph in her throat. She didn't exactly trust Amanda Sue's intentions as my cousin had proved untrustworthy in the past. She glanced at me, with that what-are-you-going-to-do look on her face. I knew she meant for me to be careful as it wasn't difficult for Amanda Sue to get herself and everyone with her into trouble.

With a flounce, Amanda Sue plopped down on the sofa and motioned for me to join her there. She patted the cushions and when I seemed reluctant, she leaned towards me with a conspiratorial look on her face. "Listen carefully, Cookie," she whispered in my ear. "We are gonna take a little walk, just you and me, and then I'll tell you what you need to do to join."

"Just what kind of club is this?" I queried. I had been bitten by her little schemes in the past and had no desire to end up in trouble, either with Mama, or Auntie Mary Anne. Danny slithered by grinning like a Cheshire cat. I wondered if he knew what our cousin was up to and whether he had a part in it.

"Do you care if Cookie and I go for a walk, Auntie Mayleen? It's kinda stuffy in here and the weather is so nice outside."

Mama thought for a moment before she answered. "I need some hot dogs for lunch from the market down on Kitsap Way. I know it's a ways to go but it should give both of you a good walk and a chance to talk. Are you up for it?"

Amanda Sue pursed her rosebud lips and tapped her cheek with her right index finger. "I'd love to get hot dogs for you, Auntie Mayleen. That will give Cookie and me enough time for the initiation."

"Just what 'initiation' are you talking about." Mama squinched up her eyes and gave Amanda one of her sideways looks. Danny and I knew exactly what Mama's look meant, but Amanda Sue just smiled up at her and flashed her dimples. Mama once opined that Amanda could charm the wimple from a Nun's head if she put her mind to it. After a bit of explaining from Mama about nun's headgear, I heartily agreed with her. And, in my own opinion (kept firmly to myself) if she couldn't charm it away, she would just yank it off and run, giggling with that sharp little tinkling sound she made—so endearing, according to her mother, but a sound that gave me goosebumps. At any rate, Amanda Sue smiled up at Mama.

"Oh, it's just a little club with a few of my friends in it. We get together now and then and go to the movies. You wouldn't mind if Leah went to the movies with us, would you? It would be on a Saturday and just the Admiral Theater downtown. It doesn't cost much."

Mama cocked her head and nodded back and forth. "I guess that would be okay, once in a while." She smiled at me and said "It's nice of your cousin to invite you. I know you'll enjoy the movies. Now, here's some money for a pound of hot dogs." She handed the money to me. "You know what kind we like, honey—the ones with the crunchy skins." I took the dollar bill and tucked it with care into the pocket of my jeans.

I glanced at the kitchen clock as we headed out the back door, Amanda Sue and me and the dollar bill for the hot dogs. It was close to 11 AM, and I knew that it would take us twenty minutes or more to walk the twelve long blocks to Kitsap Way and Cushman's market.

Holly's Sundries sits right next door to the market. I love to go there and walk up and down each aisle, looking with envy at the many interesting items on display. Although my hands long to touch the papers and pencils, threads and bits of cloth, I keep them to myself. The shop has its own special smell, of sharpened pencils and handmade beeswax candles and soaps scented with lavender and lemon. The lady who owns the store likes me, and often gives me a sweet candy or a taste of ice cream from her deli fountain. Sometimes I sweep the porch for her or perform some other little chore. It makes me feel good inside to know that I have done something for the candy or the taste of ice cream or sometimes just the length of time I spend wandering up and down the aisles. I am lonely and have a lot of time on my hands, especially on the weekends, when Robbie and Danny often do their boy things. Mama works and that leaves me alone most of the days when school is out. Although I read books from the library in town and draw (when I have paper and pencils) I am still lonely.

Now, along came Amanda Sue with her offer. I should have been flattered to be included. She and her friends were older than me, and much more sophisticated, but I was still suspicious. Once bitten twice shy, my mama always said, and I had been bitten, literally and figuratively, on several occasions by my wily cousin.

As we walked down the rutted road towards Kitsap Way Amanda Sue skipped ahead, humming to herself and pretending to play Hopscotch. She seemed to have lost interest in me, although occasionally she would slant her eyes to the right and flutter her lashes. After a few minutes, I inquired about who else was in her club.

"Well, you wouldn't know them, would you." She said it

with a little snicker in her voice. "They don't go to your school, after all. *You* go to this school in the projects; *I* go to school downtown where the normal kids live."

"What you mean by normal kids?" I demanded.

"You know, the kids who have a mom and dad who live in the same house." She smiled widely, showing the dimples on each rosy cheek, her perfect curly black hair framing that cherub's face of hers. She wriggled her nose and sniffed as if something smelled bad. "And *their* moms don't work in the bottle club."

I had a sudden urge to slap her but stayed my hand at the last minute. Assaulting her would do me no good, as she was both bigger and nastier than I, and Mama would be angry that I hadn't held my temper in check. She was trying to make me into a lady, she often explained with exasperation when she caught me rough-housing with Danny and Robbie. Mama worked two jobs to keep a roof over our heads. Days, she kept books and answered phones for the Ice Company that made deliveries to stores and homes all over the county. On Friday and Saturday nights she checked coats and hats at the Carlo Club downtown, accepting tips in a little jar at her window for her service. Those tips made the difference between no shoes and new shoes for her three kids; besides, Amanda Sue's mom spent many a Saturday night having a cocktail or two with friends at that very same club.

"That's not fair," I exclaimed, "your daddy doesn't live with you, either. He's still in California and your mom works in the shipyard!" Amanda Sue whirled around and glared at me, teeth bared and hands balled into fists. I thought she was going to hit me so I jerked backward and stumbled over the curb, falling hard on the ground. She laughed, pointing at me as I lay sprawled on my fanny on the broken black tar road in the thin winter sun.

"I don't think I want to be in your club."

"It doesn't matter," she sneered, "you're gonna join whether you want to or not!" I stared at her hard as I got back up, brushing the dirt off my jeans. Mama wouldn't like it if I had a fight on the public street, even though I felt as if Amanda Sue deserved a good smacking. We resumed our walk towards the market on Kitsap Way, although any charity I felt towards my cousin when we started out a few moments before was gone from my heart.

After perhaps fifty yards she turned to me and offered her hand. "I'm sorry, Cookie. I didn't mean to be mean. Sometimes I just can't help it! Friends?" She gave a smile that made her dimples pop, but her eyes didn't reflect it. They remained cold as their ice-blue color and mirrored the hesitant look on my face. Reluctantly, I took her hand and she pulled me up beside her. We walked that way until we came to Kitsap Way.

Traffic on Kitsap Way was known to be dangerous. It wasn't safe to cross anywhere except at the signal and we had caught it on the red. The road, descending from a rise to the west called Dead Man's Hill, was steep and curved, and the site of many accidents, not a few of which had proved fatal to the occupants of the vehicles involved. Not without irony, the local cemetery spread out over half the hill and spilled onto the relatively flat area beyond its bottom where the road straightened out due east.

After a few seconds wait, the light turned green and we crossed as quickly as we could, dodging the cars eager to make a right-hand turn. I stopped at the door of the butcher shop, fully intending to purchase Mama's pound of hot dogs, but Amanda Sue pulled me forward.

"What'ja doing that for Amanda Sue? Mama needs these hot dogs and it's getting late." She pointed towards Holly's Sundries next door.

"You wanna belong to my club or not?"

"I already told'ja no," I replied with indignation. I had my doubts that this initiation she talked about was going to be good for anyone.

"It's really easy to join," she whispered. "All you have to do is take *one little thing* from the variety store." She must have seen the shocked look on my face because she laughed and said, "It's just a little thing, and all the other members have done it. Don'tcha know that these stores expect people'll take little things? It's all worked into their bookkeeping or something. I heard my mom talking about it with Auntie Nor. She works at the Woolworths, you know, and people take stuff from there all the time. It's called shoplifting and all the kids in town are doing it."

"My mom says stealing is wrong, no matter what you call it or where you do it! Even if it's just an apple from someone else's field, it's stealing and it's *wrong*." I remember the lesson about stealing from Sunday School and reminded Amanda about it. "'Thou Shall Not Steal,' Mandy. It says so in the Ten Commandments that Moses carried. I won't do it."

I yank my hand away from hers as if a bee has stung me and I stand as tall as possible with my hands on my hips and I stare up at her with her beautiful blue eyes and that innocent smile and those sweet dimples. Mama has taught me that stealing hurts other people, even if we do not know the other people. The lady who owns the variety store is my friend. I do not want to hurt her. Amanda Sue says I am an idiot. Her mama does not mind if she steals and my mama will not know about it if I do not tell. I know what is wrong and what is right. It is wrong to steal and it is wrong to lie and I will not do it just to belong to somebody's club—even Amanda Sue's!

"And the Bible says 'you shouldn't sleep with other people's wives,' too. That doesn't stop your daddy or mine from doin' it."

That puzzled me. What was wrong with sleeping with someone? Danny and Robbie and I all slept together in the same room—occasionally in the same bed if Robbie were having bad dreams.

Quick as a snake my cousin Amanda Sue snatched my hand and bent it back, hard against my wrist. Her peaches and cream face turned tomato soup red and she spit in my ear "You are **GONNA** go in there and steal something, and you are **GONNA** belong to my club and you better not tell your **MOTHER,** either!" With each emphasized word she pressed my hand harder. No matter how I tried, I could not wrest it from her grip. Tears streamed down my cheeks and little globs of snot dribbled from my nose.

"Well," she hissed. "What do you say."

I said okay as I wiped my nose and eyes on my shirt sleeve. She released my hand, smiled broadly, and motioned towards the door of Holly's Sundries.

"I'll just wait here until you're finished," she smirked.

The lady at the counter smiles at me as I open the door and enter. "Having a nice day?" she asks. I nod my head and try to smile, then stroll down the aisle closest to the door as casually as possible. When I get to the end of the first row of shelves, I hear the bell on the door ding. The lady at the counter says hello and chats with whoever has come in. I can hear them chattering as someone picks out candies and asks for a pint of hand packed ice cream—chocolate, the kind with swirls of dark syrup through it. I turn around the end and continue along the second aisle until I come to the sewing things. I look for something small and surreptitiously pocket a packet of needles, the kind Mama puts in the old White treadle sewing machine she uses to make dresses and pinafores for me to wear to school. I can feel the blood rise in my face and the packet of needles seems to weigh me down. As quickly as I can, I skip back to the door, waving at the counter lady as I leave. "Come back soon," she says to my back. "I need the porch swept."

The minute I cleared the doorway and the door swung shut, Amanda Sue yanked me down the sidewalk. "Well, didja do it?" she hissed. I produced the packet of sewing machine needles and proffered it as proof of my theft. "Not much," she chortled, "but enough to be a thief! Well, I didn't think you'd do it, but you're in."

The packet of needles lies in my hand, small and white, with black swirls surrounding its black print. "Machine Needles, Singer Size 90-14, Qty 5". Not weighing as much as a penny, that little packet feels as heavy as the anchor from one of the big navy ships that Amanda Sue's Mama works on in the shipyard.

"Don'tcha want 'em? I tried to thrust the packet into Amanda Sue's hand.

Amanda Sue shook her head. "Na, that's not something I

want. You can keep 'em."

Slipping the object of my guilt into my pocket, I encountered the dollar bill for Mama's hot dogs. I nearly bolted into Holly's Sundries to pay for the needles but stopped myself at the last moment. Instead, in silence, I entered the butcher shop next door and quietly asked for a pound of wieners, the kind with the crunchy skin.

Amanda Sue chattered brightly on the twenty minute walk back home, but I didn't say a word. I walked with my shoulders hunched together and my head down so that no one on the sidewalk could see the big red T branded on my forehead. *"If Daddy were here," I think to myself, "I could tell him about what my cousin has made me do." I feel dirty inside and I know that God is probably angry with me. Daddy would hold me close and help take away my guilt. I cannot talk to Mama. She has so much on her mind.* Did Mama and Daddy just forget that Danny and Robbie and I need both of them? I prayed every night that God would send my daddy home.

On Sunday after church, Mama let me walk down to Holly's Sundries by myself. She was a little puzzled since I had been there the day before, but when I explained that the counter lady needed the porch swept, she relented. Mama was proud of me for doing little chores for other people. How could I tell her that my real reason was to return a packet of needles I had stolen at the direction of my cousin! I sneaked into the store, slipped the packet from my pocket, and deposited it back on the shelf. Then I swept the porch for the counter lady and the sidewalk in front of the store, as well. When she offered me a candy, I refused, blushing, and told her I did not deserve it. Before my brain could engage, I heard my mouth telling her what I had done the day before, and that I had returned the purloined needles. I begged her not to tell Mama, as she had enough on her plate without being shamed by a daughter who was a thief. She laughed and told me it would be a secret between us. I had paid my debt by returning the needles and confessing my crime. Relieved, I ran all the way home, but I never returned to Holly's Sundries without my mother.

CHAPTER 10
In Which I Receive My Just Desserts

The following week Mama had a telephone installed. We were on a twelve party line, but at least we were connected to the world again. Danny called his friends first thing and gave out our number. Mama let the family know but asked that no one tell Daddy. "I don't know how long that will last," Mama exclaimed when she was finished telling OurGrandmother. "I almost didn't let her in on the secret but figured *someone* would give your daddy the number."

One of the first callers was Auntie Mary Anne. "Amanda Sue would like Cookie to come down on Saturday and go to the matinee with a group of her friends, is that okay with you? If you put her on the bus, I'll meet her at our stop and the kids can all go together. I'll make sure she's home before you have to go to work." Much to my horror, Mama accepted the invitation before I had a chance to refuse.

"I don't understand you, Cookie. Here you are, cooped up all weekend and now you don't want to go to the movies with your cousin?" I couldn't tell her the truth—that I was ashamed of letting Amanda Sue intimidate me into becoming a thief. Notwithstanding that I had returned the item, the fact remained that I had stolen it in the first place.

On Saturday, Danny and I boarded the bus together. He planned to meet a few of his friends and hang out downtown. He practically shoved me off at the Callow Avenue bus stop in Charleston where Auntie Mary Anne and Amanda Sue waited.

"Where's your club member friends," I queried Amanda Sue as we walked up Fifth Street towards the downtown theater.

"Oh, they're meeting us there," she smirked. "They had a few 'chores' to do to keep their memberships up to date."

I felt the skin on my back grow cold, goosebumps rising at the thought of what those 'chores' might entail.

In due course, Amanda Sue's three friends joined us, each of whom had brought their 'dues'. These included a bright silk scarf, the kind girls tied around their necks to accessorize a white blouse, a pair of dangle earrings, and a small bottle of cologne. Amanda Sue scrutinized each offering, making sure they still had price tags attached, before proclaiming that they would suffice for the week. She lowered her eyelids and peered at me from beneath her long, black lashes, as if reminding me that membership required sacrifice.

Danny and his buddies followed us into the Admiral Theater along with most of the kids in town, it seemed. He tapped me on the shoulder and whispered in my ear; "What'ja doin', Leah! I saw that funny business goin' on with Amanda Sue and her friends—looked fishy to me. Think I'll tell Mama what you guys're doin'."

"I'm not *doing* anything, *Daniel*," I hissed back at him, little bits of spit shooting out and hitting him on the side of his head for a change. He wiped his face on his shirt sleeve and gave me his patented beetle-brow glare.

"Well, **she's** up to no good, and I know it. So better watch yourself, **Leah!**"

I paid for my ticket and joined Amanda Sue and her friends inside the lobby. Amanda Sue snatched my arm, demanding to know what Danny had said.

"None of your business," I responded smartly, "just some brother stuff."

"Well, you better keep your mouth shut about our club. Boys aren't included."

"And I am excluding myself," I thought silently, "as soon as this movie is over!" Unfortunately, I had no control over the festivities on today's theater agenda.

I followed Amanda Sue and her little group of toadies down the aisle as close to the front of the theater as possible, winding up in the center of row five. From here, I had to crane my neck to see the screen, but at least, with my glasses, I could tell what was going on. I settled in, expecting to watch the cartoons, the serial, the previews and the news, followed by a Gene Autry spaghetti western. The cartoons and serial screened first, but before the previews, the lights came up and the theater manager took the stage. He quickly set up his microphone and announced that all children who had a birthday in February would receive a free ticket for a future Saturday afternoon matinee.

Amanda Sue immediately brightened and stood up, motioning for all of us to stand with her. "Come on," she hissed "he don't know when your birthday really is. We can all go up and get us a ticket. Come on!"

She grabbed me by the wrist and dragged me out of my seat.

"I'm not going up there," I said sharply. "You know my birthday is at Christmas time and yours was last week."

"Too bad," she said. "You're coming with me up on that stage. And as for the rest of you," she turned to the three standing on her left, "you already paid your membership dues this week so sit back down. **Leah** hasn't. She comes with me." They sat, but I could hear them mumbling about not getting their free tickets. Amanda Sue tossed an evil look in their direction, and with that, she pushed me out onto the aisle and hustled me into the line of kids waiting their turn on the stage. In stunned silence I let her manipulate me up the stairs until I stood in front of the microphone, telling everyone in the theater that my name was Leah and my birthday was on the 26th—technically not a lie. My mouth was so dry that the words barely croaked out, and as I turned to leave, ticket in hand, my eyes met Danny's. He stood at the bottom of the stairs and his demeanor boded me no good.

"Well, this will break Mama's heart, Leah, to know what a liar you are—and in front of the whole town, too. Daddy will never take us back when he hears about it. Give me that ticket, right now."

"Are you gonna give it back to the theater?" I asked with a trembling voice. Amanda Sue threw her head back, black curls bouncing on her shoulders, and laughed until tears trickled down her rosy cheeks.

"Of course, he isn't, you dummy. He's gonna keep it for himself."

"*I* didn't steal it, Leah—*you* did. Me'n my buddies'll come next week and I'll have money for popcorn! You better hope that man from the newspaper didn't take your picture. Mom'll whip you for sure if you show up on the front page of the Sunday edition. With a kid like you, no wonder Daddy left."

I was stunned. Not only had Danny taken the ticket (secretly, I was glad that Amanda Sue could not demand it) but I might now cause Mama a public humiliation. I knew in my heart that my parents' breakup had something to do with Daddy's friend, but a little part of me now stood ready to take the blame. I remembered what Daddy said when he realized I had overheard his telephone call on New Years' Eve. It was, therefore, with a heavy heart that I sat back down and watched the movie. Danny met me outside when the lights went up and escorted me to the bus. I mounted the bus steps and rode home in silence with my brother.

In the end, Danny didn't tell Mama about my transgression at the theater. In truth, he couldn't, as he had plans for the ticket and, I guessed, that made him a thief, too, if somewhat after the fact. Never again did I appropriate something that did not belong to me, whether from a store or another person. "Thou Shalt Not Steal", it says in the Bible, and I believed in those Ten Commandments from God. By confessing my crime to Holly at the Sundries Store, my conscience was technically clear, but deep in my soul, the theft of that needle packet smoldered. The theater ticket was another matter, and I did penance for it by giving my movie money to another kid the next time Mama let me go. I waited outside the theater 'til the kids got out.

By definition, I was a thief, a sinner, and as such could be responsible for the breakup of my parents' marriage. It was my fault, and I bore that burden alone.

CHAPTER 11
In Which We Flee for our Lives

On Valentine's Day Daddy made his next move. February 14 was my parents' wedding anniversary and instead of celebrating, Mama was taking care of hats and coats at the bottle club and (probably) flirting with Lee. Danny and Robbie were asleep in their bedroom and I was guiltily reading a library book under the covers lit only by Mama's bedside flashlight when a commotion outside attracted my attention. Someone pounded loudly on the front door, shouting my name. The someone sounded a lot like Daddy, but he was slurring his words. A red light rotating round and round shined through the bedroom window spreading an eerie glow across the wallpaper.

Danny must have wakened and crept silently into Mama's room as I heard a voice close to my ear whisper; "Jiggers—the cops!" I gasped in fear as I pulled the covers over my head, the image of being led away in handcuffs and the sound of 'thief, thief, thief' bouncing back and forth behind my eyes.

Presently the pounding stopped and Daddy (we were certain it was Daddy) told someone that he just wanted to say goodbye to his kids.

"Where do you suppose he's going," I queried.

"I bet the cops are gonna take him to jail," Danny answered solemnly.

"But why would they do that?"

"Cripes, Leah, how would I know!" Danny blurted out in exasperation.

The commotion outside eventually calmed down and the red lights went away, apparently taking Daddy with them. Danny and I cuddled together in Mama's bed, talking quietly and waiting for her to come home.

Mama arrived home in yet another police car.

"Your Daddy had a problem." Mama spoke carefully. We had pelted her with questions when she arrived, flustered and red-faced with tear streaks evident on her cheeks. Now she snuggled between us with the covers pulled tight up to our necks, an arm around each of us. Robbie still slept peacefully in his little twin bed in the next room.

"He had too much to drink and he said some things that scared me."

I could sense that Mama was searching for just the right words to describe the situation without alarming us. "The police will keep him safe until he is sober."

"But what did he say, Mama," Danny pushed for more details.

"Well, honey, he said he wanted to hurt himself, and I was afraid he might do something rash. He told the police he wanted to say good-bye to his children."

Danny gasped. "You mean he was gonna commit suicide?" This was a new word for me and when I inquired as to its meaning, Danny gave me one of his "I can't believe you are so stupid, Leah," looks. "It means kill yourself, doesn't it, Mama?"

"Yes, Danny, it does, and Daddy and I may be having a rough time, but no one wants Daddy to do such a drastic thing."

We talked, the three of us, softly asking and answering questions, until dawn warmed the room with pale light and I fell asleep.

Daddy spent the weekend in jail, and before they released him on Monday morning, we were gone—packed up lock, stock, and barrel. Mama's friends were certain that Daddy was dangerous, although it was hard for me to believe that he could hurt the people he loved. Lee had found us a place to live far from where Daddy might look for us.

"People do stupid stuff all the time, Leah," Danny explained patiently when Robbie was out of earshot. "Don't you listen to the news or read the newspapers?"

Danny was in Junior High and thought he knew everything. The curriculum included Current Events which required him to read the paper every day and keep track of things going on in the world. Basically, this made him an authority on such happenings, he informed me curtly, which included the stuff that people did to their families. Recently someone had killed an entire family in Kansas, tying up the parents and children, and then shooting them with a shotgun. Danny followed the elements of this crime avidly and kept me informed in such detail that I almost accused him of making it up. His morbid curiosity alarmed Mama who threatened to quit taking the newspaper. It didn't help that Daddy owned both a shotgun and a rifle.

At any rate, by Monday afternoon the four of us were

settling into yet another place, this one so far off the beaten path that Daddy wouldn't be able to find us. Some of Mama's friends from work pitched in to move our things and pledged to help Mama pay the rent until she found a job, something not necessarily easy to do in Shelton. Danny reacted with an outburst that left Mama reeling.

CHAPTER 12
In Which I Learn about Trains and Rats,
and Things that Go Bump in the Night

"I just get settled in school, back with my friends, and you yank me out again," Danny spoke quietly, but with considerable venom. Mama's face looked stricken.

"It can't be helped, honey. I need time away from Daddy and as long as the family knows where we are, he can find us."

"Well, what's the matter with that! I wish you would just make up your mind so we can all go back home again. It wasn't so bad living with Daddy! At least we knew what was gonna happen most days." He stomped outside and slammed the door.

Home was now a tiny two bedroom unit on the ground floor of a six unit apartment building, one of several that dotted the grassy slope separating the highway from the railroad tracks running to the lumber mill in Shelton. The road swept from the north straight past our cluster of buildings, down a long, steep hill into town, approximately two miles away. The scraggly fir trees scattered about the complex did nothing to protect us from the unremitting rain. It was just as dark and gloomy outside as inside the tiny apartment. Paint peeled from the walls and the toilet constantly threatened to overflow at the slightest flush.

Danny kept to himself, muttering his way through homework and plotting his weekend escapes down the long road to town and its lone movie theater. Robbie clung to Mama, not wanting to stand at the school bus stop even if I held his hand. Things that disrupted our lives always bothered Robbie more than anyone else and I regretted that I had made his last summer before all the trouble started so miserable. I longed to take the walk up Quaker Hill to Annie's simple cabin and sit by the fire, piecing together fabric quilting blocks. We'd sip chamomile tea brewed from the plants I had helped Annie pick and dry, and she would listen with her heart to the happenings in my life.

The days were growing slowly longer and giving me more opportunities to slip out of doors after I returned Robbie from the school bus. As long as I was present to help with dinner and my homework was finished before bed, Mama seemed not to care what I did with my time. She was moody and difficult to approach, and, for the first time since they began, she made no comment on my restless nights and numerous nightmares.

I had encountered the train on our first full week at the new apartment. Thursday afternoon the school bus was late, so I did not deliver Robbie and get my clothes changed until shortly after 4:00 pm. As I slipped outside, I heard the rumbling of wheels on the track that ran a hundred yards beyond the fence that separated our apartment complex from the green field extending to the trees, running as far as the eye could see to north and south. The thrumming of the powerful engine ran up my legs and seemed to settle in time with my heartbeat. I could feel and hear it long before it rounded the bend north where the road disappeared into the forest.

I eventually discovered that the train made two trips a week south to deliver logs to the mill and north to return the empty cars. Loggers rode in the single passenger car or in the caboose with the brakeman. I became a regular every Monday and Thursday at 4:02 pm when the train rounded the bend and the engineer blew his whistle. I would dash off the bus, hurriedly deposit Robbie on the sofa and change out of my school clothes in time to greet the train. Occasionally, the engineer would wave at me as the big steam engine puffed by.

That train defined my time in Shelton—helping me to delimit the endless sameness of each week and divide it into chewable chunks. I came to know the face of the brakeman who hung from the caboose and often gave me a salute. I played at counting the cars and imagining where the huge logs had made their homes before being harvested to become houses for humans. I longed to hop aboard and often pictured myself loping along beside the caboose, the brakeman holding out his hand to help me aboard. I would travel off to places far away from Mama and Danny and Robbie and the dark, narrow apartment with the leaking toilet and nasty-smelling gas stove that stood on legs in the cramped kitchen.

One of my chores is taking the garbage sack out to the incinerators that squat in an alcove outside the main building. I enter through a small pathway and distribute the garbage into individual bins according to type. The area is dark, dank, and stinks of decomposing vegetation. On more than one occasion I accidentally trap a feasting rat, most of whom are not amused at having the single entry-exit spot blocked by a small, blonde human. One particularly large black Norwegian variety, roughly the size of a small house cat, leaps at me from the dark, snatching my neck with its cheese yellow chisel teeth and making a nasty slash before dropping off as I run to the back door shrieking so loudly it wakes the graveyard shift mill worker on the second floor. Mama swabs the cut with Peroxide and dabs it lavishly with iodine while Danny laughs and dances around outside the minuscule bathroom, delightedly reciting the various symptoms of bubonic plague in loving detail. After that, Danny became the appointed garbage man, ultimately making me pay miserably for the rat attack.

As the dank late winter plodded inexorably into damp spring, I made not one friend at school. My class was mixed third and fourth graders, most of whom had attended the same school together since kindergarten. They were not much interested in the new girl who had already finished the reader they were just starting. We shared two to a desk and my desk mate was a third grade boy whose name I could never remember. Every day I drifted slowly to my seat beside the anonymous blond-haired boy and picked up "If I Were Going" and read the same stories and poems I had already mastered at my previous two schools. It is no wonder that the teacher sent home more than one note to Mama regarding my solitary persona.

"What has gotten into you, Cookie?" she inquired, not unkindly, after the third note. "Don't you like your new teacher? You know, I just can't handle another problem—you are my rock! I count on you, at least, not to give me any trouble. Danny isn't adjusting well at all, and Robbie cries all the time. If you fall apart on me, well—I just don't know if I can take it!"

I felt guilty at failing Mama just when she needed me the most. Consequently, when the music director asked for volunteers to dance in the upcoming springtime parade, I raised my hand, much to the amazement of my teacher!

Each school day the volunteers met for an hour's rehearsal, learning the choreography performed to Tchaikovsky's Dance of the Flowers. I ended up as a violet crocus costumed in crepe paper and starched cheesecloth. My male partner wore a bee outfit, complete with antennae and stinger. Mama said the whole thing was a little too Freudian for her taste. Before I could ask, she raised her hand and laughed that I would 'get it' far too soon! I thought the whole thing was stupid—flowers, bees, and butterflies dancing down the main street of Shelton—ushering in the chainsaw wielders and axe throwers honored at the festival.

On the designated Saturday, I rendezvoused with all the other woodland flora and fauna at the designated gathering place, costumed in my designated floral costume. Just as our little group began to dance and sing our way down the street, dodging the accumulated detritus from the mounted Sheriffs' Posse we followed, the heavens opened up and drenched us to the bone. Within minutes, crepe paper petals began to bleed violet and green and yellow and red rivulets down our faces and legs and arms. The stiffly starched cheesecloth drooped and bee and butterfly wings sagged as our costumes slowly melted, leaving us in our assorted undergarments. We valiantly struggled through the complicated dance steps as giggles from those still standing beneath umbrellas reached our ears.

Suddenly Mama swooped down on me, covering my dissolving costume with a blanket. "Enough's enough, already," she laughed as she scooped me up and carried me to the cover of a nearby store awning. "You've been a really good sport, honey, but now it's time to go home." She held me close as I shivered, sharing her warmth with me.

I don't remember how we got back to the apartment—perhaps someone offered us a ride—at any rate, by dark my throat was closing up. At midnight, Mama came to bed and wrapped her warm arms around my shivering body. She had dosed me with aspirin and Mentholatum, but without one of Daddy's Tee shirts, the old standby remedy didn't work as well. Mama said it was all in my head, not unkindly, but with some exasperation in her voice. Now she snuggled close, pressing herself against my back.

"Mama," I croaked as quietly as possible, "can I ask you something?"

"Sure, Cookie—anything you want."

I liked it when she used her special nickname for me. Tonight, it made me feel unique.

"It's kinda personal."

"That's okay, honey. You're entitled to know what's up."

"Remember the Sunday when OurGrandmother came to Park View and you two had the fight?"

"Yeah, honey, we disagreed on a few matters, I remember."

"Well, when she left, she took a good, long look at your tummy—that's all, and it was so flat. Now, it's getting round—not that I mean you're getting fat, or anything, but I kinda wondered why."

Mama sucked on her teeth, a little habit she had developed recently. I snuggled closer, wiggling my fanny up against her warmth, and waited patiently for Mama to speak.

After a few moments she whispered in my ear; "I'm going to have a baby in the summertime. Maybe it will be a little sister for you."

"Does Daddy know?"

"I don't know—probably, by now he does. I found out shortly after we moved back to Bremerton. Your grandmother guessed—part of why we argued that day—and she's probably told Daddy by now. That's one of the reasons she wants me to go back to Daddy, new girlfriend or not."

"I'll help you, Mama. Don't go back if you won't be happy. I can stay home from school after the baby comes and take care of it for you. That way you can go on working, and Danny can help, too. He can get another paper route. We'll work it out somehow, Mama. You can count on us." I was making a commitment for Danny that I had no right to make, but surely, he would want to help Mama.

For a moment I thought Mama was laughing, although her pillow muffled the sound, then I felt her cheek on mine, wet with hot tears.

"That won't be necessary, honey. You belong in school, but I'll never forget your offer."

CHAPTER 13

In Which I Dream of the Spirit World and Mama has a Revelation

Mama was fairly advanced in her pregnancy when Daddy arrived at the door of our ratty Shelton apartment, towing a trailer behind his borrowed truck. He had come visiting the previous weekend, wooing Mama with flowers and a nice meal at the family diner downtown while Danny, Robbie, and I shared macaroni and cheese at the small kitchen table.

"I betcha Mama's havin' steak," Danny moaned sorrowfully. Robbie smiled and made smacking noises, all the while stirring his gelatinous mac and cheese about on the plate. "Maybe she'll bring us home a doggy bag."

Robbie pouted. "We don't got a dog, Danny," he pointed out, gesticulating with a forkful of dinner.

"He means maybe she'll bring us home the leftovers to share—*if* we clean up our plates..." I dealt Robbie a fierce big-sister glare, motioning him to eat his bite before it fell onto the floor.

Danny laughed. "Probably Daddy'll have her leftovers. He can sure eat a lot, our Dad!" He spoke with pride as if overeating were a talent he wished to emulate. He was so pleased that Mama and Daddy were speaking that he had actually volunteered to babysit Robbie and me while they went into town. I wasn't so sure about this family reunion. Mama had cried half the night. She thought her sniffles went unnoticed, but my ears were keen. At one point, I rolled over and patted her on the shoulder. She lay quietly not acknowledging me, then blew her nose and snuggled into the blankets. I knew she was especially tired, as she (we) had not slept well the previous night, nor the night before that.

What occurred two nights before was one of those times that stand out in a child's life. I suppose this was the sort of thing that gave OurGrandmother the 'willies' about me, although I never told her of it.

We were out of the loop, so to speak, here in Shelton, with no telephone access unless Mama begged a call from the office manager, or we went into town to use the payphone booth squatting in all its green glory adjacent to the bus stop. Consequently, Mama was unaware that her daddy had suffered a stroke while out plowing and was hospitalized in Tacoma. Auntie Nor seldom contacted him, and OurGrandmother was quite likely preparing to celebrate with a Scottish Celidh at word of his demise.

The day began with Robbie deciding he didn't want to go to school. Mama had spent a deal of time that morning French braiding my hair (a fruitless endeavor in the best of times) using lots of WaveSet, all the while Robbie danced about kicking the table legs and making a general nuisance of himself.

"Stop that, Robin!" Mama made a swipe at him with her rattail comb as he stopped his round of the kitchen. She had her left hand tightly round one braid, and the motion yanked my head, causing tears to form in my eyes. I knew better than to protest, as such actions usually caused that same rattail comb to smack me smartly. Robbie deftly outmaneuvered her. Danny laughed behind his hand, catching my eye as he stood, unseen by Mama, in the small living room next to the kitchen. He was in Seventh grade, almost a grownup in his eyes, and pretty much did as he pleased.

At last, the braids were in, and Robbie was settled and out the door, dragged by me towards the school bus. Mama stood at our doorway, arms crossed, seeing us off. I remember watching her from my window seat. She turned towards the door, rotated back again, and blew me a kiss. Then the bus lurched forward and we were on our way to town, Robbie still grumbling by my side. He was having trouble with his Second Grade reader, and I spent the half-hour ride to the elementary school helping him sound out the words phonetically, rather than learn them by sight as the current school curriculum decreed.

In the afternoon Mama was unusually quiet. She went about preparing dinner without comment on our day at school, ignoring Robbie's whining and Danny's constantly changing the radio station, something that would usually result in chastisement. We ate in silence as well. After cleaning up the dishes, Robbie and I sat at the table practicing sounding out the words in his reader; Mama looked on with pride and Danny made rude remarks under his breath. He passed by once on his way to the refrigerator and an after-dinner snack, passing his wet finger across the back of my neck. I heard him purse his lips and felt a glob of spittle drop on the top of my head.

"Stop that," I whispered as I shoved his hand away. "And quit spitting on me." Mama ignored the interchange and continued reading her paperback. The book had no cover. Auntie Nor brought them home from her job at Woolworth, where old paperbacks were stripped of covers and dumped into the waste bin. Mama received them gratefully as she couldn't afford to purchase new books and seldom checked them out from the Bookmobile that came twice a month. As her pregnancy advanced, Mama spent more and more time sitting beside the one lamp in our living room, reading novels without covers.

Mama seemed preoccupied—almost dream-like in her demeanor, appearing to read. When I asked her if she were okay, she nodded without speaking. Something was bothering her—I knew it. I hoped it wasn't a problem with the baby.

At nine, Mama shooed me off to the bed we shared, and I was fast asleep when she came in quietly and slid in beside me, adjusting the covers to give us as much warmth as possible. The apartment had no heat at night, and the winter had been cold and damp for the most part. I felt her spoon me, wrapping her arms around my tummy and pulling me close. I felt the bump that was my (hopefully) baby sister move against my back. Mama mewed softly, settling in with a soft breath against the back of my neck. At peace with my world, I fell asleep in her arms, and dreamed of the farm and Annie Marsh, far away on her hill.

In my dream(?) I awoke suddenly to bitter cold. The room felt like the meat locker where Daddy stored his winter's kill in a rented bin. My breath floated in white mist, spreading out into the room that glowed with a low, blue light. I could feel

Mama sitting up, her body pulling the covers off and letting that frigid air reach me. Shivering, I rolled onto my side and lifted my head, supporting it with my hand. Mama stared, eyes wide open and unblinking, at someone (thing)—an *apparition?* standing, standing? at the foot of the bed.

At first, I was frightened, but quickly realized that the misty figure was my grandfather—Mama's daddy, and, therefore, could not possibly be a threat. He stood in the swirling blue light, almost solid, smiling down at the two of us. Mama breathed in short, quick puffs, not moving. I lay quiet as if I were still sleeping, although I knew this was no dream. My grandfather stood before me, although in what manner that was possible seemed unimportant.

Then he spoke. His voice, soft and mellifluous, floated from a mouth that did not move, nor did it mist in the room. "Mayleen, my little flower, I have passed from this mortal life."

Aha, I think. This is what a soul looks like. I am neither frightened nor disturbed by his demeanor. Mama remains frozen in place, almost like a statue, though she breaths.

He continues; "I wanted to tell you myself. Don't worry about my passing. It was quick and I was quite prepared to cross, but you had not heard of my stroke. Remember that I always loved you best. I shouldn't have had a favorite, but I did." He raises his hand to his mouth and blows her a kiss, then turns to me and winks. I smile back. "And Cookie, I am counting on you to help your mama. She may not remember this in the morning. Things are going to change for all of you now, and she is going to need that listening heart of yours more than ever." He faded then, quickly swirling away with the blue mist and the room rose several degrees.

Mama sighed and lay back down. I pulled the covers over us and quickly fell into a deep sleep, dreaming of my grandfather and his little dairy farm and happier times.

In the morning, Mama failed to mention our visitor. As we sat down to our cereal, someone rapped on the back door. Danny rose with a snort, annoyed at this disturbance, and opened it to the Office Manager's son with a message for Mama—she had a telephone call and would she come. Mama jumped up so quickly her chair fell and Danny kept her from following it to the floor. She grabbed her jacket and nodded to us to finish at the table, leaving for the office without closing the door behind her.

"What was THAT all about," Danny huffed as he shut the door and sat back down to his CheeriOats. Robbie wiped his nose on his sleeve and took another swig of cocoa. I shrugged, although such a call bode no good. If it had anything to do with the previous night's spectral visitor, we would soon find out.

Mama returned with red eyes and nose; it was obvious, even to Danny, that she had been crying. "It was your daddy on the phone," she explained after a trip to the bathroom to bathe her eyes and blow her nose. She sat at the table, coffee cup in hand. "Auntie Nor gave him the number." She paused and took a gulp of coffee, sputtering into her napkin as the hot brew hit her mouth.

For once, Danny waited patiently for Mama to continue.

"Grandpa passed away last night," she managed to get out before the tears welled in her eyes again. "Daddy wanted to be the one to tell me."

Danny puts his arms around Mama and holds her close while she cries softly. I sit there, not knowing what to say, totally unsurprised by Daddy's revelation, but quite shocked by Mama's response. She actually acts as if she does not know—as if last night has not happened. I think for a moment that I have dreamed our encounter with my grandfather's specter, and then recall his admonition to me. My mama does not remember, but I do, and I will never forget how he looks into my eyes and smiles.

So, we now sat at the little kitchen table awaiting our parents and the hopeful advent of a doggy bag with steak.

Presently the front door squeaked open, spilling Mama and Daddy into the tiny front room. Robbie ran squealing to Daddy who swung him up into the air, smiling. Mama sat down in her soft chair as Danny gleefully removed a brown bag from her hand. "Smells like steak, huh?" he smiled. Mama smiled back and waved him to the kitchen. I could hear him shuffling the bag open.

Daddy deposited Robbie on the floor where he clung to his daddy's leg, a huge smile on his face. I knew the boys missed Daddy. Robbie was his little man and Danny resented being the man of the house in Daddy's absence. I, however, remembered the arguments and hurts and disappointments that drove my parents apart, especially Daddy's betrayal with another woman.

Daddy knelt down and put his arms around me, snuggling close with his five o'clock shadow. He smelled of steak and horseradish sauce and Prince Albert tobacco, and aftershave— all the daddy smells I had missed in the last months. "Do you forgive me, Cookie?" he whispered, so low that I almost failed to hear it. "I miss you and your mommy and your brothers. Will you take me back?"

I thought he should be asking Mama that question but figured he already had, so I nodded my head in response and whispered back that I had missed him, too.

He stood up, looked over to Mama, and nodded his head.

"I have an announcement. Mama has agreed to come home this weekend. I found a great old house in Tacoma, where everyone can have his or her" (Daddy turned and winked at me with a smile) "own bedroom. Robbie and Cookie are only three blocks from school and Danny can walk to the Junior High. How does that sound?"

*I look to Mama. Her face wears no emotion, but she is nodding, too. Maybe it is for the best. How could we cope with a new baby in this little apartment so far from town? I will miss waving to my friend the engineer after school, and I will try to make new friends at yet **another** school. I have none here, other than the engineer and the brakeman. If Mama is happy, why should I not try? And in the summer, I will have a sister, if I am lucky. If we cannot return to the farm, I will attempt to be happy in Tacoma.*

Shortly after this night when my parents reconciled, we moved into a huge, old Victorian house in Tacoma's north end. Neither Daddy's girlfriend nor Mama's old beau Lee was mentioned again. While Mama was setting up the living room area, she opened the old lampstand and discovered Amanda Sue's (previously Shirley Anne's) broken doll. Daddy mended her arm, and although I eventually returned her to Amanda Sue, I spent several months playing with her in peace. She ended up smashed to pieces in the road outside OurGrandmother's apartment on Cambrian Street in Bremerton when Amanda Sue threw her there in a fit of anger.

I finished Fourth Grade at Grant Elementary School—the fourth school in one year—reading *"If I Were Going"* for the fourth time. My teacher, a tall, skinny, and (I thought) ancient old maid thought me brilliant because I so quickly memorized all the little poems in the reader.

OurGrandmother's piano was back home, proudly sitting in the big old dining room of our Tacoma house. I started playing again, practicing every day when I came home from school. Not that I played well without lessons, but I was learning, teaching myself from Danny's old piano books that Mama had kept. I learned the magic language of music— chords and their progressions, the different scales, and making the music dance from the keys to my ears. Sometimes, I believe that piano saved me—oh not my life, but my soul. And every day Annie sat beside me on the bench.

In the summer, my brother Tommy was born. Somewhere in the passage of Fifth grade to Sixth, Daddy resumed his roving ways. That Mama also found herself back in touch with Lee, was a secret between Mama and me, a secret I kept for decades. Two years later Ricky joined the family.

During the years of not so peaceful coexistence, we seemed to move all the time, resulting in my having attended fourteen schools by the time I graduated high school. Somewhere my box of private papers disappeared. With the box went all my un-mailed letters to Annie. I had stopped writing them when my parents reconciled, confiding, instead, directly to God in my silent bedtime prayers. Each time we moved I found it more difficult to make new friends—friends I would soon leave behind; and in each new house, I would dream of the farm where life now seemed ideal, and of Annie, waiting for me in her little hilltop cabin on Quaker Hill. These childhood memories ultimately became too painful; I buried them deep, deep inside and the dreaming stopped.

Eventually, my parents' relationship reached détente. It lasted until she fell in love and ended their marriage years after I had moved away from home and had children of my own. Even then, Daddy blamed me for the breakup. Perhaps this blame had its roots all those years ago when I accidentally interrupted his New Year's Eve phone call—he always viewed me with suspicion after that night, although I never told my mother; or maybe he needed a scapegoat to ease his conscience. Maybe it was partially my fault, I reasoned. The problem with Jerome had certainly dealt some kind of near-fatal blow from which none of us ever recovered, possibly the proverbial straw. At any rate, over the years Daddy became convinced that I wanted him out of our lives. Nothing could have been further from the truth. I loved him with all my heart, but I had listened to my mother's unhappiness with that same heart.

The truth is, I loved them both—but she needed me more.

CHAPTER 14
In Which I Learn the Quality of Diplomacy and How it Applies to Friendships

Our new house in Tacoma's north end was a huge old two story Victorian mansion. Built well before the turn of the twentieth century, it had originally housed a local founding family. The house sat on a corner lot surrounded on two sides with lawns sloping rather sharply to sidewalks separated from the streets by parking strips; an alley ran north and south along the spacious back yard housing a huge old elm tree, and white picket fencing separated it from the house directly north. She was the matriarch of the entire neighborhood. A lovely front porch with white railings intersected a cement walk to the street. Double doors with stained glass insets to each side opened into a short hallway with dusty Burgundy colored velvet panels separating the hallway from a formal parlor to the left. On the right, glass paneled doors led to a library filled with light from huge windows overlooking the porch.

Fourteen-foot ceilings dwarfed our slightly shabby dining room furniture cowering in the center of an ancient rug. The dining room adjoined the parlor, separated by huge sliding doors. A bifurcated staircase spiraled down, splitting just beyond eyesight with a straight portion sloping to the kitchen—obviously for the servants of past days. Two bedrooms opened off the dining area, separated by a huge walk-through closet. A butler's pantry lined with glass doored dishware cupboards and sideboards for food led into the kitchen with doors to the bathroom, large pantry, back porch, and side stairs to the second floor. Another stairway dropped to the basement below. Here were stationary tubs for laundry, an inside clothesline for rainy days, and the huge coal burning furnace that heated the entire house. It sported the luxury of a stoker holding enough coal (Danny's job) to feed the furnace for an entire day and night. A bin for coal storage hunkered under dual windows to the side yard with chutes for delivering it from a service truck.

The curving stairway terminated upstairs in a long hallway leading to four bedrooms and a play area. A second bathroom with a huge claw-footed tub snuggled between the playroom and the stairs.

Mama gasped in amazement (perhaps in awe at the amount of work she was taking on). Daddy's negotiation with the owners included repairs and refurbishing leading to reduced rent. If all went as planned, Mama and Daddy would heal their rift and we would be a family again.

The house, lovely as it was, came with a few 'conditions', one of them being a roomer in an upstairs bedroom. His name was Bill Gardener and he had lived in the house for forty years, apparently passed along to owner and tenant alike. Bill took his meals elsewhere but required a room cleaning and bed change each Saturday. This chore fell to me, and I was not pleased.

On Monday, I began my fourth school of my fourth grade year. By some stroke of fate, the class had just begun a new reader—"If I Were Going". I had practically memorized it by now. My teacher, a tall, skinny grey-haired "old maid", as Daddy said, was extremely impressed with my ability to memorize great portions of the text! I guess in my case, four's the charm.

Settling into yet another neighborhood and school had its rewards and its drawbacks. There existed a world of new friends ahead, but always in the back of my mind lay the possibility of moving on and losing them again. I still wrote to Abby but never received a reply, and Mama eyeballed me every time I asked for a stamp.

"Darn it, Cookie," she would admonish me. "You never get an answer from her. Why do you waste your time?"

"She's my friend," I would reply. "And I don't think she has very many friends." My nose twitched as I recalled the smell of Abby's clothing. It reflected the house she lived in and its lack of both privacy and modern plumbing. "She's gotta know that *someone* loves her, Mama."

Mama sighed and acknowledged that it was so, then parted with yet another stamp for my envelope. "At least it shows you know how important friendships are. I am proud of you, honey. It's just that I know you are disappointed when you don't get a reply."

Mama laid my new baby brother Tommy tummy down on a diaper covering her lap, rubbing his back in a soothing circular motion that seemed to please him, as he rewarded her with a decidedly gooey burp. I had prayed hard for a sister, to no avail! Daddy was pleased, but Mama seemed resigned to having only one daughter, as she vowed never again to go through the whole thing.

Summer was at an end, and fifth grade loomed ahead. I hoped that a few of the friends I had made in the last three months of fourth grade would share my class, but we never knew until the first day. Mama had not had time to make school clothes, busy as she was with the new baby, so I had to be content with hand me downs from Amanda Sue. My cousin Jerilynn's things never fit, as Aunt Barbara failed to take into consideration that Jerry was twice my size, even though I was two grades ahead of her in school. Mama said we would make do. New shoes that fit were more important than new dresses and sweaters.

Danny had spent the summer vacuuming up every slang term he came across in writing, radio, and on the lips of his hip friends. He had wasted no time hooking up with all the top seventh graders at Jason Lee Junior High School and was looking forward to eighth grade. On the pretense of dusting, I took the opportunity to do a little snooping and found the list of 'cool' words he was busy incorporating into daily use.

Robbie, now staring second grade and thinking himself quite the man, ran around shrieking "cowabunga" at every opportunity and startling Tommy awake just as Mama had put him down for his nap. Danny had taken to referring to me as his nerdy sister. I retaliated with DDT (drop dead twice) and he returned it with "What, and look like you?" Tears welled in my eyes and I made for my hiding place in the upstairs playroom. Hard as I tried, I could never get the best of my big brother Danny!

I sit at the old desk in my upstairs bedroom, lodged

between Danny and the bathroom, cattycorner from Bill Gardener the roomer, and look out my window at the neighbor's upstairs window. It is nice to have a room of my own, but I do not feel comfortable yet. I do not feel comfortable using the bathroom next to me as the door has no lock and I risk being interrupted by our weird roomer while I am on the toilet. Danny is not here to snoop so I quit my new bedroom and sneak into the playroom and my private hidey hole.

This old Victorian house held a secret. Beneath the windows was a crawl space about two feet wide between the inner and outer walls. The windows on this side of the house were inset about 8 inches from the outside, leaving a lovely windowsill on the inside. A small access door hidden inside the bottom cupboard of an old ceiling high cabinet led to the crawl. A small child like myself had plenty of space to hide amongst the cobwebs and dust. I suppose the crawl gave access to electrical wiring although if it ever needed fixing, the electrician would have to be a midget!

This alone time, and I do not have much of it, is mostly spent in remembering the farm and daydreaming about visits with Annie at her little house on Quaker Hill. It seems like forever since I last saw her, but two and a half years is a third of my lifetime. I picture Pete on his black mare Velvet and imagine him sweeping me up behind him. We gallop off across the open field, Velvet's mane whipping Pete's face. I grip his waist tight . . . Mama's voice from the bottom of the stairs rouses me from my reverie. "Time to set the table, Cookie," she shouts. I leave my dreaming and crawl out of my secret place. Mama needs me.

On Labor Day, with school scheduled to start on

Wednesday following, we went out to the Vanac family farm in the Valley and showed off Tommy to Daddy's family. We picked up Daddy's mama, my sweet Bohemian grandmother, at her little house on 34th street. She had moved there after Grandpa Jan 'went home', as she always referred to his passing. Great Uncle Matthew took care of managing the farm for her, with her boys (Daddy aside) pitching in when needed. In the late summer and after school all the cousins took turns picking and weeding and generally helping with harvest.

This is my family. I am a Vanac in heart and soul, and dream of having Vanac as my last name, instead of the one I bear. I have begged OurFather to let me have Daddy's last name. I want so desperately to fit in with my friends and not have to explain why Danny and I don't share the same name as Robbie and Tommy and (eventually) Ricky. From the day Daddy brought me home from the hospital I have been his forever daughter.

OurFather was only concerned about Danny's education and that he might marry and have a boy child to carry OurFather's family name. If some man found me suitable for marriage, and OurFather had his doubts there, my name would change forever. It made no sense to me that he refuse to consider the only thing I had ever asked from him. He refused because he could, was his answer.

I thought deeply about names and what they mean to a person—how they tie us to family. I was part of Daddy's family, and they had accepted me as such since my birth. I identified with their values and who they were as both a family and citizens of my homeland. My Vanac uncles had served with pride in the various services during WWII, and grandma and grandpa had gold stars in their window to proclaim the same.

OurFather's brothers had served also, but Danny and I were not close with them during our early years. So much strife and bitterness over OurFather's actions had kept us at a distance.

We drove out Valley Road past the little cemetery where Grandpa Jan lay at rest. The road wound alongside the river, past the cannery where Aunt Barbara worked, then crossed at the old wooden bridge, ran through town and out to the fields and farms beyond. We finally pulled in at the driveway used jointly by the two family farms. Daddy parked our new Ford Tudor well away from any harm from other (older) vehicles. I secretly missed Elizabeth but had to admit this new car rode a whole lot smoother! We called her Elizabeth Two.

As soon as Daddy stopped her, he hurried around to the passenger door to help Mama and Grandma Vanac out. Cradling Tommy in his arms, he escorted his two ladies into what was now Great Uncle Matthew's house. Danny, Robbie, and I squeezed ourselves free of the back seat and ran to join the cousins and friends gathered in the back yard. There were blonde, blue-eyed cousins and dark haired hazel-eyed cousins and brown haired brown-eyed cousins and friends whose black hair and beige skin and dark eyes with epicanthic folds told of their Japanese ancestry. This was our last outing before the long school season, and I intended to make the best of it!

My daddy was a first generation American. His parents, my stoic, mustachioed grandpa, and my cuddly, grey haired grandma, immigrated from the Austro-Hungarian Empire prior to WW1. Grandpa Jan Vanac, who eventually American-ized his name to John, came as a four-year-old from Bohemia with his parents to farm in the Puyallup-Sumner area of Western Washington. His Uncle Matthew followed. My Grandmother Maria, barely six weeks old when Grandpa's family left, was affianced to Jan, an arrangement not uncommon between affluent Bohemian families.

While Grandpa grew up in America, Grandma attended Convent school in Austria, becoming a refined and well-educated young woman. I don't suppose she ever believed she would end up on a small farm in Edgewood, Washington, but a few weeks after her twentieth birthday she found herself on a ship destined for Ellis Island.

After she cleared customs with the help of a family friend who traveled to New York to meet her, Maria was on the train for Puyallup, Washington. Within days of arriving, she was married to John, a man she knew only from family stories and a few letters. Uncle Joe was born ten months later, followed within the year by Daddy.

I am not sure that she ever really found a fit in farming life, but nonetheless, she arranged for her younger sister Barbara to join her in the new world and marry Grandpa's brother Emil. This made for a confusing array of 'double cousins', who all looked alike, talked alike, and bore family names like John and Joe and Barbara and Mary. The two families lived on adjoining farms in Edgewood.

Two other farms bordered Daddy's family farms—both owned by industrious Japanese-American families who had immigrated about the same time as Daddy's grandparents. The entire northern fence line of Daddy's family's farms was shared by the Sakato and Nakamura farms. The four pieces of land were occupied at approximately the same time in the late

1880s, and amid different languages and attempts to become assimilated, the families formed a bond.

Daddy's family soon became naturalized citizens of the United States of America, unlike their Japanese friends, who were prevented by federal law from applying. Their children, the Nisei, were first generation Americans and citizens by birth. By 1941, the Vanac, Sakato, and Nakamura families were firmly entrenched into the third generation, two of them born and bred in the Puyallup Valley and firm friends and partners in the land. The kids in my generation chattered in three languages, English, Bohemian, and Japanese, attended school together, and played and worked in harmony.

I would not be born for another nineteen days when the Japanese government sent its forces against the United States at Pearl Harbor on the Hawaiian Island of Oahu early on Sunday morning, December 7th, 1941. The events set in play that day would have a profound effect on my family, ending fourteen months later when Mama and Daddy married.

I do not remember a time when OurFather lived with us. After all, he left my mother when I was three months old. I was and forever would be Daddy's only daughter, who regretted that I did not carry his last name. During the Depression years, he had taken an apprenticeship in The Navy Yard in Bremerton, sending most of his pay home to help his parents and siblings on the farm. By that fateful day in December, he was a Journeyman precision machinist and fast friends with OurFather.

On that same day, the fate of the three Japanese American families who would influence my life balanced on the edge of a knife. Within a few weeks, all three would be sent to Camp

Harmony as it became known, the first step in their journey to internment camps for the duration of the war. Three generations of Sakatos and Nakamuras and two and three quarters generation of Kusakas, never mind that most of them were American citizens, were at the Western Washington Fair grounds in Puyallup, living in barns made to house livestock.

And at Pearl Harbor, the father of another I would come to know was dying aboard a naval ship, trapped beneath the water and the fire and the bloody carnage of war.

The things that influence one's life do not necessarily begin only after she or he is born. Fate sets in motion the circumstances that influence the paths we take.

CHAPTER 15
In Which I Believe in Myself and Teach a Lesson

School started the day after Labor Day, a knee-high fog greeting Robbie and me as we opened the back gate onto the alley and turned right towards the school. Danny no longer walked with us. He was in Eighth grade at Jason Lee Jr. High, several blocks in the opposite direction from Grant Elementary. The sky above promised blue and sunshine to come. Robbie was still a little boy that year, a third grader who looked up to his big sister in fifth. We held hands and skipped, singing together.

Mama was hanging her first load of laundry on the lines Daddy had strung in an open backyard area—Tommy's diapers and little shirts and nighties with a drawstring at the bottom to keep them from riding up at night. Although one of Daddy's sisters had gifted three months of diaper service, OurGrand-mother did not approve. The diapers were harsh, she snorted, and probably filled with other people's germs, although they smelled of bleach and looked okay to me!

Mama sighed and stopped the service.

At school, I left Robbie with a group of his friends and went

128

to my assigned classroom. This year I had my first male teacher, Mr. Knutson, who smiled with his eyes as I entered. He was tall and handsome with blue eyes that twinkled and dark blonde hair. From his name, I surmised he was Scandinavian. He motioned me to a seat in the front of Row Three.

A small girl of obvious Japanese heritage sat next to me, smiling shyly from behind her hand. "Cookie," she murmured, catching my attention. I smiled back! What luck! There sat Mieko Kusaka—we had shared the first part of Fourth Grade together at Washington Elementary before my sudden departure to Bremerton.

According to Mama, I had collected Mieko. Although it was true that I tended to gather up unfortunate kids and mother them, Mama was wrong about Mieko, whose name meant "Beautiful Blessing" in Japanese.

Mieko's family is one of the first groups of Washington Japanese ordered to report for internment. They grow strawberries on Bainbridge Island, beautiful, plump fruits filled with sweet juice—unlike the mostly tasteless berries of today. Her parents, both Nisei and therefore American citizens by birth, are married right out of high school. They move in with Mieko's Kusaka grandparents, her father continuing to work the family land, her mother helping with the house. Midori Kusaka is eight months pregnant in April 1942 when the call to leave Bainbridge Island comes.

Whether the Kusakas ever met the Sakato or Nakamura families in Camp Harmony I never knew. The Kusakas were assigned to Manzanar near Tule Lake in California. Mieko was born in Camp Harmony two weeks before her parents were relocated. The Sakotos and Nakamuras went to Minidoka near Hunt, Idaho, where they spent the remainder of the war.

It soon became apparent to Daddy's family that someone needed to take care of the land while the Sakotos and Nakamuras were gone. No one knew how long the war would last, only that it now involved not just Japan, but Germany and Italy as well. Daddy's brothers were soon off to Navy ships and Army posts while he stewed at his position in the Navy Yard, unable to join them. Those left behind struggled to tend four farms. Agreeing amongst themselves, the family scraped up enough money to pay property taxes when the State came to take possession. In the event our Japanese-American neighbors did not return, the family would claim the land for the taxes paid.

Fifth Grade in Mr. Knutson's class held another surprise for me. Harry Adamsky scurried through the door just before the bell rang, sat down behind Mieko and did a double take when our eyes met. He smiled and waved then took a spit wad from his mouth and stuck it into Mieko's hair.

"Saw that," Mr. Knutson said in a voice loud enough to startle the now assembled classroom. "Take it out of her hair, now!" Harry did.

Mieko blushed, jerking her head forward and flipping her short, black Dutch bob. The whole class laughed, not at Mieko, but at Harry, his face a deep brick red.

Harry was a redhead with a mop of curly hair and a face full of freckles. We met in kindergarten at Park View school in Bremerton, spending three years in the same classrooms. We had a lot in common, both coming from Shipyard families with members in the armed forces. We also both had stepfathers we loved. Harry's father had died at Pearl Harbor when Harry was just two months old. His mother later married an Ensign she met while working at the NCO club, who was raising Harry along with two younger sisters. Although the spit wad in the hair was one of Harry's little jokes, I also knew he did not like kids with Japanese parentage. I suppose I couldn't blame him under the circumstances of his father's death.

In retrospect, the Gods, or the Force, or whatever we call that universal spirit of life that flows through and connects us all, must have conspired for me to be reunited with two such different friends. I knew that Harry was usually kind, notwithstanding his propensity for spit wads and practical jokes. Mieko was sweet natured, intelligent, highly motivated, and appeared placid, but if pushed, she would defend herself fiercely with words and the occasional punch to the midsection.

Mieko did not talk about her family. I knew that she lived alone with her mother who worked as a clerk at a local Pharmacy. When we spent a Saturday together at her house, Mieko's mama served us tea in traditional Japanese dress— Kimono and obi, and raw fish! This was my first experience with sushi, and I ate it, as Mama had trained me well. *"We eat what is on the table, Leah, especially in other people's houses!"*

Raw tuna is not nearly as good as a tuna sandwich.

It was Daddy who told me about Mieko's father. The 442nd Regimental Combat Team was a fighting unit composed almost entirely of American soldiers of Japanese ancestry who fought in World War II, their families confined to internment camps. Beginning in 1944, the regiment fought primarily in Europe—in particular, Italy, southern France, and Germany.

It was the most decorated unit for its size and length of service in the history of American warfare. The 4,000 men who initially made up the unit in April 1943 were replaced nearly 2.5 times. In total, about 14,000 men served, earning 9,486 Purple Hearts. The unit was awarded eight Presidential Unit Citations (five earned in one month). Twenty-one of its members were awarded Medals of Honor. Its motto was "Go for Broke".

"And Mieko's father was one of those soldiers killed in action," Daddy told me while Robbie and I sat with him on the front porch steps.

I put my elbows on my knees and cradled my chin in my hands. "Was he a hero?"

"All the men who die for our country are heroes, Cookie." Daddy took a pull from his pipe and blew blue rings into the air. Robbie flicked them with his fingers and muttered "Cowabunga" under his breath. That night I lay awake pondering my two best friends.

The first months of school had been difficult for the three of us. Harry spent every recess and lunch hour tormenting Mieko, notwithstanding three trips to the principal's office and several times-out during class. He didn't seem to care that his mother was most annoyed that her eldest child was developing the reputation as a bully.

"Why do you call her those names," I asked him one day during lunch break. Harry had 'accidentally' dropped his milk carton on Mieko's lap as he sat down between us at the table, muttering a rude comment sotto voce.

"What did he say," Mieko asked me. "Did he talk bad about my dad again?"

I just shook my head and took a bite of my peanut butter sandwich.

One afternoon as Harry and I walked home together I asked him why he hated Mieko. She wasn't even born when the war started.

"Her dad killed mine." Harry's face scrunched up and tears welled in his eyes. "Them stupid Japs bombed the ships and my dad drowned. For what?"

"Mieko's dad was born here just like you and me, Harry," I snorted. "He didn't have anything to do with Pearl Harbor."

"Doesn't matter. He's a Jap and so is she."

Later, at recess, I sat sharing an apple with Mieko. "Why don't you let kids know about your dad?"

"It's private," she whispered. "They can think whatever they want. They have moms and dads that tell them lies and nothing I can say will change their minds."

"You're just *stupid*, Leah" Danny laughed. "You kill me. You think that everyone should get along. Just stay out of it or you're gonna lose 'em both!"

Mama agreed with Danny's appraisal of the situation. "Sometimes people just can't be friends. Don't get your heart broken, honey. Just like them both, but separately." I had tried that for months, now, and it didn't feel right to me.

Finally, I approached Mr. Knutson. "Well, you do have a conundrum there, Leah. Sometimes it's just better to let sleeping dogs lie, but you appear to have tried that approach. It's still pretty close to the war for most people to rethink their prejudices." He paused for a few moments. "However, if you are willing to take a risk, maybe you can make the whole class look at this in a different light. The local newspaper is running an essay contest for fifth and sixth graders this spring—with citizenship as the subject. We just learned about it this week. Maybe you can enter and use it as a teaching tool for all of us."

"But Mr. Knutson, I couldn't write something good enough to win."

"You don't have to win, Leah. The school is going to have an assembly and the best essays from our school will be read. I bet you can write one good enough for that." He smiled at me and sent me home to do some thinking.

Mama was against it, as she thought I risked losing my friends. Danny laughed at the thought that 'crazy Leah' might get her essay read at school. "Glad you don't go to Jason Lee," he snorted. "I wouldn't want anyone thinkin' we was related." He clipped me on the back of the head as he sauntered out the door.

Daddy thought for a few minutes. "It's up to you, of course, but—Cookie, I think it's a really good idea. Sometimes the best lessons come out of the mouths of babes."

For a moment, I thought Daddy was calling me a **babe**!

So, I entered the contest. With the help of the library downtown and my Uncle John Vanac who had contacts from his army days, and the encouragement of parents and teachers, I wrote about Pearl Harbor, and the internment camps, and the 442nd Infantry. I wrote about sacrifice and forfeit and what it means to be a citizen of this great country, even when the country appears to desert you. And in the end, I won.

Before school let out for Easter vacation, the principal read my essay at assembly. I was sick at home with another kidney infection, so I missed the big fuss, but Mama and Daddy were there. Mr. Knutson took the stage to receive my award, then announced to the whole assembly that we had two heroes of our own—Harry's father and Mieko's father. After explaining what he meant, he invited them up on the stage to applause.

When I got back to school a week later, my two best friends met me at the schoolyard gate. Harry had his arm around Mieko's shoulder and they both wore smiles. In my heart, I knew that Annie was smiling, too!

Mieko died in an automobile accident when she was twenty-four and Harry passed away last year. We mostly kept up through Facebook the last few years. He got a little maudlin there at the end. He had cancer and knew he hadn't much time. Maybe that's why he wrote the letter. He had thought a lot about our early years, he said and had concluded that sometimes the most important words are the ones you don't say. Diplomacy takes courage, he wrote, but when friendships are at stake, the risk is worth taking.

CHAPTER 16
In Which Danny Learns a Lesson about Commitment

During that first year back in Tacoma, Danny entered Jason Lee Junior High School approximately twelve blocks east of our Steele Street Victorian house. He walked to classes every day, then went on to diving practice at the Y after school and took the bus home in the late afternoon in time to cover his paper route for the local newspaper. Daddy worked at the machine shop down by the docks during the day and spent most nights at the Union Hall where he served as the Business Agent for the Machinists Union. Mama had her hands full with Robbie and now baby Tommy, whose birth had drained her greatly. She had not planned on new babies coming along in her thirties, but Mother Nature apparently had had other plans for her. Tommy became my baby the day Mama and Daddy brought him home from the hospital on an unseasonably hot July afternoon.

Robbie is jealous of little Tommy. Mama says he has his nose out of joint because he is no longer the baby of the family and is expected to act like a big brother. She sighs as we do the laundry in the huge basement below the house. Twin stationary tubs snuggle against the south wall of an established laundry area far enough away from the coal stoker for our huge furnace for Mama and me to operate the wringer washer in safety. We have two laundry lines along the south wall where clothing and diapers can dry on rainy days, although hanging inside makes the dry garments and diapers smell of coal soot that causes me to sneeze.

Mama retrieves clean diapers from the washer, skillfully feeding them through the wringer into the first stationary tub full of warm rinse water, then I shift the wringer and thread the now soap free garments through it into the second water filled tub. Mama warns me to be careful with the ringer, as it operates on electricity, and is heavy-duty enough to wring out Daddy and Danny and Robbie's jeans. I am very careful after seeing Mama have her arm sucked in up to her elbow before the two ringer parts that look like padded piecrust rollers pop apart and release it. The double rinsed diapers are a third time wrung, now into the basket that I carry over to hang next to the north wall or lug up the stairs and out through the kitchen to the laundry lines in the back yard and hang them, carefully snapped in place with springy wood clothespins while Mama gets the next load into the washer. It is hard work, but necessary.

Daddy is seldom home for dinner, now. The two jobs keep him jumping, he tells Robbie and me on the weekends when he has some free time. I don't think Mama is very happy, but she tries not to show it to us kids.

In December, OurFather and **NINE**-a came to Tacoma to have a 'talk' with Mama and Daddy concerning Danny. The four adults sat down in the library that served as a front room in this old Victorian style house. Mama had me serve the coffee and donuts she had prepared, then sent me up the stairs with Robbie and Tommy. Danny supposedly was in his room listening to the radio and doing his homework. Instead, he sat on the first stair around the staircase corner, listening to the adults, homework awaiting on his desk in front of the window overlooking the front porch roof.

Danny hides his ashtray and the smelly Camel cigarettes he smokes at night when he is alone in his room under the outside window sill where Mama does not see them when she goes into his room. He tells me not to squeal to Mama as he will 'get' me if I do. I smile at him and say that the cigarettes are our secret and ask for a puff. He says gah, no, Leah! My sister will not smoke! I smile at him and he winks at me and says he is always looking out for me. I smile back and do not tell him that I think of it as him trying to be what he thinks a man should be.

After I had Robbie settled in the upstairs playroom beating up my small Barbie collection, I joined Danny on the stairs, bouncing Tommy on my lap. We were experts at keeping tabs on adult conversations from our observation posts on the stairs. Today the adults were discussing the possibility of Danny returning to Bremerton with OurFather and **NINE**-a for the upcoming school semester.

"And if he likes it," OurFather leaned forward as he spoke, "he can start Highschool in September. That should relieve some of the strain on the two of you and give us some time with my son."

"And what about Cookie," Daddy interjected with sarcasm. "Of course, you will continue to send her support money."

Danny snorted so loudly I had to put my hand over his mouth to keep the adults from hearing. Mama's head jerked around, but she didn't say anything. "He don't pay any support for either of us, as far as I know," Danny whispered in my ear, little bits of spit hitting the side of my head. I nodded. It was well known that he refused to 'pay for a dead horse', as he called the fifty dollars monthly child support as ordered by the courts.

"Of course, Hal. We will be happy to send fifteen a month for Leah's expenses if Daniel is living with us." I wished I could see Mama's face, but the sliding door that separated the Library and the Dining Room where we sat on the stairs suddenly shut tight, blocking our view and muffling adult voices.

"Well," Danny huffed. "That's the story, it is? They want me to go live with them." He rose from his seat on the step and stomped upstairs. I heard his door slam hard at the end of the hall.

As I carefully got up to tend to Tommy, the library door slid open and Mama appeared. She followed me up the stairs, giving me a quick squeeze in the hallway. When I came out of the playroom with the now dry baby, she and Danny were headed downstairs. Mama paused for a moment and asked me to prepare a bottle and put Tommy down for his nap. I should then join the grownups for some talk.

At the end of the day, Danny agreed to spend the second semester of eighth grade in Bremerton with OurFather and NINE-a. Mama would deliver him the weekend before school term began the first week in February.

"Now you understand, Daniel, that you have committed to

spending the entire semester with your father. No matter what happens, you will not be able to move home until school lets out in June. Do you agree?" Danny nodded his head.

"Well, that settles it, Mayleen. The boy is mine." OurFather's face lit up with a smile that gave me "the willies", as OurGrandmother used to say about me.

"Until the semester is over, he will live with you, Eldon. That's the agreement. Further arrangements, if any, will be negotiated then. Make no mistake. My attorney will draw up papers with the agreed upon details that you will sign before he leaves this house."

Danny and I talked late into that night, he laying on his bed and me sitting bedside on the rug. "I guess it will help Mom and Dad if I go over there for a few months," he opined. "One less mouth to feed, and *he* will at least send a little money to take care of you."

"But Danny, do you really want to live there?"

"No!" He spat the word out, spraying globs of spit. "I just want to be outta here and doin' something for the family. Gol, Leah! I love you guys. Maybe things'll get better without me buttin' in all the time."

I thought about this in my own bed down the hall. Life would definitely change with Danny gone; what would I do without my big brother? All my life he had been there for me, except for the two periods that OurFather had kidnapped him and taken him to California. Granted, he teased and made jokes at my expense and tried to run my life, but I loved him and he loved me. *And (face it Leah) you will miss him when he is gone. You will even miss his wet fingers on the back of your neck, and the big brother teasing and his warm spit on your cheek when he sneaks up behind you and whispers in your ear.*

On the weekend before the new semester started, OurFather appeared at the door prepared to take Danny and his boxes of possessions to their new (temporary, I prayed) home on Madrona Street in Navy Yard City. Mama tried to keep a stiff upper lip, but I could see how hard it was for her to prevent the tears from slipping down her cheeks.

"I was supposed to deliver him, Eldon," she whispered through gritted teeth.

He answered with a smirk that **NINE-a** didn't want her anywhere near the Madrona Street house. His little moustache wiggled as he squished his upper lip back and forth, apparently in an attempt to quell his mirth.

Danny promised to call once a week, but OurFather quickly put the kibosh on that, as "long distance calls cost money, Danny, and I am not made of it, regardless of what your **mother** thinks!" Mama winced but gave Danny another hug and promised that she would call him. Danny smiled with his mouth, but his eyes looked sad and a little leery at what lay ahead.

After OurFather's car pulled out onto Steele Street and headed for 6th Avenue and the route back to Bremerton, Mama disappeared into the back yard. Daddy stomped about for a bit muttering in Czech, then went inside and got a beer for himself and Mama. He directed me to keep an eye on 'the boys', which I did.

As soon as the door slammed shut behind Danny my life changed. Part of me was back under my Chestnut tree on Stewart Avenue in Bremerton across the street from the barrage balloon, already awaiting Danny's return. In all the world, no one was closer to me than Danny.

CHAPTER 17
In Which a Tumble Becomes a Turning Point and the Last of Us is Born

Two weeks after Danny left with OurFather Mama slipped and fell down the sloping lawn that ran along Eighth Street on the south side of our property. Daddy was packing his fishing things into the trunk of the car readying himself for the beginning of fishing season and his first trip for the last few years off with his brothers on Opening Day. Mama was still in her nightgown and the blue chenille bathrobe and matching slippers Daddy had given her for Christmas when she ran out to give Daddy a kiss good-bye, Tommy in her arms. As she started down the slope that dropped from house to street level, she slipped on the damp grass. Instinctively, she threw herself backward in an attempt to prevent injury to her seven month old baby boy. In doing so, she twisted her ankle—resulting in a snap so loud Daddy actually heard it. Her face turned white as one of the new set of sheets in the upstairs linen closet.

Daddy dropped the box he was carrying and bolted up the slope to where Mama lay moaning and gripping Tommy to her chest. "My God, Mayleen! Your foot is nearly backwards." Daddy shuddered and took the baby from her. I had been watching from the back porch and almost beat Daddy to Mama's side. Tommy began to cry as I took him from Daddy.

"Go inside and make sure he's okay, will you honey? And then get back out here. I need you to help me."

Baby in arms, I ran into the house. Robbie appeared out of nowhere and helped me up the back steps. After a cursory examination revealed no problems with Tommy, we put him in his stroller and Robbie took over. "You go help Mommy, please Cookie? You can trust me with Tom." He squatted beside his little brother and nodded. "We'll be fine, won't we. Cowabunga!" I gave him a quick smile and flew back down the hill to my parents.

A few neighbors had assembled to help Daddy, who directed Mr. Bonner from across the street to please call an ambulance. Mama mumbled something as I leaned over her. "Tell Daddy that I'll be okay. Don't need an ambulance." But it was evident that her ankle and leg were badly injured.

When the ambulance arrived, they loaded Mama onto a stretcher and carried her in. Daddy got into the car, discarded fishing gear thrown onto the sidewalk notwithstanding, and followed. Robbie and I took the boxes and rods and Daddy's duffle bag back into the garage and wheeled Tommy up the hill and into the house.

We waited. I fed the boys, changed Tommy, and put him down for a nap. And we waited. Finally, just as I was thinking about what to fix for dinner, the back door flew open and Aunt Dot came in. She swept me up in her arms and held me tight, whispering into my hair that everything would be okay.

I burst into tears at her touch. Don't cry little Cookie, she says as she wipes away the tears with her thumb. I will take care of you and the boys until your daddy gets home. "Is my mommy gonna be ok, Aunt Dot?" I ask, and she tells me that Daddy will answer my questions when he comes. I ask if she is alive, and Aunt Dot laughs softly. "Yes," she says to me. "Your mama is alive and was talking to your daddy when I left to come here." I remember the long weeks that Aunt Dot cares for us while Mama has surgery on her back, and Mama's long journey back to health as my sweet auntie holds me close.

I cried until no more tears would come.

Two weeks later Mama came home. She had a cast well above her knee and could bear no weight on that side of her body. She was confined to a huge wheelchair that bumped into everything in the house. Daddy found a caretaker who came just before Robbie and I headed for school and left when I got home. From that moment until I set off for school the next morning, I was mommy to my boys and hands and feet for my mama. Robbie tried his best to help, but he was, after all, only in third grade.

Danny was furious when he found out that no one told him about Mama's fall and ankle surgery for a week. Daddy said he didn't need to know, that it would cause problems and Mama didn't want to 'rock the boat'. It didn't seem right to me. I tried to call him collect so the charge wouldn't show up on the phone bill. **NINE**-a refused to accept the call, so I wrote him a letter and sent it to Grammy B's house, snitching a stamp from Mama's desk and replacing it with three pennies from my piggy bank. He immediately made plans to return home but was stopped by OurFather. "Your home is now here, young man," he pronounced, nose to nose according to Danny. "And here you will stay until I let you visit. Do you understand?"

The first weekend after Mama came home from the hospital, Danny slipped out of the Madrona Street house on Saturday morning before anyone else was up and hitched a ride to Tacoma. He cried when he saw Mama's leg in its thigh high cast with the little square hole over the inside ankle bone where stitches over the surgical area required daily attention. Mama held his head to her chest and whispered in his ear that he had agreed to stay in Bremerton for the semester, and he must hold up his part of the bargain. Daddy took him back late Sunday afternoon. Although both sets of parents grilled him, he never revealed how he found out about Mama, and Grammy B kept her own silence. She knew how to listen with her heart, too.

Over the next few months, Danny hitched rides to Tacoma at least every other weekend, with either Daddy driving him back on Sunday, or OurFather picking him up. Neither household was happy about the situation but worked it out. When school let out in June, Danny packed his bags and walked down the hill to Gramma B's house. OurFather followed, demanding that he return, but Danny faced him down. He had promised only to stay for the last semester of the school year and was going home to his family. That I-want line was solid on both his face and OurFather's, according to Grampa B as he escorted OurFather from the premises and Gramma called Mama in Tacoma. OurFather threatened Mama and Daddy with police and the courts but in the end, was bound by the written agreement both parents had signed.

Years later I discovered that OurFather used this disobedience on Danny's part to renege on the fifteen dollars a month child support he was court ordered to pay for me, once again reminding me that the child without a spout meant nothing in his eyes.

Mama's ankle recovered slowly, but by the end of summer, she was on her feet and back in charge of the household, albeit she had begun working as a cashier at the Piggly Wiggly market a mile or two up Sixth Avenue from our house. Tommy was a real firecracker—talking and walking and becoming a person. Laundry was easier as Daddy found a 'deal' on an automatic washer that he installed in the pantry area off the kitchen. I still hung the clothes either in the basement in inclement weather or outside on the old lines, but now diapers were a thing of the past. I started sixth grade, Robbie went into fourth, and Danny began his freshman year in high school at Stadium, a little too far to walk, but fortunately, city bus close. Daddy was now full-time and on salary as the Machinist Union's Business Agent, no longer simply a machinist.

Things are going smoothly for our family I think as I let myself in at the back door after school on a slightly gloomy Friday afternoon shortly before Thanksgiving. Robbie is outside in the back yard with Tommy, pretending to be policemen with their wooden pistols made by Daddy, running back and forth shooting at the bad guys according to Tommy. As the door shuts softly behind me, I hear Mama's voice talking to someone, but I do not see Mama. I walk through the kitchen past the little half bathroom in the hall that runs to the dining area and my parents' bedroom and see my mother staring at her reflection in the mirror over the little sink. I stand quietly, listening to her say that she is pregnant and there is nothing she can do about it. She is going to have another child, and she is not happy.

I startled at this piece of information and Mama turned her head. "Leah." It was a statement, not an inquiry. "Did you hear what I was saying?"

"Yes, Mama."

"You will not repeat what I said, do you understand me? This will be a secret between us until I have a chance to talk with Daddy."

I understand that this is an order, not a request. I do not answer her with my mouth, but I nod my head. She sighs softly and her shoulders relax My eyes tell her that I am listening with my heart. I will not ask the question I see lurking in her eyes as she stares into the mirror.

Richard was born in August. I had prayed for a sister, but in my heart of hearts, I knew this baby would be another boy. He had blonde hair and blue eyes and was a bubbly little brother from the start, and except for coloring, looked exactly like Daddy!

I see my parents and the smile on Daddy's face as he brings his new child into our home. Mama is happy—her eyes filled with relief. Daddy hums to baby Richard as he places him in my arms and hugs Mama. "Do you have a song for your new brother, Cookie?" he asks. I smile back at him. Daddy leans forward and kisses my cheek, then sings in his beautiful baritone voice—"You're the end of the rainbow, my pot of gold—You're Daddy's little girl to have and hold—and the only daughter I will ever have."

Perhaps there is hope for our future after all.

Interlude

The following year we moved yet again, this time to a farm at the southeast edge of the city—a small acreage with room for a cow and calf, a hog, chickens, and eventually my first personal horse. Mama changed jobs to a grocery store not too far from our 'new' old farmhouse, Danny started his senior year at Franklin Pierce High School, and I started as a freshman. Robbie entered this year in middle school, and my two little brothers stayed behind, watching us hustle down the road to meet our respective school buses and lusting for their own school days to come.

Danny learned to drive this summer of his sixteenth year and OurFather has seen to his wish for a car, but he didn't offer me a ride to school. "Gah, Leah," he exclaimed—"What would my buddies say if they saw my little sister in the back seat?" After school he often spent part of the afternoons drag racing with these same buddies, using the back roads for a track. We were both careful lest Mama found out about this little hobby.

My cousin Sharon lived not too far from us and we spent many hours riding our horses bareback down the pole line road that ran through the small farms and growing neighborhoods bringing electricity from a dam on one of the rivers flowing from Cascade Mountain Range. She was two years my junior but we were close. I also met Marnie who became my best friend and confidant through high school and college.

Daddy is preoccupied with his job as Business Agent for the Machinists Union. He tells Mama that it keeps him busy many nights after work. I am not so sure, as I have heard phone calls sometimes at night. My little room is on the ground floor of the old farmhouse, next to the kitchen where the phone hangs on the wall. All the other bedrooms are upstairs. Daddy gives me 'that look' on mornings after the calls. I smile and keep my mouth shut. Does he think that Mama does not know?

OurFather insists that I become a member of Job's Daughters, an organization for daughters of Masons. This means I must ride the bus downtown to the Masonic Temple in Tacoma twice a month or more for functions, carrying a formal outfit in a plastic bag. I am not keen on high heel shoes and prefer my western boots, but they will not 'do' says **NINE**-*a. At some of the meetings I play the piano; it makes me feel like I fit in with these girls from elite North End Tacoma homes.*

On some meeting nights, Mama rode the bus with me into Tacoma then met with friends, or later drove us in her car after Daddy fixed up a second hand vehicle for her to get to and from work. *Mama spends her spare time writing letters to her old Bremerton friend. She sends me down the road to mail them in the public box by the school bus pickup. "Our little secret, Cookie," she says and I smile.*

Danny graduated high school in June following our move to the farm and immediately enlisted in the Navy. School was different after Danny left. I was big sister to Robbie again, trying to keep him out of trouble. I joined the yearbook staff, rising to editor over the three years left until I graduated and went off to college.

I started writing poetry during that first summer at the farm before school started, sitting atop the pasture hill beneath a tired old pear tree, pouring out pieces of my heart in blank verse and rhyme.

I hide the book away from prying eyes—especially Mama's. They replace the many unmailed letters I wrote to Annie before her memory slides into that tiny black hole where all the hard times from the past are stored. Daddy spends less and less time at home, Mama does the same, and they do not talk.

I separated myself from them during my last two years of school, concentrating on what lay ahead. I needed space to grow and that space caused a widening between my parents and me. Not that it was a bad thing. I had won scholarships and had been accepted at a university in Seattle. The burden had begun to lift.

And I begin dreaming...

CHAPTER 18
In Which I Remember My Past and Consider My Future

By the time I finished high school Anne Marsh was long relegated to some deeply hidden place where memories of the heart never tarnish, nor grow old and dog-eared. Consequently, I was quite surprised when a recurring dream about someone called Hatchet Annie and a place called Quaker Hill began interrupting my sleep.

I stand at its base, poised at a footpath sloping gently upward through tall grass and meadow flowers. The rising moon hangs like a lemon slice against a dusky twilight sky the texture of crumpled velvet punctuated by a scattering of early rising stars. Grass clings to my ankles leaving wet dew-streaks on my scuffed leather sandals. The path glows white in the moonlight, covered, as it is, with dust ground fine as flour by countless passing feet. I kick off my sandals and let the dust puff between my toes, reveling in its silken texture, cool, soothing, almost damp to the touch. I venture up the path, feeling for it with my bare feet rather than watching where I am going; that path is as familiar to me as my face—I simply cannot lose my way. Unfortunately, I cannot remember just where the pathway leads.

I climb steadily, pausing occasionally to catch my breath and admire the view. Somewhere in the hazy valley below, children call to one another—laugh, shout, then grow silent as one by one their parents call them in. Lights dim on porches— kitchen windows glow with warmth. I smile in the growing darkness, surprised that my eyes that see the valley so clearly cannot make out my destination.

As I near the top my perspective changes—I am five years old again, a blue-eyed "only girl" towhead with a pageboy haircut, wearing a sundress made by Mama from a flowered feed sack. My left hand clutches the handle of my old red wagon in which sits a dented milk can. The sun rides high in a hot summer sky dotted with hawks (makin' lazy circles, I snicker to myself)! I am on my way to fetch milk from Smith's Dairy— and (oh-my-gawd—how could I forget) Hatchet Annie lives just over that hill. My heart leaps wildly, restrained against my bodice—my hands grow slick with cold sweat.

Without warning, the bent figure of an old woman hunched almost double with a load of firewood appears before me. The old woman stops for a moment and adjusts her load. She wears a long-sleeved black blouse and a long black skirt falling to her ankles, regardless that the hot summer sun is beating down. A white shawl across her left shoulder folds back upon itself, providing a sack of sorts that holds a small hatchet partially shielded by her floppy straw hat from which protrudes one long grey braid snaking over her shoulder, accenting the pin tucking on her blouse front. Bare feet peek from beneath her dampened skirt—black boots, laces tied together, drape over her right shoulder. She has obviously come from the creek and has seen me spying on my brother.

My hand chooses this precise moment to lose control of the wagon handle. CLANG! The old woman looks up from her modifications, raising her face to me, her snapping dark eyes drilling into mine. She accuses me with a frown.

I had been at college for a year and two full quarters when the dreaming started. The dreams disturbed me less than the sudden return of a nightmare that had plagued my childhood, although they filled me with no less dread.

I am in the wood below our back pasture. The day is sunny, early spring, but light filters in diffuse streams through the tall trees and splats in bright pools on the mossy forest floor. I am picking wild flowers—trilliums—for Mama and I am humming to myself as I search for additional tri-leafed white blooms. In my dream, I am crouching beside a mossy log in a sunlit circle when the light abruptly disappears and hands grab me, one on my shoulder, the other across my mouth. I am jerked onto my back and into blackness.

I awoke screaming loudly enough to jolt my roommate Jenny upright in the bottom bunk. Jenny slept like the proverbial log and could easily sleep through our wind-up alarm clock that sounded like the firehouse bell and was audible, according to our hallmates, up and down the second floor of Blaine Residential House at the University of Washington.

"Whoa," she muttered. "What the heck was **that** all about!"

"Gol, Jen—I don't have a clue," I replied. "Haven't had that dream since I was a little kid." I breathed deeply, trying to banish the wave of terror that still washed over me.

Jenny turned on the little light that hung by curved hooks over the headboard at each level of our wooden bunks. "Are you okay?"

I sighed. "Yeah. Wish I knew what it means. Maybe I should ask Professor Davis after class." She was my first year Psych teacher. She had mentioned dreams in one of her lectures, but we had not yet studied their significance.

Jen shared this part of my schedule. She snorted and commented that if I brought it up in class, Ms. Davis would probably make a quarter-long study out of it. We both laughed and she turned out her light. I could hear her snuggle back into the blankets and soon she was snoring softly. I lay awake for quite a while, searching my childhood for some meaning attached to this nightmare. Finally, I drifted off and thought no more of it until it became a nearly weekly occurrence.

We had entered the thousand days of Camelot—handsome young First Family, age of lunar explorers and Cuban crises. Viet Nam still waited in the wings and no one had yet heard of a flower child. I attended college in Seattle, lived on campus, and worked part-time to supplement my scholarships. My older brother had set me up (as he had so many times throughout the years) with yet another of his friends—this one a classmate named Kurt. We became friends during our high school years and recently Kurt had tendered and I had accepted his marriage proposal. Shortly afterward the dreaming began.

"I'm going to get to the bottom of this," I sputtered with exasperation after awakening three nights running. Kurt began to notice dark circles beneath my eyes and my roommate grumbled that the tossing and turning kept her awake. Consequently, on Friday after classes, I rode the bus from campus to the pier and caught a ferry cross-Sound to Bremerton. Kurt met me on the Peninsula side. He lived in nearby Port Orchard with his family while he pursued an apprenticeship at Puget Sound Naval Shipyard. My future in-laws had invited me for the weekend—something I considered both a lovely gesture and an opportunity for further inspection (theirs and mine).

Asleep that first night in the guest room, a tiny walk-in closet sized room off the bathroom, scarcely big enough for a twin bed and a lamp, I dreamt again of times past and my first encounter with Kurt.

CHAPTER 19
In Which a Song and a Slap Carry Lasting Consequences

When World War II ended the barrage balloon that had protected the Bremerton Navy Yard and (in my mind) our little house across the street, disappeared; in its place building commenced on a new church. I was sorry to see the fenced area and its huge balloon leave, especially Chief Ginty and his crew of sailors who tended to it. I especially missed what I considered my only chance to coax a uniform top from the back of one of the sailors! Mama said I should be happy that the war was over and the sailor boys and their shirts could go home to their families.

Construction on the church advanced at a snail's pace, leaving many hours during the long summer days for neighborhood kids to play in the piles of sand, collect 'slug money' (the round metal knockouts from electrical boxes) and walk the framework of the choir loft on dares, much to our parents' dismay! We were already attending Sunday School held in the basement of the nearby Lutheran Church. Mama and Daddy became friends with Pastor Pool and his family who had moved into the parsonage catty corner from us and next door to the church construction site. Katherine and Frank, Jr., the Pool children, were high school age. Danny and his cohorts followed Frankie's every move. He was rebuilding an old car as a hotrod for himself now that gasoline was not so severely rationed. Katherine babysat us when Mama and Daddy took in the occasional movie or attended a dance. Katherine read books to us and let us stay up late! She wore her hair in pin curls with a scarf wrapped around her head neatly tied in a knot above her forehead, blue jeans rolled up mid-calf, saddle shoes, and one of her father's white shirts! She was studying for her driver's license and I worshipped her.

Mrs. Pool (Florence to Mama) taught my Sunday school class. She was a stout woman, gray-haired and a little florid. Her bosom sailed ahead of her like a ship on high seas, and she favored floral print dresses with large white lace-trimmed collars that lay on that bosom like foam. Her shoes, stout, sensible brown lace ups with a two-inch heel, stuck out from her stubby legs like wooden blocks. They fascinated me, for some reason, and I couldn't keep my eyes from them, which is why, perhaps, I lost custody of my senses.

"Leah, can you tell us what your family does together?" Mrs. Pool's question caught me completely by surprise as I had 'misplaced' the morning's subject while daydreaming about sailor shirts.

During a previous question and answer period at Sunday School Mrs. Pool had asked everyone in the class to tell what we did on Saturday night, just to get us acquainted, I suppose. I told the class that we had a bathtub so big that we all took a bath together. Mrs. Pool told Mama who explained that the three of us kids took that bath, not the whole family. Mrs. Pool should, therefore, have been warned about asking me offhand questions.

I jerked my eyes from Mrs. Pool's stubby shoes and groped for an answer. "We sing a lot," I muttered.

"Lovely," purred Mrs. Pool, apparently thinking that nothing can go wrong with singing. "Can you sing one of your favorite songs for us?"

For the life of me, the only song I could think of was one I learned from my daddy—a little ditty about two hens and a rooster. When Mama heard me singing it to my dolls, she had washed my mouth out with soap. Regardless, I opened that same mouth and out flew Daddy's ditty. Mrs. Pool gasped, my classmates giggled—I turned bright red and knew I was in for a repeat soaping!

Sometime before autumn, Mrs. Pool forgave (or forgot) my past musical transgression as I was often asked to sing little solos at Sunday school, and sometimes, even at the grownup's service! Mama dressed me in white pinafores and Patent leather Mary Janes, polished with love and Vaseline by Daddy. As a general rule, Daddy did not attend services, but he made exceptions at Christmas, Easter, and whenever I sang.

"You're gettin' stuck up, Leah," Danny hissed one Sunday after Mama again forced him to sit through adult services to hear me sing. "One'a these days it's gonna backfire on you and I'm gonna be there to see it!"

Christmas services were always a special event at church. On Christmas Eve all the Sunday school classes joined to put on the Christmas story. We had a manger with straw, neat cutouts of sheep covered with real wool, tall camels, and all the kids took part. One year we acquired an actual donkey for Mary to ride. As Joseph and the pregnant Mary approached the crèche, the donkey cocked its tail and made a large deposit adjacent to the organist. She leapt to her feet, startling the donkey, who abruptly deposed Mary. Joseph laughed so hard he backed into the cluster of wooly sheep, laying the whole flock flat. The donkey was banished back to its barnyard for subsequent performances!

The Christmas morning before my sixth birthday was very special for our family. In October, Pastor Pool asked Danny and me to sing a duet at the main service—something that neither of us had done before, and something that Danny didn't want to do now. "Ah, mom," he groused, "why can't Leah do it alone? She likes to get up in front of all those people and scream her lungs out."

Mama squinched up her eyes and gave him a stare. His face slowly turned red as he glared and took a step backward. She grasped his shoulders, stopping his retreat. "You will sing this duet, young man. You will sing it and smile as you sing. This is an honor."

Danny faced the inevitable with one last comment. "At least Leah likes to sing in public—I don't!"

"Well," soothed Mama, "perhaps you won't be asked again." Danny's face lit up. "You think?"

Mama could see where his thoughts were taking him. "Young man, you'd better not be planning something." Danny smirked at me over Mama's shoulder. "Not me, Mama, not me—I promise you!"

"You'll do just fine with your sister, honey. I know I can

count on you—both of you!" She gave him a squeeze and a pat on the fanny, then turned and winked at me.

In the weeks before Christmas Danny and I practiced our duet daily. It was nice, for a change, to have someone by my side. The particular song had been selected by Mrs. Pool—one that lent itself to a duet. We practiced singing verse one in unison with the chorus as a duet; verse two was a solo for Danny. Again, we sang the chorus together. Then it was time for my solo—verse three, with duets on the chorus. The final verse and chorus we were to sing together—all in all, a nicely balanced performance. Mama got busy with her sewing machine, whipping out a suit for Danny and a new dress for me.

As the big day grew closer Danny became increasingly reluctant, forcing Mama to drag him across the street for our final practice. The organist gave us our cue and we launched into our performance, which went off without a hitch. Mrs. Pool was very pleased, as was Mama.

On Christmas Eve Mama washed my hair and set it in pin curls with gel from her green bottle to "give it a little body", as she always said. I liked the WaveSet smell, and the way the stuff oozed off the comb as Mama dipped it into the bottle, but I didn't like sleeping with all those metal pins in my hair. The results, however, were worth the effort. Mama always reminded me that we must suffer for beauty—at least that's what her mother said. I waited with eager anticipation for Santa's visit and the Christmas morning church service. Danny rolled around all night in his bed, mumbling under his breath.

And so, Christmas morning found Danny, dressed to the

hilt with his hair slicked back, standing side by side on the rostrum with his loathsome little sister and facing a full house. Mr. Pool had given his sermon on the meaning of Christmas and the birth of baby Jesus. The collection plate had been passed and the choir had sung. The time was ours—Danny's and mine, as the organist began to play.

The duet began splendidly, with Danny and I in perfect harmony. He sang his solo verse and we blended the chorus without flaw. As I started verse three, something unthinkable happened. I was not alone. Danny was singing—singing loudly—singing **my solo**!

I turned in disbelief and stamped my foot. Danny ignored the stamp.

"This is my verse," I hissed, jabbing his ribs with my elbow. Danny kept on singing.

I watched my arm, hand attached and outspread, rise in slow motion towards Danny. The congregation sat spellbound as the hand made contact with my brother's cheek. **CRACK!** Danny's face went deep red, except for the outline of a small palm and five fingers on his left cheek. The sound rebounded through the sanctuary. Collectively, the congregation took a deep breath. Without missing a beat Danny grasped the offending hand tightly in his.

In the stunned silence that followed, I heard only two things—my mother's tiny "oh, dear!" and my brother Danny, still singing. As he came to the chorus, I instinctively picked up the duet. We finished the last verse and chorus as we had begun, letter perfect.

Danny yanked me down the stairs in silence. "I will never sing another duet with **her**, again," he declared as he delivered me to Mama, and he never did!

CHAPTER 20
In Which I Meet Kurt and
"The Great Krespen" Determines
My Future Husband

Kurt and I met for the first time in the Mission Covenant church basement, Bible School, first day. Place, time, date, impressed indelibly in my Book of Life.

The church is across the street from where I live with Mama and Daddy, Danny and Robbie, in Bremerton. Kurt and I are both five years old. Kurt has a thatch of dark blonde hair, freckles across his nose, and ears that stick out at the sides of his head. He wrinkles his brows and his blue eyes go up and down rapidly as he watches me from across the room. Then his tongue peeks out from between his lips. He retracts it when he sees Mrs. Pool, the Pastor's wife, looking at him, but pokes it out a bit, clamped between his front teeth when she turns away.

*When I return to my spot at the raised sandbox, I feel someone put his finger on my neck. I spin around and find myself eyeball to eyeball with little blue eyes and his tongue. He runs away and Mrs. Pool tells me that he likes me. I do not think he likes me. I do **not** like him!*

Mrs. Pool said that Kurt had a crush on me, whatever that meant, but I thought he hated me, and the feeling was mutual. Although I was glad when Bible school gave way to Sunday school and the long, hot summer, I secretly looked for the little blonde boy every Sunday. He was not a regular after summer, but his family did attend on holidays.

By the time I reached dating age, my older brother Danny had solidly established himself as a purveyor of male companions for his only sister. These consisted of Danny's buddies, who, in his eyes, could do no wrong. This did not, however, mean they met *my* approval. They consisted of a pack of scraggly Maynard G. Krebs lookalikes with fast hands and smart mouths. I occasionally acquiesced to his arranged dates, providing the proposed venue was relatively interesting and the male friend suitably dressed for the occasion.

Since Danny was 'cool' and a 'wheel', and I was as square as they come—honor roll, student council, editor of the yearbook, school newspaper, and Quill and Scroll member—I was supposed to be honored that any of his crowd would date me at all. My brother certainly had an elevated opinion of himself, but I loved him, nonetheless.

When Danny graduated high school, he enlisted in the United States Navy and found himself aboard one of the ships at Eniwetok during the United States hydrogen bomb tests. He returned, somewhat worse for the wear physically but still my big brother, about the time I entered my senior year at Franklin Pierce High School in the south end of Tacoma. I was no longer Danny the Wheel's little sister, but a person in my own right—perhaps not a Wheel, but open to all my classmates. I had few close friends, but these I trusted implicitly.

Danny had entered an apprenticeship in Electronics at Puget Sound Naval Shipyard in Bremerton that supplied him with a new crop of male friends who must have a date with his little sister Leah. I had handled my own dating for three years, thank you Danny, and did not appreciate his interference yet again. Since, at the moment, I was between dates, he persuaded me (reluctantly) to meet his best buddy for a movie two weekends hence. Kurt, who lived in Port Orchard, was "a really nice guy", and Danny just knew I would like him. Some niggling voice whispered in my ear that Danny's face was a little controlled and I should possibly inquire further into motives. I decided to let it go for the present. After all, anything can happen in two weeks.

The following weekend Marnie, my best friend since ninth grade, joined me for a double feature at the Temple Theater on Saturday afternoon. We had been waiting to see Exodus, and it was in its third week. The lines should be short enough for the afternoon matinee.

"Besides," Marnie drawled dramatically, "'The Great Krespen' is performing during intermission. You can ask him about the impending date with Danny's latest best friend."

"Okay, I will," I laughed back at her. "Maybe he'll pull my question out of the fish bowl."

I close my eyes and take myself back to the Temple Theater on a bright Saturday afternoon. Marnie and I wait in a fairly short line, moving slowly with the drift of teenagers and the occasional parent to the ticket counter, and then into the theater lobby. On a table opposite the refreshment area sits a large glass fish bowl half-filled with slips of paper on which theater goers have left messages for the Great Krespen. Go fill *out a slip, Marnie says and pokes me in the ribs. I pick up a pencil and begin. Marnie peers over my shoulder and reads aloud what I put to paper. "Will it work out" I print in block letters. I put my initial L at the bottom as Marnie snorts and stage whispers in my ear, "If he pulls that one out of the hat you sure didn't give him anything to work with." I tell her I know, dummy, I want him to work **at** it! Then the aisle curtains open and people stream out. I fold the paper in half and drop it into the fish bowl. Marnie pulls me forward and we go find ourselves a seat.*

We sat through the first flick, a spaghetti western with Clint Eastwood, I believe, and endured previews of coming events before the House lights came on. "Well, here comes the 'Great Krespen,'" Marnie hissed into my ear. "And he's got the famous fishbowl with him!"

Indeed, a tall, slender middle-aged man dressed in a black tuxedo and dramatic, red-lined black cloak strolled quickly across to center stage accompanied by his assistant toting a small table and the bowl half full of paper strips. While the assistant, a small, dark-haired young man, arranged table and bowl in the exact center of the stage, the Great Krespen (we all assumed that it was he) popped his cuffs and dramatically swooped about flaring his cloak. Finally, he settled at the table and announced in a low and conspiratorial tone that he was about to begin.

"No chance he's gonna pick yours outta that bowl," Marnie giggled. "Mom says he's a hoax and all the ones he pulls out are fake." She mussed my hair and I swatted her hand away as the Great Krespen inserted index and middle finger into the bowl, extracted a folded paper, and dramatically unfolded it.

"Is KJ present in the audience?" A gasp went up from the balcony and we turned to see a rather chubby older woman stand and wave her hand.

"Probably his wife," snickered Marnie.

"You ask of your health." The Great Krespen paused dramatically, the heel of his left hand pressed to his forehead, eyes closed. "You have had tests, but do not yet know the results, yes?" The woman nodded. "Fear not, dear lady. The results will be encouraging."

He reached for another folded paper, going through perhaps three more before he announced that the one he now held would be his last for this intermission. "Here it comes, here it comes." Marnie poked me in the ribs. "It's gonna be yours."

"Is L in the audience—I am seeking L." A young man rose, but the Great Krespen motioned him down. "This L is a young lady. I can feel her presence. I believe she is also called Cookie."

I gasped! "Marnie! He means *me!*" I stood so quickly she had to reach out and steady me.

"Ah. She is here. You ask of a young man, is this not true?" I nodded. "And you wonder—will you like each other, no?" I nodded again. "You have met—in the past. And you will remember." He paused and an odd look passed quickly across his face. "The answer is yes. And although the path is not clear, you will marry him."

I sat down with an audible thump.

"Well, that was interesting," interjected Marnie. "Thought you said this was another one of Danny's buddies from the Ship Yard."

"He is—and I swear his name doesn't ring a bell. Oh well,

I guess I have to take the date with this one—or I'll never know!" I did the spooky face and wiggled my fingers. Marnie burst out in laughter, causing the Great Krespen and his assistant who was busily removing both table and bowl from the stage, to stop and stare disapprovingly in our direction.

And so, as they say, no good deed goes unpunished. My brother actually introduced me to a nice young man named Kurt with blonde hair and ears that stuck out slightly, and though he never brought the "Famous Christmas Duet" episode up to me again, he did allude to it in a toast at our wedding. He told Kurt that as we went through life together, never, never sing a duet with me. Kurt acknowledged that he was safe in that regard as he couldn't carry a tune if it were nailed to a board!

One Saturday afternoon several years later when I was very pregnant with our first child, Kurt's mother and I sat drinking coffee at her kitchen table, chatting about old times and things Kurt and I had done as kids. We were joined by Kurt's Aunt Lucy B.

"Hey, Pearl," she said, "do you remember the summer all the kids went to bible school at that church in Bremerton?"

This was not necessarily news for me—Kurt and I had discovered while dating that we shared that early history. But what she said next raised the hairs on the back of my neck!

"And at the Holidays we went for Christmas service?"

Uh-oh, I knew where this was leading. Think fast! Before I could open my mouth, my mother-in-law laughed, her face beaming with delight. "I sure do. You're thinkin' about that little girl and her brother, aren't you!"

"Yeah," chortled Aunt Lucy. "I still remember the sound of

that slap as she nailed him across the face!"

"I remember feeling really sorry for her mother," Pearl responded.

I could feel the blood trying to decide whether to drain from my face or rush to my hairline. I actually contemplated fainting, but before I could put action to thought, Kurt's mom turned to me with her cherub cheeks and twinkling eyes.

"You went to that church when you were little, didn't you, Leah? Did you know that girl? Whatever happened to her?"

Trapped! What in the world was I going to say? For a microsecond, I saw myself levitating from the chair and fleeing the kitchen. Then reason took over. I gulped.

"I did know that little girl, Mom. You could say we were really close. Actually, she grew up and married your son."

Kurt's mom's mouth flew wide open. Aunt Lucy B. threw back her head and gave a huge whoop of delight. I bit my lip and waited for the axe to fall. I always felt Kurt's mother was still trying to make up her mind about this girl who had taken away her son. Kurt was the first of the three sons to marry and the middle child. We had caused quite a stir as this upset the family tradition of the eldest marrying first. On the bright side, after four years, I was pregnant with the first grandchild. Maybe she'd go easy on me.

"Oh, my," exclaimed Pearl when she could finally talk. "Oh, my—I did so think that child was a brat. I remember telling the boys in great detail what I would do to them if they ever embarrassed me like that! Kurt told me I didn't have anything to worry about since he didn't have any sisters!" She started to laugh, so hard that tears rolled down those rosy cheeks. Then she reached across to where I was sitting and took my hand in hers. Looking deep into my eyes she smiled. "And to think she grew up to be my very own, very dear daughter!"

CHAPTER 21
In Which I Visit Yukon Harbor and Meet the Aunt and Uncle

"You geared for me to drive you up the Hill?" Kurt's grin spread across his face and his eyes sparkled. Both of us felt that a visit to the old farm might put some meaning to my dreaming.

"Ready for an adventure, huh? Well, I think maybe I'd like to do this one alone."

"You mean I should drive you there, find a place to park, and plan on reading a while?" He was deep into "Studs Lonigan", a book he called his 'little vocabulary builder.'

"That sounds good, but how about we hold off until tomorrow? If the weather's nice we can take a picnic and find a quiet spot out by the lake on our way back."

"Okay by me."

He was being agreeable about this weird dreaming thing, I thought. He usually pooh-poohed anything off-beat, keeping his feet firmly grounded in a mixture of practicality and old wives tales learned at his mother's knee. I loved him dearly— he was the perfect foil to my usually fey approach to life.

We had hoped for a fairly quiet evening with his parents

and younger brother, but after dinner, Kurt's Uncle Clyde and Auntie Lynn came along to look me over once again. We had met before under less than optimum conditions.

On a decidedly wintery evening, Kurt set out to introduce me to his favorite Uncle and Aunt who lived at the little community of Yukon Harbor nestled in a sheltered cove on the shores of Puget Sound. Kurt spent many childhood days and nights camping and fishing with Uncle Clyde at his cabin on a little island in the middle of Stewart Lake in British Columbia, and Auntie Lynn, who had no male babies of her own, cosseted him exclusively. His two female cousins, several years his junior, accepted him as a pseudo brother and had adjusted accordingly. He loved his auntie and uncle and wanted their endorsement of his life mate perhaps even more than he wanted his parents' approval!

Consequently, this particularly nasty winter evening found us at the top of Yukon Harbor road, staring at slippery, frozen ruts carved into two feet of snow. The road, cut through from the main highway only the summer before, fell in a sweeping curve that dropped steeply to the harbor below. Uncle Clyde's log home huddled at the end of a long driveway attached to the new road just where the curve straightened into its final drop. A full moon reflecting from the brilliant crystal snow made the night almost bright as day, casting long indigo shadows from a few sparse trees acting as retainers for the narrow, steep road. Since the county had not seen fit to install guardrails, one wrong turn, one departure from the frozen ruts, could send an automobile plummeting down the slope to disappear in the deep underbrush below.

Kurt huffed with relish, anticipating this demonstration of

driving skill with which he intended to dazzle me. His breath puffs lingered in the still, icy winter air.

"Can't we take the long way, honey?" I put on my silkiest wheedling tone.

"Not on your life, Leah. That'd take more'n twenty minutes. There's the light from the windows—see?" He pointed downhill towards a tiny pinpoint of yellow nearly hidden deep below the sloping road. "Saddle up—I'm gettin' cold!" Kurt stuffed me into the passenger seat and bolted for the driver's side, slipping on the icy footing. "Gonna be a little tricky," he chuckled, as he slammed the door shut and dropped the still-running car into gear. "Hang on!"

Which I did—onto the edge of my seat! As this was before seat belts, I braced my feet against the floorboards and prayed.

Kurt's Ford Victoria sticks, failing to gain traction against the frozen rut. Kurt rocks us back and forth until our momentum carries us forward, slipping gently as we start our descent. I bite my tongue and hold my breath as we gain speed and Kurt attempts to keep us in the middle of the road. About halfway down we skid to the right, hop out of our snow furrow and head directly toward the drop off. Kurt whistles, I scream, and the car comes to a stop, bellied out on a snowplow pile, with my side hanging over the edge. It teeters for a few seconds, threatening to continue its plunge down the slope, then slowly settles into the snow.

"Whoo-whoo," laughs Kurt. "We nearly lost it that time. What an entrance that woulda been—right onto their front porch!" He turns towards me, his broad grin fading at the sight of my wide eyes and ashen skin. "Everything okay with you, Leah?"

Everything is not okay, thank you very much. I have wet my panties and can feel the warmth spreading out over the (thank you, God) plastic car seat cover. I grit my teeth, smile at him, and say nothing.

"Well, I'd better hop down and ask Uncle Clyde for a hand. Coming with?" I hesitated for a moment, contemplating the state of my underwear and jeans. "You can wear my parka if you're cold," he offered, leaning across the driver's seat with an outstretched hand. I grunted my assent, grabbed his hand and slid out into the frigid night air. Kurt snatched his parka from the backseat and swaddled me, thankfully failing to notice the slowly widening dark splotch on my jeans.

I follow my prospective spouse in silence as we slip and slide down to Uncle Clyde's driveway, then skate its full length to the house. Auntie Lynn greets us at the door with hugs for Kurt and a nod for me, the 'woman' who is her rival for Kurt's affections. We hurry down the dark hallway into the yellow warmth of a huge fire ablaze in the living room fireplace.

Uncle Clyde gave me a squeeze and stood back to appraise me. "This one's a keeper," he pronounced after what seemed an hour. "Take off your coat and stay awhile."

I started to comply, then remembered the state of my clothing and kept the huge parka tight around me.

Kurt's Auntie Lynn is heavy set with dark hair and brooding eyes the color of swamp water. She is Norwegian and proud of it; lutefisk, blood pudding, and pickled herring are her peanut butter and jelly. Uncle Clyde is a mixture of English and Irish, with the Irish part most pronounced. Blue eyes sparkle in his ruddy gnome face surrounded by a nimbus of gone-to-white hair. His ears stick out from the hair fringe in friendly greeting, rosy and ready for listening to little girls and big boys. The ears remind me of Kurt's.

"What's up, son of my sister." Uncle Clyde motioned for us to sit. "Where's that little blue bomb of yours?" Kurt's eyes swept the ceiling as if searching for inspiration.

"Well, we had a small problem comin' down the hill. I was hopin' you'd haul out the jeep and help me extricate her."

Uncle Clyde emitted a deep chuckle and grinned so broadly all his even, white teeth showed.

"Guess you ain't the best winter driver yet—a course, ya didn't have all those years in Alaska to practice like Auntie and I did!" Clyde and Lynn had lived for many years in Fairbanks, close to his brother Lloy's family. Kurt's mother had three siblings still living, Uncle Clyde, who was older than she, Lloy, who still lived in Alaska, and Floy, his twin sister from Kent, who were younger.

While the men traversed the snow and ice, bravely mushing to the defense of Kurt's old Ford, Auntie Lynn kept her eyes on me.

"You have a problem with taking off that old parka?" she inquired bluntly.

"I'm still a little cold, thanks, so I think I'll keep it on, if you don't mind," I answered politely. "May I use the bathroom?" She ushered me down a dark hallway, motioned to the door, and retreated to the living room.

A careful inspection of my nether garments revealed their still damp appearance. I could be excused the wetness by explaining a fall while skating down the hill, but the moment I got anywhere near that blazing fireplace, the true nature of the stains would be apparent to all. Sitting on the furniture in my current condition would definitely fall under Mama's category of a visitor no-no. If Auntie Lynn had been one wit more welcoming, I might have scrounged up the courage to confess the problem, but as it was, I neatened myself as best I could, zipped the parka, and returned to the inquisition.

Auntie Lynn eyed me as if she suspected I concealed one of Annie's little hatchets. "Have a seat," she motioned.

"I think I'll stand," I countered.

"Known Kurt long?" she inquired. In fact, I had known him since we were five—something we had recently discovered and had not yet revealed to the family.

"Actually, yes and no," I replied enigmatically.

She tossed me a smile the way one tosses a bone just beyond the reach of a chained dog. We remained in silence for several moments—neither of us willing to speak. We were both stubborn women, although she had had a lot more years of practice than me!

Just as I was about to give in the door flew open. Kurt and Uncle Clyde burst through—laughing, rosy cheeked, and covered with snow.

"Woman, how about some coffee and a wee sip of that peach brandy you have hidden away," Uncle Clyde demanded jovially as he and Kurt divested themselves of coats and boots, shouting over each other with details of the automobile recovery. Kurt, on the pretense of snuggling close to me, put his icy fingers on the back of my neck and nuzzled my cheek with his decidedly frigid nose. "Whydja still got the parka on," he whispered softly in my ear.

"Please don't ask—I'll tell you later," I murmured in reply. "Let's just get outa here!"

"Soon, soon," crooned my intended.

We retired to the kitchen where I found myself trapped at the table between Uncle Clyde and the wall. After several cups of very thick coffee and more than one sip of schnapps, Clyde raised his head and sniffed.

"What's that smell?"

I felt my face go beet red.

"Gawd, Lynn, has that dog a-yours gone and peed in here again? Jeezus Keeerist!" Clyde leaped up from his chair and inspected the cushion, testing it with his hand. The dog in question, a little brown mutt of indeterminate heritage, jumped from Auntie's lap and dashed guiltily towards the hallway. In the ensuing hubbub, Kurt and I made our good-byes and sidled out the door.

As soon as we were safely up the driveway, Kurt slowed the car and turned to me.

"Now, what's all this stuff with the parka?"

"Well, it wasn't dog pee that Uncle Clyde smelled," I confessed. "It was me. I wet my pants when I thought we were going over the edge!"

Kurt laughed so hard I thought we were going to have another accident. He pulled over to the side of the road and slapped the steering wheel with glee. When his seizure of merriment concluded he shook his head. "Why didn't ya just ask Aunt Lynn for something to wear?"

That was such a logical solution for a man.

"In the event that you should wet yourself while laughing at my predicament, I have no doubt you would head straight back to that house and ask for clean underwear," I snapped sarcastically.

Kurt stopped laughing. "Well, maybe I wouldn't now that I think about it. I guess that was kinda tough on you, wasn't it. You couldn't exactly march through the door, introduce yourself and ask for a change of shorties, or whatever you ladies call 'em." He directed the car back out onto the road. We rode along in silence for a few minutes.

"I promise I won't tell, Leah. My family can get kinda carried away with the teasing."

I leaned over and kissed him on the cheek, pleased that this man of mine was one of the good guys.

"Just promise me one thing," he continued.

"Anything, honey," I avowed, "Anything at all."

"Get my parka cleaned before you give it back!"

I promised!

Uncle Clyde seemed to like me—Aunt Lynn was still withholding her opinion pending further developments. As long as she lived, I was never certain she had finished her evaluation.

At any rate, we now sat around Mom's kitchen table, drinking thick, boiled coffee and moose milk, a mixture of moonshine rye whiskey and cow's milk. My panties, thank you, were dry as a bone!

By ten PM, I buzzed like a pinball machine. Kurt and I slipped outside for a quick kiss in private, then walked hand in hand up the dirt road until the moonlight cleared our heads. When we returned, the uncle and aunt had gone home, everyone else was in bed and the house was quiet.

We sneaked in, kissed goodnight, then crept as silently as possible to our separate bedrooms—he with his younger brother, I in the tiny, unheated spare room. His mother (whom I was directed to call mom) had slipped a welcome hot water bottle between the chill flannel sheets. I doubled my knees up into my nightgown so that my feet were covered, then wrapped them around the hot water bottle and quickly fell asleep.

At three in the morning, I jerk awake, remembering Anne Marsh (AKA Hatchet Annie) with perfect clarity. Memory-snaps flash like a giant slide show across my mind—a montage that carries me back to my childhood. How could I have forgotten Annie? Relief floods through me. I had begun to think the dreams were a sign of some deep inner conflict requiring psychiatric intervention, or so it seemed after my Beginning Psychology class. Sorting out the details could wait for morning, so I snuggled Anne's memory close to my heart and fell into a dreamless sleep.

CHAPTER 22
In Which I Recall Old Friends and Make New Acquaintances

Kurt's family rooster rousted me at dawn! He had a particularly harsh and raspy intonation resulting from an unsuccessful throttling at the hands of his previous owners. Perhaps he had sounded even more unpleasant before this vocal reorganization. His present living arrangements were tenuous, at best, and only his obvious age and overall sinewy body kept him from my prospective mother-in-law's Sunday stewpot.

"You could boil that bird for three months and a knife would still bounce off-a the gravy," she had remarked the last time I spent the weekend. We debated the stewpot solution for weeks after the rooster attacked her as she tossed scratch into the enclosed chicken yard. He flew straight at her face, spurs first. Only her quick thinking and accurate aim with the feed bucket saved her a good scratching.

"I gotta give him credit for guts," she marveled. "I hit him so hard he ended up on the other side of the fence, but he staggered to his feet and had the nerve to try and peck me as I closed the gate." She shook her head at his audacity.

On this beautiful Saturday morning, he woke us all to an unblemished springtime sky. I stuck my head out the open bedroom window, breathing in air redolent with green growing things and freshly turned leaf mold. What a wonderful morning—perfect for reclaiming part of my childhood! Brimming with enthusiasm, I pulled on my jeans and added a sweater over my shirt before hurrying through the kitchen and out into the farmyard.

"Want to get the eggs while I feed?" Mom (I already thought of her as 'Mom' although the official date was still months away) turned the little wooden peg that held the wire and wood frame chicken yard gate closed. I could see our friend the rooster lurking beside the hen house, partially hidden from view.

"Yeah, I'll join you!" I picked up a good-sized piece of kindling and hurried before she closed the gate. "Watch out Mom—he's coming around the hen house now!" She brandished the feed bucket and the rooster veered, eyeing me as he back-pedaled.

"I wouldn't try it, Buster," I muttered as I hefted my kindling strip and swished it menacingly through the air. It made a lovely whistling sound that turned the rooster in his tracks. He stayed impressed just long enough for me to duck into the hen house and collect seven still warm oval brown eggs. *One nest holds a broody hen who protests with pecks on my wrist as I gingerly slip my hand between body and straw. The trick is to extract the eggs without jerking at the pecks— anything but a smooth exit risks cracking them on the nesting box. This morning I am successful.*

Mom and I managed a trouble-free exit, laughing as we

Troubled Skies Over Quaker Hill

caught the rooster unawares. She was a nice lady, my fiancé's mother. Laughter crinkled up the corners of her mouth and turned her cheeks to apples. She had naturally curly hair, prematurely white, cut short, and no-nonsense, like herself. Wire rimmed glasses slipped down her nose and she periodically yawned to readjust her dentures, letting them click back into place. She was down to earth and practical but suffered no fools. No one would ever accuse her of tact nor doubt her genuine love and concern for friends and family. I liked her. In time I came to love her dearly. She had three sons, good strong 'Skandehoovian' men all, but not the kind in which a person confided. With my upcoming marriage to Kurt, I slipped easily into that spot she had reserved for the daughter she never bore.

Back in the kitchen we quickly served breakfast—her specialty oatmeal, referred to by Kurt and his brothers as 'Ma's wallpaper paste,' had been gathering strength on the back of the cook stove while we tended to chores. Pearl didn't believe in measurements, hence the finished product's high tensile strength and propensity to stick to one's ribs. Kurt facetiously demanded a knife and fork instead of a spoon.

I declined oatmeal, settling for coffee and cigarettes shared with 'Dad'. I had trouble warming up to this highly opinionated Swede who seemed uncharacteristically talkative. Sharing a smoke with him was safe as long as I kept any personal opinions strictly to myself. He talked at me about some pet peeve while I sipped morning's version of the world's strongest coffee. Mom ground her own beans—"No new-fangled store bought fancy named cans for me. They're cheaper by the hunnert pound bag!" she expounded as she sat

181

the old granite pot to grumble all day long on the wood stove, adding water and additional tablespoons of coffee as needed. Consequently, by evening the contents snarled ominously from mugs chipped through years of use. Newcomers learned to drink deeply without flinching if they wished to gain the status of family member.

Kurt helped me clean up after breakfast, much to the disgust of his younger brother who viewed dishes as 'housework, fit only for Wimmin'. Ryan was twelve and suspected I had brainwashed his brother.

"Everyone knows that girls are only after a guy's money," he announced when told of our coming marriage. I jokingly inquired as to just what money he had in mind, but he was ready for me. "He must have money. He's got a job, don't he?" Who can argue with such logic!

As we washed and dried bowls and mugs, we decided on ham sandwiches and fruit for lunch, sluiced down with lemonade. I debated asking Mom for slices of berry pie, but Kurt opted for molasses cookies, instead. "Ma's piecrust is hard as Bakelite, but her molasses cookies are the best!" His matter of fact analysis of his mother's pastry skills took me by surprise. Pearl, overhearing him, responded tartly; "Don't hurt my feelings none. Just leaves extra for the rest of us." Since he had more experience in the matter than I did, we settled on the cookies.

As Kurt loaded the food basket and lemonade into his car, along with a blanket and his trusty book, I changed into clean slacks and shirt. I pulled my hair back in a ponytail secured with a rubber band and decorated it with a scarf.

The tiny bathroom mirror revealed how much I had

changed since my family left the farm. My platinum bob had darkened to honey blonde—my eyes were hazel, not green. The nose looked about the same, still tiny and slightly upturned at the tip. My ears remained small and flat to my head. A serviceable face, I observed—not beautiful, certainly, but attractive in its own way. I had a few freckles, just a fine dusting across the bridge of my nose, and fair skin that burned too easily.

"She'll never recognize you, will she?" I queried my reflection. "You sure don't look eight anymore." I guess I expected Annie to be the same, that Quaker Hill existed in some time warp where no one aged or sickened (or died) and nothing ever changed.

"What's taken' you so long in there!" Ryan's pounding on the door waked me from my reverie. "I gotta go, ya know!"

"Hold it, Pooper!" That was Kurt. The pounding stopped.

"Leggo my arm, Kurt. I said, leggo my arm." Ryan's voice rose an octave. "You're hurtin' me. MA!"

I opened the bathroom door and stepped around them, gesturing broadly that the room was free. "Sorry, Ryan."

"Well, it's about time!" Ryan yanked his arm free and stomped into the bathroom. "Thanks for nothin'," he huffed. Using the bathroom at the family homestead was never private as the door opened directly from the living room. Family and guests sat in their chairs and sofas or around the oil burning stove crouched in the corner and guessed at how long the occupant would take, just what they were doing, and whether the sound of faucets would indicate a hand-washing, however so brief it may be.

I sighed. "I don't think he's ever going to like me, Kurt."

"Don't worry about him, honey. He'll come around."

I hoped I lived that long.

The dashboard clock read 11:00 AM by the time we finally backed down the long, narrow driveway. Kurt whistled tunelessly as he maneuvered his light blue Ford Crown Victoria out onto the gravel road, eventually blending in with busy weekend traffic where the gravel went to blacktop. We rolled down the windows, reveling in the unseasonably warm sunshine kissing our skin.

"Sing for me, will you?" Kurt liked my voice. His mother quipped that he couldn't carry a tune nailed to a board, but he knew what he liked, and I gladly obliged. I sang and we laughed at his attempts to join in.

Kurt was an unusually quiet young man, tending to relax and open up only when we were alone or with close friends. His wry sense of humor and quick brain set him apart from his family, exacerbating his unfortunate tendency to stutter with excitement.

I was the odd man out in my own family, the keeper of family secrets, and resident bookworm. I felt inferior to my gregarious brothers who had no problem making and maintaining friends, preferring to keep my feelings to myself—experience had proved that sharing them gave others a way to hurt me. I trusted with difficulty and not very often, revealing little about myself to casual acquaintances and very little more to friends and family. My family position was holding up the sky that so often had nearly collapsed and destroyed us. I worried that when Kurt and I married there would be no one to carry on that job. Every night I prayed that in the morning I would awake on the other side of the rainbow where skies were always blue and the mysteries of my past were remembered. Over there, my family would be happy and free of strife, and Kurt and I would be free to create our own tomorrows.

Out of the blue, Kurt tapped my knee and broke my reverie. "Do you think she's still living there?"

"I don't know," I responded, "I hope so. I hope she's still alive. She seemed so ancient when I was a kid."

"All grownups seem ancient when you're a kid." Kurt smiled.

"Honey, I know she was a lot older than my parents—she had grown grandchildren!"

My good mood blew out the window, leaving me silently contemplating possibilities. "Maybe I shouldn't go back. If I leave everything alone, I can imagine her as she looked the last time I saw her. Now that I've remembered, those dreams'll probably go away. At least they won't bother me anymore."

Kurt laughed. "Too late, baby. Here's your old neighborhood. Which way do I go?"

When I lived here, one took the road uphill past the elementary school, turned left at the top, then drove a long looping route through trees and fields to reach our farm. Recently the road that had dead-ended at the Darling's place a half-mile past our driveway had been cut through, completing the circuit. As the crows flew, we could practically spit on the place from here.

I sighed. "Take a left up Hickey Road—quick before I change my mind. I can't back out now."

Hickey Road ran straight west and up the hill, disappearing into mixed forest. Low income housing flanked its short flatland portion. Years ago, I walked barefoot through the woods on the old footpath that connected our dead end road and the rutted dirt and gravel one-laner snaking its way past the Holy Roller church and rusted out car skeletons. Mama often sent me down the far side of the hill to the little grocery store in Park View, clutching a few coins tied up in the corner of a handkerchief and a short list—usually bread and peanut butter.

Originally Park View served as wartime housing for Navy families. After the war, its duplex units were converted into low income housing, now well populated with small children and dogs. I liked walking through the cool woods and down the hill to Park View's paved streets. Many of the children I passed were classmates. I'd wave but didn't dare stop to talk. Mama kept track of the time and didn't hesitate to send Danny hunting for me if I took too long.

Small children and dogs still cluttered the tiny grassless yards, cracked sidewalks and streets now liberally scattered with potholes. Kurt skillfully maneuvered his prized Ford Vickey through the bustling residential area while avoiding possible hazards.

"Phew!" he exclaimed. Have you ever seen so many potholes in two short blocks? That place needs some serious road work. Say, where do we go from here?"

"Huh?" his words startled me from my daydream. I looked up just in time to see what was left of the church. "Stop here for a minute." We pulled into a deserted parking lot, pausing next to a partial sign.

"What used to be here?" Kurt leaned past me, opened the glove compartment, and retrieved his sunglasses.

"When I was a kid, everyone called this place the Holy Roller Church. I don't know what denomination it was then, but from what's left of that sign I'd say it was a Pentecostal church until recently." We turned to face the deserted remains of a structure newly gutted by fire.

"I remember walking down through the woods after school one day, going to the store for Mama. I had Robbie with me and he was running on ahead, you know, playing hide and seek and jumping out to scare me." Kurt and I got out of the car. I headed for a path head just visible to the rear of the ruins.

"There's the trail! This is where it came out on the dirt road!" We walked a few yards up the trail until it made a turn. "We heard the noise from here."

Kurt took my hand and pulled me down next to him on a trailside log. He could see how involved I was in remembering that long-ago day.

"Well, don't keep me guessing—what happened?"

"Robin came bolting around the corner and ran right into me. His eyes were just like an owl's in his little, white face. I didn't have to ask him what had scared him—I could hear it myself—low-pitched, rhythmic voices punctuated by loud shrieks, in some unrecognizable language. We listened for a few minutes, then crept around the bend. Through the open windows and doors, we could see a woman writhing around on the floor, making these animal sounds and talking weird stuff. I'd heard kids at school talk about the Holy Rollers and how they fell down at church and rolled on the ground—but none of my friends mentioned the voices."

"What did you do?"

"What d'ya think? We turned around and ran for home, screaming all the way. Mom thought the whole thing was pretty funny, but she didn't make us go back."

We laughed.

"You wanna leave the car here and take the path?" The woods looked cool and inviting, offering us a little privacy.

"Maybe later, honey. Right now, I'd like to find the old farm and see if Annie's still on her hill."

From the church, the new road paralleled our old path. I was glad about the old path—it gave me hope that other childhood landmarks might have survived. The two road sections connected fifty feet beyond what had been the Darling's driveway. I recognized the big, brown-shingled house as soon as I glimpsed it from the road. It was surrounded by lilac bushes covered with huge purple blooms and grown to nearly the size of small trees. Someone had converted the enormous pasture between road and house into an orchard filled with blossoming apple trees that covered the field with a fluffy white canopy. I could tell from fluttering curtains at open windows that someone still lived in the apartment over the detached four car garage.

It is springtime and another shower has scrubbed the trees and fields clean and bright. I sit at the crest of our eastern field looking down at the Darling's side yard. Linda and Jimmy have chased Bobbie and me over the fence once again. For some reason, they do not like Bobbie who lives with her mother Jana in the apartment atop the garage that houses both of the Darlings' cars.

One of the Darling's cars is old, like our own Elizabeth—a model A Ford, bottle green and black, with two doors instead of four. The other car was new—so new that the interior still smelled like the factory and the chrome was so shiny you can see your face reflected in the bumpers. *It is a shiny maroon Chevrolet coupe and it belongs to Linda and Jimmy's father.* A bucket of soapy water sat beside the coupe parked in the packed dirt driveway. Jimmy had a hose in his hands and was using his fingers to direct a stream of frigid water straight from the well our way. We laughed because the water fell short and splashed mud on Linda's clean, white socks and shiny patent leather Maryjanes.

Jimmy throws the hose on the ground, kicks over the pail of soapy water, and screams "Bastid, Bastid, Bobbie is a Bastid" at the top of his lungs. Bobbie's face turns the color of broken bricks and tears trickle down her chubby, russet cheeks. I have asked my daddy what that word means and he tells me that it is someone whose father and mother are not married. I ask him why that should matter. He says that it is not a nice thing to say about someone and that someday I will understand. He also tells me that Jimmy and Linda are wrong, but this bit of information does not stop them from hurting Bobbie's feelings.

Bobbie says her daddy is dead—dead in the war against Japan in a place called Guadalcanal.

Every day Bobbie's mother Jana goes to work at the shipyard where my daddy works. She wears two-piece pajamas—not the kind you wear to bed—a matching jacket and pants, and her long, red curly hair is pinned up on the top of her head in a bandana. She carries a black lunch pail. Bobbie is all alone after school.

This gave Linda and Jimmy lots of time to tease her. Linda

was Robbie's age and didn't know any better, but Jimmy was one of Danny's friends. He is in the same grade as Danny, although they do not share a teacher. He was old enough to know better. *When I ask Danny to tell Jimmy not to call Bobbie a bastid, he laughs at me and tells me I am not saying the word right—it is **bastard**, and I better not let Mama hear me saying it, or she will wash my mouth out with Life Buoy soap.* Then he told me to stop sticking up for wimps and losers. *Bobbie is not a loser, I tell him. She is my friend and it is **HIS** friend who cannot say the word. Danny gives a shrug and stomps off.*

Jimmy and Linda's mother called them into the house, and Bobbie and I waited until the sun hid behind a rain cloud. When we were sure that no one could see us, we crept silently down through the pasture grass and slipped carefully under the barbed wire fence. *I hold the wire while Bobbie crawls under, then she holds it for me. As silently as two little girls possibly can, we approach Mr. Darling's shiny new car. I take the side nearest the fence and pasture, Bobbie takes the side next to the garage apartment.* Quickly we dipped our hands into the mud puddles that have accumulated in the dirt driveway. We used the soft, squishy mud as finger paint, applying it with quick strokes to the maroon surface of the new Chevrolet Coupe. Bobbie giggled as she used her finger to print "Jimmy is a bastid" on the side of Jimmy's daddy's shiny new car.

"Roberta Walker—what on earth are you doing?" I hear a voice shout from above. From my side of the car, I can see Bobbie's mama in the open window of the garage apartment. She can see Bobbie, but she cannot see me! I drop to the ground on my haunches and stay as quiet as I possibly can. "You stay

where you are, young lady. Don't you dare move!" Bobbie's mama Jana disappears from the window and I take the opportunity to crawl under the fence and hide in the tall grass on the other side.

Bobbie's mother knocks on the Darlings' door and stands there talking to Mr. Darling and pointing towards the car. I cannot see what Bobbie is doing, but I can hear a little voice inside me that says I should get up and return to the car and stand beside her. I do not move.

Now Mr. Darling is talking loudly at Bobbie and her mother. I can hear Bobbie crying—great gulping sobs that cover up what the grownups are saying. Then Mr. Darling asks if she has done this on her own. I cringe, hunching down in the pasture grass to make myself invisible. I know that when Bobbie says my name that I will run away as fast as I can. I am a coward!

Bobbie says nothing.

I cannot believe that she has taken all the blame!

Now Jana moves to the garage. Now she returns with a piece of kindling in her right hand. She snatches Bobbie by her arm and whacks her across the back of her legs. Bobbie makes a grunting sound, low and heavy in her small throat. Tears well up in my eyes as the kindling strikes her again and again. Bobbie does not cry—she just makes that same sound each time the wood thunks against her legs, but I am crying, and I cry all the way home to my warm, brightly lit kitchen.

I shuddered at the memory as tears welled in my eyes— not that Bobbie and I had done such a thing, but that I had not stood up and taken the blame along with her. What would Annie have said if I had ever told her of this particular afternoon with Bobbie? Kurt pulled to the shoulder and stopped. From here, I could see the still open pasture sloping gradually uphill to the west from the fence line adjacent to the Darling's driveway. It appeared to surround a white shake house perched at the top. "There it is, Kurt, "that's the house I lived in. This pasture," I gestured, "was part of our property. Daddy turned the cows out here."

I looked more closely at the expanse of fresh, springtime green dotted with buttercups and dandelions. "Look—the path's still there!" I pointed out a narrow brown ribbon meandering in the general direction of the wooded lot to the north. "We took that path through the trees to get to school; and there's the barn! You can just see the roof! I can't believe how much everything looks the same from down here." I pulled my head back into the car.

Somewhere nearby a chainsaw buzzed in irritation, its high-pitched screech wailing up and down like an angry wasp. I hoped somebody was bucking dead wood, not clearcutting some back lot acreage for pulpwood.

Kurt eased the car slowly up the hill along the pasture, keeping the wheels on the gravel shoulder. As we leveled out the wood and wire fence gave way to an overgrown hedge that effectively screened the house from view. Daddy had always kept the hedge framing the little farmhouse's front yard and boxing it off from both road and driveway neatly trimmed. This hedge ran wild and undisciplined.

"Don't miss the driveway, honey. It would be an easy thing to do," I admonished Kurt as he carefully navigated up the poorly maintained road. Hedge branches had encroached on the rutted dirt drive, turning it into a dark and narrow tunnel.

Kurt pulled completely off the road and stopped, killing the engine. "You wanna walk down from here, 'cuz I'm not gonna drive the car through that!" He flapped his hand in the general direction of the hedge.

I sighed and contemplated the driveway dappled with dark shadows. "Will you come with me? I'd like to see the old place again before I try to find Annie's cabin."

Kurt opened his door and stepped out on the deserted road, not bothering to look for traffic. We had neither seen nor heard another vehicle traveling Hickey Road. He walked around the car and held the passenger door for me. I took his hand and stepped out into the shadows.

We walked in the ruts, he in one, I in another—ruts worn deep by years of tires. Short grass grew on the berm between them, punctuated occasionally by rocks that showed evidence of scrapes from a bottomed-out vehicle. Obviously, the drive needed more attention than a general trimming of overhanging hedge and trees.

I remembered the drive as long, sloping from the road all the way to the barn, widening out at the back door area into a well-maintained farmyard kept neat and tidy by my mother. Today's driveway ended at a carport that looked like an afterthought tacked onto the rear porch. Weeds and tall grass clogged any space not in constant use. A ratty-looking path led from the carport down to the barn, silvered with weather and time and badly in need of repair. I could smell years of manure and straw and strong animal urine. We looked at each other. Kurt leaned close and whispered that he thought we should get out before someone took a potshot at us. I agreed with him, but before we could retreat the back door flew open and a smallish in-her-thirties woman popped down the stairs. She held a broom at half-staff and appeared startled.

"Whatcha doin' here!" She lowered the broom and put her hands on her hips in a belligerent stance. "Well, cat got your tongue? I'm waitin' for an answer, you hear me?"

Kurt placed himself between the woman and me.

"We don't want to cause any trouble, ma'am," I answered, peeking out from behind Kurt. "I lived here when I was a little girl. We just wanted to see the place one more time. See how its changed, you know. Take a look around if you don't mind. I'd sure appreciate that!"

"Well, I *do* mind. You can both get back up that driveway. We're private people down here—don't need no one snoopin' into our business. Sure don't need no one snoopin' 'round in our house. Get out now, before I call my husband."

I had already decided to pass on any invitation to a guided tour inside as a sour odor of bad cooking and worse housekeeping oozed through the open doorway.

"We're on our way, ma'am. Sorry to bother you." Kurt took my hand and jerked me towards the drive. He stepped out firmly with a no nonsense stride that dared me to argue his decision. I had no intentions of that. I felt her eyes burning holes through my shoulders all the way up the driveway.

"If she's an example of the local folks, I don't feel very good about you looking for your Annie all alone." We were back in the car and finished with a fit of nervous giggling. "I'm sure glad she was holding a broom and not a rifle."

"A-men to that!" I shuddered. "You'd think she was hiding the Hope diamond, or something! Didja get a whiff of that house?" I didn't usually make judgments about people based on first impressions. This woman was an exception.

Kurt looked at his watch, then pointed out the time. "I'm gettin' hungry, honey. Let's eat our lunch somewhere and look for Annie's hill later."

We retreated down the road to the burned-out church and took our lunch up the trail. Once we passed the curve, the trail opened out into an area of sparse grasses and dried fir needles. Kurt spread our blanket in a sunny spot while I set out sandwiches, cookies, and lemonade. We sat in the little clearing not 100 yards from Hickey Road, eating our lunch and feeling completely alone.

After lunch, Kurt pulled out his dog-eared paperback and settled down for a rest. He quickly became engrossed in Studs' life and appeared to forget all about me. I waited a little while before interrupting him.

"Kurt, I can see you're interested in reading."

"Hum-hum," he acknowledged without raising his head. "Don't bother me, I'll lose my place."

"If you'd like, I can take the car and go find Annie's place. It shouldn't take me long." I was taking a calculated risk, here, since Kurt didn't let anyone drive his car. If he were really deep into Studs Lonigan, he'd give me the keys without thinking.

He looked up from his book and rolled his eyes at me. "Not on your life! Either I drive you, or you walk." Apparently, he had reconsidered his opinion of the neighborhood. More likely, he was so deep into Studs he'd forgotten Mrs. Personality. Actually, walking was worth consideration. This clearing was within spitting distance of the Darling's place. If the path still went through to the west, I'd come out on Hickey Road near the orchard.

"Okay, I'll do it! I'll walk. It's still early afternoon and the weather's great! Give me a couple of hours, then drive on up the road until it curves north just beyond the old farm. That's where the trail should take off for Annie's cabin. I'll meet you there." Kurt grunted, checked the time, and waved me off with a kiss. I grabbed my sweater in case the afternoon grew chilly and struck off down the trail.

My luck held. Within five minutes the little trail spilled out at the Darling's place. I walked briskly past the orchard, noting a new mailbox as I passed the driveway. "Baker" it read in neat, sensible black letters like the neat, orderly rows of blossoming fruit trees. I wondered how the Bakers felt about their unpleasant neighbors.

As I passed our old farm, I heard children's laughter and couldn't resist peeking through the untidy hedge. Several equally untidy children squabbled over broken toys on the scabby weed patch that passed for a lawn. One small urchin caught me watching and hurled epithets from his snot-encrusted upper lip. As I hastily withdrew and quick-stepped past the driveway entrance I heard Mrs. Personality's grating voice:

"Whatcher yellin' them words out here for, ya durned fool kid? I swear your mouth'll be soaped for that!"

"Gee, Ma—you don't wanna do that! Some preevert was peekin' through the hedge at us!"

"Run get your father. We'll see about perverts!"

Without thinking, I stepped across the irrigation ditch running along the shoulder and hid behind a fence post overgrown with blackberry vines newly in leaf. "This is stupid," I thought furiously. "Why am I hiding like some criminal?" Before I could act, someone tapped me on the shoulder.

"What'cha doin', lady. Lose the crystal outta your watch? Or were ya just spyin' on my kids and needed a place to hide!"

I stepped from behind the post with as much dignity as I could muster. "Of course not!" I responded, choosing to ignore his accusation. "I lived on your farm when I was little—I just wanted to see what the place looked like now."

His demeanor changed. "Oh, my old lady said some people came by wantin' to look around. Guess she wa'nt too friendly, was she? Well, ya caught her on a good day, otherwise she'd a took the broom to ya." He snickered, pulled his upper lip back from his yellowed teeth, and spit out the side of his mouth. "Ya still wanna see the place, I'll be glad to show you around mysel'." He raised his eyebrows and leered.

I declined the offer but accepted his outstretched hand to help pull myself back across the irrigation ditch.

"How long has your family lived here, Mr.—er—"

"Just call me Jack. We don't own the place or nothin'. Just hangin' out for a little before we go back t'the South."

I thanked "just call me Jack" for his help and edged down the road. For a split second, I thought he was going to lunge for me. Our eyes met and held, then he stepped aside and let me pass. I managed a casual retreat without looking over my shoulder. After all, it was broad daylight, barely mid-afternoon—a marvelous April Saturday on a public road.

I had gone perhaps four yards when the sound of scuffling feet and raspy breathing at my elbow drew my attention. I lifted my arm and peered below. One of Jacko's moist-nosed brood stared up at me through thick black bangs.

"My Dad wants to know where ya' goin' to, lady." The child wore bib overalls and striped tee shirt. Neither voice nor clothing gave me a clue about its gender. "Are you all alone?" Little Black Bangs appeared puzzled. "What happened to that guy who was wit' ya?"

It occurred to me that perhaps Mr. and Mrs. "Just call me Jack" were occupying the farm illegally, in which case I could be in some danger. "Oh," I answered airily, "I'm going just around the corner to meet my boyfriend. He's waiting in the car for me." I speeded up. "You'd better go home, now. Your father's looking for you." I waved gaily back towards Jacko and the rest of his androgynous cubs. They appeared closer than the last time I looked, although I hadn't seen them move. The urchin at my armpit tilted its head and swiped a grubby arm over its nose.

"What's your name, kiddo?"

"Ruthie—what's yours?"

Aha, a girl!

"Well, Ruthie, stop following me and go home." I tried to sound cross. Looking straight ahead, I accelerated briskly. Ruthie kept pace. I felt a tug at my sleeve, stopped, and glanced down. Ruthie let go.

"Lady, you didn't tell me your name." She had a whiny little voice. "My Daddy wants to know your name!" Little foot stamps punctuated her demand. She reminded me of Kurt's neighbor's pony—impatiently stamping its feet to hurry up the carrots and oats.

In what I hoped was a no-nonsense tone I raised my voice and again directed Ruthie to go home, expecting Jacko to get the message. I heard him chuckle behind me. He obviously enjoyed my predicament and had no intentions of spoiling the sport.

Ruthie wrapped herself around my leg and clung like a limpet.

"What are you doing? Let go of my leg!" I directed firmly.

Ruthie held on tighter, resisting my attempts to pry loose her sticky hands.

"Not 'til you tell me your name!" she whispered fiercely. "My Daddy'll be so mad at me! If you don't tell he's gonna beat me!"

I took a long look at Jacko's amused face and knew Ruthie told the truth. Fortunately, Kurt's car wheeled up beside me, horn beeping. "Get in, honey. I got tired of waiting." He leaned over and popped the passenger door open. Ruthie dropped my leg and stood up. "Who's your little friend?"

"Her name's Ruthie and I'd like you to meet her father." I gestured behind me. "Kurt, meet Jack."

"Meet who?" I gasped. The road was empty. Apparently, Jacko and his cluster had disappeared into thin air. Ruthie took one look and skittered off in the direction of the driveway, stopping to glance back at me just before she stepped into the shadowy drive. She nodded once, decisively, then disappeared.

"Looks like you had some little adventure here. Care to fill in the blanks?" I got in and sat down next to Kurt, quickly shutting the door and locking it behind me.

"Let's get out of here, first."

Kurt headed down the road and around the corner onto Quilcene Drive, then pulled onto the shoulder and stopped. "Just what was going on back there. I got the distinct impression that I busted up something interesting."

"Boy, am I glad you came along when you did. Why did you, anyway?"

"I got worried and decided not to wait."

"Kurt! If I didn't know better, I'd think you had a premonition!"

"Not me, baby. Just a hunch. Men do have hunches—how many times do I have to explain? Premonitions and intuition and all that stuff are woman things."

Kurt's entire family remained firmly grounded in the three senses—things you can touch, things you can smell and taste, and things you can see. You probably couldn't trust what you hear and never what you read. Whatever his source, Kurt had good instincts when he trusted them.

I quickly filled him in on 'Just call me Jack' and his little gang without mentioning how uncomfortable the situation had made me feel. I didn't want him to go all he-man on me and decide to defend my honor. That could seriously complicate the afternoon which was fast disappearing.

"Why do I get the impression you're editing this story for content? You're holding out on me, Honeybear, and I'm sure as hell not gonna let you go traipsing up some hill lookin' for a little old lady who's probably been gone for years with that weirdo hangin' around. I must've been crazy, lettin' you walk up here alone!" Kurt could be quite persuasive, even if a trifle chauvinistic! I agreed with him but saying so would surely give him the impression that he had the upper hand.

"Kurt, the hill's right there."

From our position along the road, we could see the path that ran due west as a narrow extension of Hickey Road. Kurt started the car and carefully backed up to the point where

Hickey Road ran into Quilcene. There we had a better view.

Annie's path wandered through knee high bunchy winter grass interspersed with fresh spring greens and weeds until it disappeared across an irrigation ditch lined with stunted cottonwoods and willows. I caught another glimpse of where it started up the hill. The old path that had once seduced me around Annie's hill was no longer visible from the road, obscured by brush and young fir trees.

"I can be up and down in twenty minutes. We'll be home before your mom has dinner ready. Okay?" I opened the door, half hoping he'd stop me. He did.

"Please, honey—not today. I know you're antsy but I'd feel better if you waited. Maybe we can get back over here tomorrow."

I knew we wouldn't, but I didn't protest. I'd come again, alone, and take my time. After all, Annie's hill and path remained, enduring the elements and withstanding the passage of time. They would stand a while longer.

I close my eyes and rest my head against the seat back, pretending to fall asleep as I search inside my soul for that dark and hidden place.

I cannot marry Kurt if I do not know myself.

We drove back to his parents' house in silence.

CHAPTER 23
In Which I Begin the Journey Home

An opportunity didn't present itself until late summer. Kurt and his brothers traditionally spent a week in August at Uncle Clyde's cabin on Stewart Lake in Canada, fishing and scratching and telling stories—dirty, tall and sometimes true— in general, the big boys' play time. They started out clean, freshly shaved, and neatly attired, only to return dirty, smelling of fish and sporting scraggly beards. They always had a wonderful time, or said they did, even with bad weather or the occasional case of poison ivy.

My family (at least the part still living at home) had planned an August trip to Disneyland timed to coincide with Daddy's union convention in San Francisco. Neighbors volunteered to feed Mama's cat and the boys' dog, take in the papers and mail and keep the lawn watered. With Kurt in Canada and my parents in California, I had no need to spend the weekend in Tacoma at home, and no desire to languish in the half-empty college dorms. Since Marnie had promised her mother a visit, she offered me her apartment key while she drove home to Oregon; I accepted.

Marnie and I were forever friends, having met at Franklin

Pierce Highschool in the far south end of Tacoma, the first day of our Freshman year. When we graduated, she went off to Nursing School and I went to the University of Washington. She now worked in Bremerton and we often spent weekends together.

I left Seattle on a hot and humid Friday evening, scrambling with summer tourists and busy commuters for a shady seat on the 6 p.m. ferry. As usual, someone had left the Seattle PI on the slick, green vinyl bench seat. I gratefully accepted this serendipity, and, with pleasure, settled myself to read for the one hour crossing.

On the Peninsula side, I shunned the busy foot traffic headed for waiting taxis and local bus stops. Marnie's apartment was a few short blocks from the ferry terminal if one knew the back ways through Bremerton's cramped downtown section.

Bremerton snuggled cheek to jowl with Puget Sound Naval Shipyard leaving little room for business section expansion. Consequently, parking spots were premium and downtown always bustled with foot traffic, whether or not department stores were open for business. On a Friday evening in summer, restaurants and the Admiral Theater did booming business with tourists and Navy personnel. Everywhere I looked sailors in their summer whites cruised for action near beer taverns and pool halls or negotiated for tattoos at tacky lower First Street dives.

The Puget Sound area did then and still does depend upon military presence as part of its economic lifeblood. When I was growing up, 'nice' girls didn't date (or have anything to do with) sailors and soldiers. Girls who did risked shunning by friends and family, only slightly less terrible a fate than 'getting in a family way.' One never said pregnant. That word was too suggestive. We all had friends, acquaintances or classmates who had disgraced their families and presented them with out of wedlock offspring or disappeared for an extended period, then reappeared looking older and much, much wiser. Marnie and I had a mutual friend who left school for a semester. When she returned, her mother had a new baby. We felt particularly sad for Ingrid and her little 'sister'.

At any rate, sailors were off limits, even if Kurt's ring had not sparkled brightly on my left hand. A few whistled as I trotted smartly past, and one called out. I ignored them all.

My walk quickly took me into the residential area immediately adjacent to downtown Bremerton. Here, most of the old, wooden single family dwellings had been converted to apartments and single rental spaces. A few houses offered room and board. Marnie's one bedroom daylight basement apartment seemed luxurious compared with some of the Spartan 'housing units' on these first few streets.

Soon I arrived at the alley fronting Marnie's place. The alley appeared deserted, except for garbage cans and a skinny, moth-eaten tabby stretched full length in a patch of evening sunlight. I struggled a bit with the key. Mr. Tabby raised his head and stared, unhappy at being disturbed. He sat up, yawned, and stretched, then wandered over to see what I was doing, rubbing up against me and bumping the back of my legs as if to encourage me to open the door. I wondered if Marnie ever fed him and made a mental note to share some dinner scraps.

The latch finally gave and I let myself in, welcoming the

cool, dark interior after late summer's heat and glare. At 7:30 p.m. the sun still hung high in the sky. Night would not fall for another hour or so. By then I had eaten a bowl of cereal, taken a cool bath, packed a paper bag with sandwich and fruit for tomorrow, and now sat in my pajamas sipping tea at the courtyard window, watching the long twilight melt into night, my thoughts on the next day's odyssey.

Lately, I had allowed doubt about the accuracy of my memories to undermine my confidence. Perhaps my family's assessment of me was correct. I was particularly susceptible to my brother Daniel. He knew my vulnerabilities intimately and went for the jugular whenever possible. One summer he managed to convince me that our parents had adopted me.

"After all," he pointed out with syrupy tones and a sad smile, "you are blonde, and both Mama and Daddy have dark hair." He pointed to his own lighter, but definitely brown thatch. "Besides, you don't fit in. Robbie 'n me are boys—Mom and Dad only needed a girl to do housework. That's why they 'dopted you."

I politely pointed out that since Daddy was not really related to me, his hair color was not part of the equation. Danny shot back that OurFather had dark hair, and so there!

"Well, at least they picked me out," I reasoned. I imagined my mama and daddy walking down rows of baby cots, searching for the perfect little girl to take home. "They just had to take what they got, with you!"

"Boy, are you dumb, or what!" Danny snorted gleefully. "No one would pick you out on purpose. I remember when you came. The people dropped you off at the door with a box of old clothes. Mama 'n Daddy wanted to send you back, but the orphanage wouldn't take you! They didn't want no blonde kid—they asked for one with black hair. If you don't believe me, it says so on your papers. I know, 'cuz I read 'em."

That Robbie was also a towhead didn't cross my mind. Danny had me convinced. I spent hours searching surreptitiously through Mama and Daddy's things seeking my adoption papers, stopping only when Mama caught me and forced an explanation. Danny's smug grin as she delivered a tongue lashing told me that once again, he had had a wonderful time at my expense.

I thought of my memory as a curse. The entire family had long ago dismissed as wild imagination my ability to remember my childhood in vivid detail. No amount of arguing on my part could convince them otherwise. These people who were my parents and siblings simply did not view the world as I did. Somewhere along the way, they had lost (or had never possessed), the ability to remember incidents and details as clearly as the motion picture images that scrolled across my mind. I saw spoken words as most people see pages in books and could repeat whole conversations with little effort.

I suppose my 'gift' caused some little discomfort to others. I knew no other way of thinking but had learned after much unhappiness to curb my revelations. I kept my memories to myself and over time doubts, encouraged by Danny, crept in.

I remembered Annie as an adult who treated me with respect and honor, who liked me as a person, and who enjoyed spending time with me. I loved her and thought of her as a second mother. I remembered her words of guidance, lovingly given and lovingly received, as well as the many conversations held before her blazing fireplace. With kindness and patience, she had instilled in me a deep and abiding faith in the order of God's Universe.

Or so I believed.

What if these were all false memories? What if I had conjured them out of thin air? I had to consider the possibility—as painful as that prospect might be—that my relationship with Annie was a product of wishful thinking. If tomorrow failed to confirm my memories, I would be forced to re-evaluate my whole belief system.

At a recent family dinner, I had mentioned a fishing trip in the Olympics and related a small incident that had occurred. No one remembered the fishing trip, let alone the incident to which I referred. Danny teased me unmercifully for hours, using the incident to reinforce his theory that I fabricated things for the fun of it.

"Oh, face it, Sis! You can remember being in the womb! You just make up this stuff so everyone looks dumb and you can lord it over us. Admit it, for once. Besides, I know for certain sure you don't remember everything!"

I went to bed that night with a semi-permanent lump wedged where my tonsils once resided. The same lump now hovered, ready to block my throat and direct tears to my eyes at a moment's notice. Tonight, it kept me sitting at Marnie's little table long after full dark, rising for bed only when laughter and sounds of rolling trash cans from the alley roused me from my reverie. I slept fitfully until dawn.

It is morning now. I rise and dress in white jeans and flowered blouse, aware that the sun shines brilliantly through the slit between windowsill and shade. It splashes Marnie's bedroom walls with rainbows as beams pass through the cut glass bud vase on her bedside table.

In the tiny bath, I wash my face, splashing cool water on eyes that droop from lack of sleep. I pull my hair into a high ponytail secured with a rubber band and wound round with a colorful scarf. The face I see reflected in Marnie's oval mirror looks oddly startled, hazel eyes pulled wide by my slightly too-tight rubber band. Freckles stand out across my nose in stark contrast to my ivory skin, untouched by sun. My reflection does not smile—the mouth lies straight and neutral, giving no clue to my inner turmoil.

In the kitchen, I make myself a cup of coffee, mixing instant powder with lukewarm tap water. I take a sip, grimacing at its bitterness. The refrigerator still squats in the corner like a giant spider, grumbling low in its innards, daring me to reach for milk to calm the tepid brew. I sincerely hope that Great Aunt Alma has had the thing fixed. On a previous visit, that same refrigerator had failed, handing both Marnie and I a bad case of food poisoning. Since my great aunt Alma actually owned this apartment house, I was fairly certain the thing was now okay. The time—what is the time? My watch ticks unconcernedly on my wrist—quite a nice watch, a graduation gift from my parents— white gold with two very tiny diamond accents.

And now it is time to leave for the bus stop. I rinse out the coffee mug and turn it upside down on the draining board, then slip into my sandals and collect my handbag. I face down the refrigerator and retrieve my lunch and a bottle of Coke, remembering to listen for the click that indicates the door is latched. Marnie's spare key lies on the kitchen table. I pick it up, open the door and step out into the alley.

Everything about this morning is crystal clear—steady and orderly, almost in slow motion. I see time spreading out before me, a nearly invisible string fanning in infinite directions, showing me all possible paths my next step can take. Behind me, the string is solidly tied to my waist and stretched, not in a straight line, but curving, up and down, sometimes nearly obscured by its twists and turns, anchored in my past. It represents all prior decisions, no matter how circuitous, that have led me to today.

I hesitate as my right foot moves forward, leaving me balancing on my left. I must choose my path wisely. The threads are so close together at this juncture that I cannot distinguish one from another. Be bold, I tell myself. Take charge of your destiny. I take a deep breath and step out.

The door slammed shut, startling me out of my reverie. Marnie's garbage can cat stared at me from atop its galvanized throne. He blinked. The tip of his tail moved ever so slightly, indicating his displeasure at being disturbed. *I turn my back on him as I head down the alley for the bus stop.*

Before I reached the stop, my bus trundled into view. I increased my walk to a jog, pulling up out of breath just as the bus door opened.

"That was close!" I smiled at the driver as I dropped my fare in the collection container. He smiled back, motioning for me to take a seat. I certainly had my pick! The bus was deserted! We lurched away from the curb before I could sit.

The squat little diesel-powered bus beetled down through town, stopping often but picking up no passengers. Of course, I had planned an early start. I supposed people might be sleeping in, or taking their time with Saturday chores, enjoying the lovely weather while it held.

"Going far?" The bus driver glanced over his shoulder in my general direction.

"To the end of the line."

He didn't reply.

I resumed looking out the window, marveling that Bremerton appeared stuck in a time warp. Houses and businesses and adults and children looked as they had when I was eight or nine. Only automobile models gave one a perspective on the current year.

Presently we chugged into Charleston, and, still without additional passengers, followed National Avenue up the hill to Navy Yard City. My paternal grandparents lived here. I briefly considered getting off at the next stop to surprise them, then thought better of it. Maybe I could stop on the way back. Today, I would allow nothing to sidetrack my goal.

We reached the end of the line before I was ready. The driver carefully reversed the bus, then opened the door, stopped the engine, and took out a thermos container. "You gettin' off here or are you gonna ride back to town now. If so, you gotta pay the fare." I demurred but made no move to exit.

"You often have runs up here with only one person?"

"Usually last run of the night. Hardly ever on a Saturday morning." The driver poured coffee from his thermos and took a careful sip.

"Ah, that hits the spot!"

He eyed me, speculatively. I gathered my courage, checked that my handbag still hung at my shoulder, walked down the aisle and off the bus.

Across the street, Park View Elementary School sat in

solitary silence. Rows of windows marched across its long frontage, all of them with shades pulled to various levels. The shades resembled eyelids, shielding the windows from impolite inquiry. The low, squat building with its rambling parallel wings called me like a siren. I had spent three school years hidden behind those windows—kindergarten through second grade—and still remembered (I thought) its entire layout. "Well, why not take a look!" I said to myself. Carefully checking both ways for traffic, I scooted across the road.

The school sat atop an artificial rise a good distance from the road. A broad expanse of carefully maintained lawn surrounded it, transected in places by wide cement entrance walks broken at intervals with shallow staircases. Someone had taken an eye to scaling both walkways and stairs to little people. I took the stairs two at a time, hoping the doors were unlocked.

I was in luck. Janitors worked away inside, busily preparing classrooms and hallways for returning students. Someone had propped one-half of the large double entrance doors open with a full mop bucket. I stepped over the bucket with care and quietly slipped inside. Instantly the smells of chalk and wax, pep (a mixture of liquid paraffin and sawdust) used to clean the hardwood floors, and Lysol and pine cleaner from the lavatories assaulted my senses.

To some people, sights and sounds bring back old memories. For me, it is smells—they act as time machines—instantly transporting me into my past. I grew giddy as memories rushed at me from all directions. Fortunately, a stack of chairs waited for distribution just outside the Office. I sat down.

I am five years old on my first day of school. I am standing next to the Principal's office, holding Danny's hand as tightly as I can. We have enrolled late. A hall monitor (a sixth grader, I learn later), takes my hand from Daniel's and leads me down the far right hand hallway to a classroom halfway between the main hall and an exit door. I look back over my shoulder, hoping for some encouragement from my brother, but he is gone. She stops at Room 110 and points to it. "Here's where you go. Don't forget where your class is, little girl."

I stand before the door, hesitant to turn the knob and enter. The hall monitor eyeballs me with distaste. I can tell she disapproves of how I look. I am wearing dark blue wool slacks, a red sweater, and sturdy brown oxfords. The long pants are a concession from the school board, arranged by Doctor Haller in hopes of preventing future illnesses by keeping my legs warm.

"What're you waiting for?" demands the hall monitor. She yanks my hand from the doorknob and opens the door. "Get in, will ya?" She shoves me through the door and shuts it behind me.

All eyes in the classroom turn in unison. I (who want so desperately to fit in) can tell in an instant that I do not. Every other little girl is wearing a dress or jumper, bare arms, bare legs, little patent leather Mary Janes. I look like a boy with my long pants and sensible brown shoes and short, blonde Dutch Bob.

"Can I help you, ma'am?"

Someone placed a hand on my shoulder. It startled me out of my reverie. I turned to face a smiling wrinkled warm-brown man. He had a full head of curly, almost white hair, and strong, capable hands. His black eyes twinkled with humor. I knew that face!

"Mr. Charlie? Is it really you?"

"Yes'm, I am Charlie Harmon. What can I do for you?"

We stood just outside the cafeteria redolent with odors from thousands of school lunches.

"I went to school here when I was little. Do you mind if I take a peek at the old place?"

Mr. Harmon leaned close and stared intently at my face, his mouth working as he fought to capture some vagrant memory. He brightened. "I remember you!" His smile reappeared. "I do remember you. You're the little lady who couldn't eat beets! Well, whadda ya know!" He threw back his head and chuckled. "Come on in and inspect the scene of your crime." The old man pushed through the double swinging doors and politely held them open for me. I stepped inside.

I am seven years old, standing in the long lunch line in the school cafeteria, trying to quell my rising nausea. The whole school smells of reconstituted powdered eggs and julienne beets—the slimy shoestring kind floating in a dangerously pink sweet and sour sauce. I can handle the eggs; it is the beets that get me.

Our school district had obtained quantities of free war surplus food, consisting mainly of huge containers filled with powdered eggs and even larger cans of beets. The cafeteria served these two at least once a week, usually on Wednesday.

I could smell those wicked beets as soon as the cooks began preparing lunch. By ten o'clock my stomach quivered in dread. On days when I carried my lunch pail, I would wolf down my food and get out of the cafeteria as quickly as possible—at least if Mr. Anders weren't watching.

Mr. Anders, our Principal, patrols the cafeteria like a prison guard. He carries a paring knife in his right hand, using it to cut children's apples and oranges, and taps it absently against his left palm as he walks up and down between the table rows. Actually, we all believe he carries the knife to deal with children who do not clean up their plates, figuratively and literally. In those days, one always eats everything placed before them or risk **THE LECTURE** *about children starving in Armenia and/or Ethiopia. I am really quite angry when I discover that Armenia has ceased to exist as an entity when my mother is a child!*

The problem, however, was not my homemade lunches.

Washington does not permit the sale of colored margarine, and one of my jobs is mixing the packet of yellow powder with the margarine, a huge block of white vegetable fat, to mimic the appearance of butter. To me, the stuff smells awful and tastes worse. Mama usually remembers not to slather my bread with slabs of margarine, so it is only the hot lunches that cause me problems—in reality, only the hot lunches with beets!

We took our lunches in autumn and spring, but deep in winter, Mama felt a hot lunch would be healthier. I begged for cold lunches on Wednesdays, but the beet problem became a bone of contention between Mama and the school—one my mother intended to win!

If it weren't for Mr. Anders and his knife, I could have, in all probability, disposed of the beets—perhaps beneath my napkin, or onto some other child's plate—someone who actually liked them! As it was, all eyes turned to me the minute I sat down, my skinny shoulder blades a target for their eye arrows. To my ears the cafeteria, usually noisy with subdued chatter and clanking implements, became deathly still. All eyes turn to watch.

I am lifting my fork. I take a bite of runny eggs, careful to eat from the side furthest from where the sweet and sour sauce has stained the eggs pink. I swallow without chewing, quickly taking a second bite. Everyone is waiting. I can hear Mr. Anders quietly creeping nearer. He is a tall, slender man who moves like a cat—and he terrifies me! I take another bite of egg, downed with warm milk drunk directly from its waxy carton. The carton smells slightly sour.

Mr. Anders' spicy aftershave drifts like a cloud submerging him in its aroma. I can smell his approach. Now he is standing directly behind me, tapping, tapping, tapping with his little knife. I can delay no longer. In desperation, I glance at the cafeteria door, my bolt hole. Mr. Charlie is waiting there with his bucket. He knows what is coming. I know what is coming. The whole cafeteria knows what is coming.

Mr. Anders leans over and whispers in my ear; "Today you will eat those beets. Take a bite. Now!"

I isolate a beet strand from its lake of sauce. Maybe I can scrape off enough to gag down the beet. Mr. Anders's hand closes over mine, forcing the fork into the mound of beets and sauce, and lifts it to my mouth before I can protest.

"Eat it!" he hisses in my ear.

Without hesitating, I open my mouth.

Now the beets are on my tongue. My mouth fills with saliva as I struggle to swallow. It is no use. As soon as my taste buds encounter sweet and sour, while the beets are still on their downward journey, my stomach rebels. I leap from my seat on

*the bench, catching Mr. Anders by surprise and, scattering tray
and dishes, I make a wild dash for Mr. Charlie's bucket. Today
I make it before I erupt beets and eggs and milk. The entire
cafeteria explodes into laughter and applause.*

*Mr. Anders is right behind me. He grabs me by the arm and
half drags, half carries me to the office. Since it is a school
policy that children who vomit must be sent home for the
remainder of the day, I have missed at least half a day of school
each time the cafeteria serves beets. This does not make sense
to me. I am not sick—I am simply sick of beets!*

"What in the world are you remembering—you have quite
a look on your face!" Mr. Harmon's voice brought me back to
reality.

"Actually, I was thinking of the last time you had to wait
with the bucket. I relied on you to be there, and you usually
were."

"After I recognized the pattern, it wasn't hard to predict
when you'd need it. Truth be told, smellin' those beets made
me want to puke, too. I am surely glad that Ol' Anders didn't
patrol the Janitor's room, to boot! We got a free lunch in them
days, and when they served them beets, we all threw 'em in
the garbage! You was sure in a dilemma. How did it finally end
up?"

"Well, my mother tried everything. It wasn't that the
school policy was so rigid it couldn't accommodate my distaste
for beets, Mr. Anders felt it was a discipline problem. He saw
my vomiting as an assault on his authority. Giving in would
mean he lost and I won. He couldn't tolerate that."

Mr. Charlie smiled and nodded his head.

"Finally, Mama ran for PTA president and won, then

brought in professionals to talk about food intolerance. He eventually gave in—mainly, I think, because I was losing so much school, anyway, and those extra half days were adding up."

"All's well that ends well," chuckled Mr. Harmon. "You jes' look around this ol' school to your heart's content. We'll be workin' here all day." He paused, deep in thought, then continued.

"John Anders's still Principal here, ya' know. It's his last year. Just thought I'd mention it in case you run into him."

"Thanks for the warning, Mr. Charlie. And thanks for being a little kid's friend."

I spent another half hour or so wandering about, looking in on my old classrooms and taking the opportunity to duck into the girls' lavatory. It hadn't changed—the same stalls painted institutional green, the same metal mirrors hung low for tiny people. Even the huge, round granite stone sink still sat dead center on the cement floor, its base surrounded by the continuous hoop-like foot pedal. I absently pressed the foot hoop, watching warm water splash into the bowl.

Mrs. Eldon is standing at the blackboard neatly printing two syllable words for us to read aloud. I raise my hand to indicate a need to use the lavatory. I glance over at Sandy, my best friend. She is also raising her hand. Mrs. Eldon requires her students to use the lavatory in pairs, and always times us. She has us signal with a "one" or a "two" to indicate our specific bathroom needs. I raise two fingers, and Sandy follows my lead. Mrs. Eldon nods her head in acknowledgment. Sandy and I quietly leave our seats and exit the room. Outside in the hall, our eyes meet and we giggle. Mrs. Eldon will time us for a 'two', giving us a few moments to talk. Danny says that it is lying to raise two fingers and not 'follow through', in his words. I ask Mama, and she laughs, telling me that I should always try for the two if I can. It is a family joke that Leah only does a 'two' twice a week, making sport of something I consider private.

I left the lavatory and headed toward the playground exit. Coming around where the hallway turned north, I met Mr. Anders face to face. He was strolling slowly back to the main hallway, arms at half mast, right hand absently tapping on his left palm. He nodded in my direction and I nodded back. He looked smaller to me, and far less dangerous than he had all those years ago in the cafeteria with a knife in his hand!

Before I reached the playground door, my eyes found Miss Benson's first grade classroom. Of course, the room belonged to some other teacher now, but I opened the door to the familiar sight of child sized desks and Alice and Jerry readers.

I am standing at Miss Benson's desk while she patiently explains to me why I should not let Terry Easter kiss me. Terry has a crush on me, she explains. My blonde hair and blue-green eyes fascinate him. Once again, Terry has wrestled me to the blacktop at recess and kissed my cheek. He has followed me home after school. I like Terry and ask Miss Benson why she does not care that Tommy Godard kisses my girlfriend Sandy.

Miss Benson seems uncomfortable. She says that Terry is not white. I know that I say to her. He is a warm, chocolate brown to match his eyes. His hair is black and curly. When he smiles, his cheeks dimple and his eyes crinkle up at the corners. Miss Benson tries to explain that white boys and girls belong together and Negro boys and girls belong together. I point out to her that Terry does not kiss Ida because she is his sister! Besides, what has skin color got to do with anything? I like people because of the color of their hearts, not the shade of their faces.

Miss Benson sighs and sends me back to play.

As I closed the door on that little first grade class, I wondered what poor Miss Benson must have thought of her tiny rebel!

I opened the outside door onto a familiar sight—a row of swings, chains polished by thousands of little hands, swaying gently in the breeze. Someone had repainted the hopscotch patterns on the blacktopped playground surface but tetherball poles stood empty, as did the badminton posts. Tether balls and nets could wait until students filled the playground. Two little girls stood at the north wall playing Seven Up with a defuzzed tennis ball. They eyed me with suspicion as I selected a swing. When I sat down, they returned to their game, glancing over their shoulders occasionally to keep me in sight.

As I sat on the swing kicking gently with my left foot so I swayed gently, an image of Annie filled my mind. I saw her so clearly I startled and nearly fell backward off the canvas seat worn slippery by years of little fannies. How many afternoons had I run up the hill to her farm when one of the staff at this school hurt me with words. I suddenly recalled the last afternoon we spent together before Daddy and Mama took us away from Quaker Hill.

On my way to the lavatory, I overheard Mr. Anders and a third grade teacher talking in the hallway ahead of me, but around the corner. *Mr. Anders is saying something about me. He is telling this teacher that I will be in her class next term.*

He is telling her that I have caused my other teachers concerns. I carefully open the Girl's Lavatory door and slip inside. When I leave, they are laughing.

"You must give thy teachers grace from your heart," Annie soothed away my tears as we sipped our cup of chamomile tea. "Child, you are not who thy teachers think you be!"

"I'm just a little kid like the other students there, aren't I?

"Leah," she answered, "your soul is not a child's soul. Your heart brings lessons you have learned from God. Thy teachers do not know how to speak to a child of your wisdom. Be kind—for in this instance you are the teacher. Someday they will remember you with tears and mayhap have learned from the encounter." Heady stuff for a little girl, but I wiped my eyes and smiled. Perhaps Annie was right. *After all, that is the reason OurGrandmother says I give her the willies.*

I rose from the swing, taking a few steps forward, and looked west up Quilcene Road.

My nostrils twitched at hot fumes rising from the fresh blacktop. The smell finally forced me around the building to the grassy slopes in front. I selected a shady spot under one of the leafy maple trees and opened my lunch. I hadn't realized how hungry I'd been. Warm Spam and wilted lettuce has never been a favorite of mine, but today it was delicious. Even tepid Coke tasted wonderful. I drank greedily. The warm carbonated beverage swooshed up the back of my nose, burning my sinuses and causing tears to well up in my eyes.

I sat awhile, remembering some special classmates, then rose and brushed grass and twigs from my jeans. Lunch remains went into a nearby trash container, except for the second can of cola and my uneaten apple. I dropped them into my handbag for later. Refreshed, I slung the bag over my shoulder and began the next leg of my journey.

From Park View Elementary School, the old road wound up and over Clinton Hill. At its crest, Quilcene Road branched south through farmland and wood lots until it ended at Hickey Road. Unless I wished to take the shortcut through the woods (and I had no evidence that the path still existed) I faced a two mile hike. I had walked it many times as a kid and could do it now, taking it slow and easy. Once I had made my pilgrimage, I'd take the shorter Hickey Road back to Park View and the bus stop.

Halfway up I started to wilt. The hot August sky had developed a brassy glow, promising changing weather by late afternoon. Heat, acrid and dry, rose in waves from the pavement. Nothing stirred—I hadn't seen another soul since the little girls at the school playground. I began to feel like an extra in some Rod Serling "Twilight Zone" script.

Only a few houses fronted Clinton. They all sat well back from the road, buried in their overgrown yards and protected from road noise and dust. After perhaps fifteen minutes I came to the intersection with Quilcene. I paused for a moment to rest, remembering a hot September afternoon on the way home from school when Abby Bailey taught me to chew road tar.

Abby and I met in Miss Benson's first grade class. She lived with her parents and numerous brothers and sisters in a ramshackle shanty on five acres fronting Quilcene Road. I could reach her house by cutting across the Broomer's field and dodging the draft horses pastured there, or by walking the long way west on Hickey and then north on Quilcene past the row of mailboxes, including our own. Mama didn't care much for the Baileys but felt sorry for Abby. Mama said she reminded her of the stray animals I insisted on bringing home. I liked her.

Abby and I are as different as night and day. She has straight, shiny, dark brown hair that hangs to her shoulders with bangs that hit her nose. She is forever sweeping them aside to reveal large, inquisitive blue eyes in a slightly grimy face. Her dark brows express happiness and displeasure with equal ease. She is quick to laugh and slow to anger, even when the other kids tease her. Abby wears truly pitiful clothing— hand me downs from several older siblings—with no apparent regard for gender or size. Her shoes range from boys work boots two sizes too big to worn-out Sunday school shoes tied on with string. On more than one occasion she arrives at school with welts the size of breakfast sausages on the backs of her skinny little legs.

"Daddy took a belt to me," she says, and she throws back her head and laughs.

Abby always looks as if she never has enough to eat.

On the hot September afternoon in question, Abby and I walked home from school together, taking the road to avoid both her brother and mine who were determined to ambush us in the woods. We followed close on the heels of a highway department crew patching potholes and cracks in the macadam with hot tar.

Abby and I had spent a few moments hunkered down at one of the shiny tar puddles, poking its surface with twigs and pulling up the sticky stuff into taffy-like strings.

"Wanna chew?" Abby held her stick up for inspection, a

large glob of warm tar congealing on its tip.

"You got gum?"

"Na, we don't need no gum! Tar. I'm talkin' 'bout tar." She pulled the lump from her stick and popped it into her mouth. "We chew it all the time. Come on—give it a try."

I pulled my own stick up from the puddle and eyed the black, gooey mass with skepticism. Abby seemed to enjoy hers, chewing with apparent satisfaction.

"You're just kiddin' me, Abby. You don't really like that tar!"

"Sure, I do!" Abby enthused. "We all chew tar 'cuz we can't never pay for gum. Sometimes, we chew tree pitch, too!"

"It isn't good for you, Abby! It's **tar** for God's sake!"

I glanced sideways over my shoulder as if Mama might catch me "taking God's name in vain". Her remedy for "swearing" was a mouthful of Lifebuoy soap! "Into the bathroom, Missy," she'd command. More than once I sat on the toilet lid squirming as I held a bar of soap in my mouth for Mama's required two minutes. "Just think about what you said while you sit there," Mama would demand. Just before she disappeared through the door she'd twirl about with a flounce and point her finger directly at me, adding a firm "and don't squirm!"

Although Mama didn't know it, I never once considered the improper language that had landed me in my predicament—I thought about how long two minutes can be when one is trying not to swallow soap foam!

"Well, I'm still here, ain't I?" she exclaimed with exasperation.

Obviously, Abby hadn't dropped dead before my eyes, I

debated. The tar was new, so thousands of tires hadn't run over it yet. It couldn't hurt to try. Come to think of it, it smelled a lot like Lifebuoy. If it tasted as awful as it smelled, I could always spit it out. Besides, if I didn't chew it, she'd think I was chicken.

I pulled a suitable glob from my own stick and inserted it into my mouth. A few tentative chews revealed a not altogether unpleasant taste, although I don't think it would sell in Peoria. I nodded my head at Abby. We chewed as we resumed our walk along Quilcene, spitting excess saliva like tobacco juice, generally pleased with ourselves. I left Abby swinging on her front gate, still chewing the tar and spitting.

Back then, I cut across Broomer's field, which took some maneuvering as all four of their huge Clydesdale horses were loose and looking for treats. They weren't mean animals, but their very size and speed turned crossing their pasture into a contest. On this particular day I won, stopping to pet them only after climbing under the wooden fence bordering our farm. The horses badgered me into picking bunches of long, succulent grass from my side of the fence. I hand fed them the grass, then removed my thoroughly chewed tar blob and tossed it into the bushes before telling Mama I was home. No sense taking any chances.

Now Broomer's lower pasture had been subdivided for single family residences, and most of the wood lots were gone, as well, although the upper pasture and old farmhouse remained untouched. Newer homes snuggled side by side with old residences and singlewide trailers and the long row of mailboxes had been replaced by neat, single boxes at each driveway. Even the Bailey's shack and outhouse had fallen to suburban crawl.

CHAPTER 24
In Which I Learn about Other People's Houses

One Thursday afternoon as Abby and I walked home up the hill (to avoid the boys and their tricks in the woods) she asked if I could come and spend the night with her. Her mama recollected it would be nice to have a houseguest, and Abby should invite me. I could bring my things to school on Friday, if Mama okayed the outing, and I would walk home with Abby after school, returning home on Saturday afternoon before dinner time.

Although Abby had invited me before, Mama had always said that the time was not right. This evening she and Daddy talked about the invitation, the upshot being that they felt I was ready to sample how other people lived. They called me into the living room. Mama squatted down in front of me, taking my shoulders in her hands and looking deeply into my eyes, while Daddy sat smoking in his chair beside the radio.

"You do know that things are different at Abby's house," Mama inquired. "Abby has six sisters and two brothers who live in that little house with her, not to forget her parents. They are poor, Cookie. They don't have the nice things that we have." Daddy made a sound in his throat and puffed out blue smoke. I could tell he was thinking about what to say but didn't want to interrupt Mama.

"They don't have a telephone, honey, so once it gets dark, you'll have to stay until morning. Do you understand?" I nodded my head. Although Mama had never let me accept an invitation, she had allowed me to extend a few to my friends. One, a little girl from Sunday School, woke up in the middle of the night crying. Daddy had called her parents and then delivered her home at midnight.

"I'll be okay, Mama. Really, I will. And I want to see Abby's pet goat and her puppies. We never get to do that after school 'cuz it gets dark so early."

Mama allowed that it was so but thought it politic to remind me that the Baileys had no indoor plumbing. That was fairly common in our rural area, although we always had had the luxury of a toilet that flushed.

Danny came along in time to catch the last part of our conversation. He snickered as he rounded the corner into the playroom. "If you're talkin' about the Bailey house, let me tell you the whole place stinks!"

"And just how would you know that young man!" demanded Mama.

"I been over there a couple a times. Bernie 'n me were playin' ball at his place and he hit a fly. Landed next to that outhouse thing—oh, gawd! Did it smell!"

"Watch your language, young man. If Leah spends the night, she'll find out first hand." She turned to me. "Still want to go, honey?"

I was a little dubious, truthfully, but loyalty to my friend trumped better sense and I nodded my head. "Then, if it's alright with Daddy, you may."

Daddy took his pipe in hand and pointed the stem in my direction. Little curls of blue smoke slipped from the end where Daddy's teeth marks were clearly visible. I nodded again, and he cocked his head, giving me a sideways nod.

"It is up to you, Cookie. You'll do okay. And Mama and I are proud of you for sticking with your friends. Friends are important, whether they have indoor toilets or not!" Danny snorted and Mama laughed.

I did some thinking in bed that night about the outhouse thing. With my wonky bladder, I often had to make a trip to the bathroom in the middle of the night without turning on the lights, bumping into doors and chairs along my way to our bathroom off the kitchen. How would I manage in a strange house—rather, outside in the dark and possibly rainy night? By morning, I had decided to put aside the outhouse problem in my delight at spending the night with Abby.

After school, Abby and I trekked up the hill in the misty October afternoon, holding hands and sharing the burden of my small bag of nightclothes and clean underwear. Mama had put in a pair of flannel-lined overalls and a striped T-shirt along with instructions to change out of my school outfit and to fold it carefully before I put it back in the bag. My shoes, of course, were sturdy enough for any activity, albeit not particularly comfortable. She also added extra socks in case my ankles bled.

I had never been inside Abby's house. I often walked by the place to and from school when we didn't go through the woods, or on our way to Sylvia and Bernie's house further down the road, but aside from stopping and occasionally swinging on the driveway gate while talking with Abby and her older sister Anna, the entire property was a mystery. Abby opened the gate and closed it carefully behind us. "Gotta keep the critters in or my pa'll give me a good one," Abby muttered sotto voce. She glanced up and met my eyes as she struggled to get the wire hoop firmly seated around the fencepost.

Behind me, I could feel the tug of a small hand on my sash. The youngest Bailey, three-year-old Mark, blew bubbles of nose snot as I bent down to greet him. He was a likeable little guy, always smiling around the mucous strings hanging from his lips. I grabbed the hanky Mama had tucked in my sleeve and wiped his face, gesturing for a nose blow while I held it around the significant object. He snuffled obediently, then swiped his sleeve across his nostrils to finish the job. I smiled back at him, using my most motherly face. Second Grade seems so far away from little guys like Mark in his bib overalls with their full load drooping down and banging on his calves.

When Abby wasn't looking, I tossed the hanky into an overfull garbage box leaning precariously against a stack of old tires. I didn't think Mama would miss the hanky, and I shuddered at tucking it back into my sleeve!

"Come on," Abby tugged at my arm. "I wanna show you where to put your stuff!" She dragged me towards the rickety back porch, jabbering about sleeping arrangements and bunk beds and shared rooms. Mark toddled behind us, pulling at his droopy overalls.

The stench hit me as I walked through the back door. Dirty bodies and pee and rotting food and animal funk assaulted my nostrils until they were overwhelmed and quit transmitting to my brain. My eyes watered a bit as the ammonia from a pile of diapers half hidden behind the door between the kitchen and what appeared to be a lean-to filled with bunk beds. Abby dragged me through, bag banging on the backs of my legs.

"This one's ours." She pointed to an upper bunk of a tier tucked up next to the slanted roofline on the short west wall of the room. Similar bunk beds lined the rest of the walls, leaving just room for the door into the kitchen. I counted room for eight people—more, if two shared a twin-sized mattress.

"Does the whole family sleep in here?"

"Gosh, no!" she replied. "Only us kids. And Mark, he mostly sleeps with mama and pa, when he c'n sneak in."

I just had time to put my bag on the upper bunk before Abby yanked me by the arm and hurried me into the kitchen. "Let's get somethin' to eat, okay?"

Mrs. Bailey stood at the wood-burning kitchen stove stirring a bubbling pot of what looked like stew, although my nose was no longer accepting incoming messages. Without turning, she directed Abby to the icebox around the corner on the back porch. Abby retrieved a bottle of milk for her mother and an apple each for us. We sat down on the back stairs, munching and talking while the other kids came home from school and work. Eventually, Mr. Bailey arrived in his beat up old Chrysler coupe and the family crammed themselves around the long table in the living room.

The table, covered with red and white checkered oilcloth, was set with three pairs of mismatched salt and peppers at approximately one-third intervals along the center. Two huge pots of stew, a pile of soup spoons, and two plates of buttered bread slices were distributed equally—bread, pot, pot, bread—

in the spaces between condiments. As they filed through the door, everyone took a glass of water from Mrs. Bailey and found a seat on the long benches flanking either side of the table. Mr. Bailey sat at one end passing out spoons, and Mrs. Bailey ruled at the other end.

"Where are the plates," I whispered to Abby. She tossed me a quizzical look and took the pot from one of her older siblings sitting to her right. She took a huge spoonful of stew, popped it in her mouth, and passed the pot to me. I sat, stunned, pot handle in my left hand and the spoon in my right. Abby poked me in the ribs, hard, and hissed that I needed to take a bite and pass the pot along to Anna, sitting on my left.

Anna reached for the pot handle, but before she could snatch it from me I dug into the glutinous mess and gouged out a huge spoonful, then relinquished the pot. I took half the mound into my mouth and followed it with a bite of bread and butter. The pots passed along hand to hand, yielding stew at every stop. Eventually, one returned to me for further sustenance.

When both pots were wiped clean and all the bread was gone, everyone left the table without a word.

It was shortly after dinner when I noticed the little black spots on my white socks. As I bent down to brush them off, they hopped onto the floor, leaving behind what looked like specks of blood. On closer examination, my ankles revealed red bumps that began to itch like crazy as soon as I touched them. Abby's gray tabby took the opportunity to rub along my leg. As I reached to pet her, I noticed similar black specks around her eyes—specks that moved—specks that jumped onto my white socks and hopped up my legs. Horrified, I began dancing about and brushing frantically at myself.

"Aintcha never seen a flea before?" snorted Mrs. Bailey. "They aint gonna kill ya, just take a little blood!" Abby's father snickered in agreement. From the looks of the cat, however, I wasn't so sure about the loss of blood. The cat's little mouth was nearly white inside, instead of the nice pink mouths of our cats, Spick and Span. The cat staggered to the ratty-looking overstuffed chair in the corner and hopped up on the heap of clothing covering the entire seating area.

Abby grabbed my arm and pulled me towards the back porch. "Gotta use the house", she muttered in my ear, "wanna come?" I nodded and we stepped outside into the cold. Abby had a small flashlight in hand that partially illuminated our path. Up above the clear sky shone bright with stars hanging so low it appeared one could reach up and pluck them like flowers in a dark blue meadow. Our breath puffed out in clouds and Abby and I cuddled together, sharing our warmth on the short trip to the outhouse that stood about thirty feet from the back door. I could smell it, a strong stench of urine and feces, fouler even than that emitting from our pigsty.

"Sorry, Leah—" apologized Abby. "My pa ain't cleaned it for a while." Secretly, I didn't think her pa had ever cleaned it. As she opened the door to reveal the wooden seat with its two holes residing inside, I plugged my nose. This helped my stomach a bit but didn't stop my watering eyes. Abby turned off the flash, an apologetic smile on her face. "Pa says batteries cost money and we all know what's inside."

Total darkness encompassed us as Abby shut the door. We groped for the holes, pulling down dungarees and panties—at least I had panties. She giggled as I struggled to gain purchase on the bench with my clothing clustered at knee level. "Push 'em all the way down, why don'tcha." This did help a little, and I was able to finish draining my bladder.

Reaching around for something with which to wipe myself yielded a pile of slightly damp newspaper strips at my left hand. I shuddered at the thought of leaving black tracks of newsprint on my private parts, and what they would do to my white panties.

Abby was obviously settling in for a longer stay. As I struggled to pull on my clothing, she found my arm in the dark. "I know you got a indoor bathroom. But this is what we got 'n it's the only place I c'n ever be by myself." Abby's voice lowered into a conspiratorial whisper. "I gotta tell you somethin' about my brother Keith. Don't let him get near you, you hear? He tries to do bad things to me 'n Anna at night when we're in bed." She paused "And sometimes my pa, does, too." This last was so quiet I could almost believe I hadn't hear it. My brain wanted to ask her what they did, but my heart didn't want to know.

"They won't try to do anything to me, will they?"

"No," she whispered. "They stay away when Anna 'n me have friends over."

She finished her business and pulled up her pants, then reached for the turn knob, a piece of board on a nail, that kept the door locked, her hand unerringly finding it in the dark. The door swung open to the dark and the stars and the clean air of October. I took a huge breath, clearing my lungs and nose of the stench inside Abby's outhouse.

Abby and I snuggled close in the upper bunk that night. She had me crammed on the side by the wall, either to give herself more breathing room or to protect me from unwanted advances from her male relatives. I didn't sleep much as the air was close and filled with the noises of moving bodies and snoring and the occasional release of gasses that permeated the room.

Morning came early. I was cold, both as Abby had rolled herself up in the one blanket leaving me shivering in my pajamas, and that it had apparently frozen overnight. I could see frost on the nail heads protruding from the boards next to my face. I gave Abby an experimental poke with my elbow and tugged on the blanket binding. She grunted, rolled in my direction, and released her hold on it. Gratefully, I pulled it over me, snuggling close to her and absorbing the heat from her body. She put her arm around me, pulling me closer to her. "I'm glad you're here," she mumbled. "Thanks for spending the night."

It made me wonder again what happened to her when I was not there—and if I told Mama about my visit, it was unlikely that she would allow me to spend another.

Abby's mother roused us shortly for breakfast. At least this time the table held individual bowls for cereal. Abby and I downed Cheerioats, milk, and toast with butter before we dressed and ran outside to feed Abby's goats. We had milk from our cow, but the Bailey's had two milk goats that Abby cared for. Anna was responsible for actually milking them, but Abby saw to it that they were turned out to pasture during the day and returned to their shed overnight. This kept them safe from marauders. One had been attacked by an eagle during the late summer and still bore the scars. The little nanny was just too heavy for the eagle to lift.

We played outside until our stomachs began to grumble—well into the afternoon. As we ambled back towards the house, I heard a honk. Daddy was parked up by the fence. "Go get your stuff, Cookie. Mama wants you home a little early," he called. I waved at him and ran to the house for my bag. Abby loped alongside and whispered in my ear that maybe she could come stay with me tonight. For a moment I considered the possibility, then told her no. We had a family outing planned for Sunday, but I would ask if she could come next weekend.

Abby sighed deeply, her shoulders sagging. "Thanks a lot for having me over," I put my arm around her and gave her a hug. "You are my best friend." She brightened and hugged me back. "You're my best friend, too."

I turned from her, took my bag from her hands, and ran to the road where Daddy waited. I thought I saw tears in Abby's eyes, glistening in the late afternoon sun, as I waved good-bye. Then Daddy stepped on the gas and we were gone up the road to home.

Mama popped me into a hot bubble bath as soon as I hit the back door. Danny plugged his nose as I went by and made gagging noises. The bath felt wonderful. Mama washed my hair and rinsed it twice. She applied ointment to my fleabites, slapping my hand when I reached down to scratch at them. "Leave those alone, Cookie," she admonished me. "They'll leave scars."

After a wonderful dinner of macaroni and cheese and green beans from our garden and canned by Mama, she asked me about my stay. I stood next to her at the sink, drying the dishes. I wanted to tell her the whole truth, but Abby's voice as she whispered about her brother and her father held me back. I didn't deliberately lie. If Mama had asked me directly, I would have told her, I rationalized, but this was a time to listen with my heart...

"It was interesting, Mama. The outhouse was awful, and Abby's bed is small, but Mrs. Bailey made stew for dinner and homemade bread." I left out the part about everyone eating from the stewpot. It didn't seem right to let Mama think badly of Abby's family.

I never returned for a night at Abby's house, although she spent many weekends at mine over that winter. Although she loved our inside toilet, the best part of her stay was having a bath in a real tub, with hot water and bubbles. Mama would wash her clothes and often found something of mine that I had outgrown and sent it along home with her.

I also didn't share with Annie anything about my friend Abby. I had listened with my heart to her story and protected her the best I could. Telling Annie felt like betraying a friend who had suffered too many betrayals in her short life.

The following summer we left the farm. We did return to the area and lived in Parkview for a while when Mama and Daddy had their little problem as the family called it, but Abby and I no longer shared a class or the long walk up the hill. She had a new best friend who I hoped protected her on weekends as I had done.

In later years I learned she became pregnant at age thirteen and left school. I often wondered if the baby's father was her brother—or, her own father. I hoped not. That seemed too cruel. She deserved someone to love and to return that love. But life is neither fair nor unfair—it just is. Sometimes believing in God can get us through the bad patches. And sometimes, the bad patches are all we have. I hoped that Abby had found peace.

My memories of Abbie left me with a sadness that brought me back to reality and the passing hour.

Quilcene Road was not as well maintained as Clinton. Potholes and cracks dotted its patched blacktop. Blackberries grew wild over fences, spilling out onto the shoulder, canes heavy laden with fat dusky black Himalayans. Risking a few scratches, I picked a handful to eat along the way. The berries were sweet and full of sticky juice—not as tart and flavorful as the smaller Cascade berries, but welcome, nonetheless.

I detoured to the blacktop only after blackberry runners snagged my feet, nearly tripping me up. Behind me Clinton hazed in the distance; ahead lay the intersection with Hickey Road. Five more minutes brought me to the foot of Annie's hill.

I stand here now, unable to move. Time hangs suspended. Again, I see Destiny's paths fanning out before me. All paths but one lead up the hill—that one (a coward's path) leads backward, down Hickey Road. If I choose to follow it, I may never know the truth about Annie. I may never know an even bigger truth about myself—whether my memories are real or merely products of my overly vivid imagination (or wishful thinking). I reject that path. The only possible choice for me is up Quaker Hill. If I do not know myself, I cannot marry Kurt.

I step forward and the spell is broken.

CHAPTER 25
In Which I Confront My Past

Journeys back to childhood places are never as we have imagined them. In our child's eye, they remain always as we last saw them—whether neat and tidy or disheveled with pain, the past is yesterday and tomorrow has not yet come. We have only today to find our inner truth.

I cannot marry Kurt if I do not know myself.

And I have come home to find out who I am.

The neat little path I remembered was now overgrown with Scotch Broom, the sloping meadows of wild flowers choked with Russian thistles and bracken ferns—spear ferns we called them when I was little. If one could pull them up without breaking them, they made a passable spear—long and straight with a flat, pointed root to serve as a blade. I can still hear my mother, voice raised in righteous indignation; "You, Danny. Put that fern down. Right now, I say. Do you want to put out your eye?"

The little path didn't appear to be much traveled, although I could see the lower, more circuitous path around Quaker Hill had grown into a good-sized by-way, enlarged over the years by horseback riders and bicyclists. Both had left visible indications of their passing. I started up the hill, picking my way carefully to avoid sharp stones and holes—pitfalls that could easily trip me up and send me sprawling. I snorted as I remembered the idyllic barefoot stroll of my dream. Without shoes, my feet would be cut to ribbons!

Footing improved as I encountered branches and cross paths—new additions since my childhood excursions brought me this way. Obviously, someone still used most of the path on a fairly regular basis. My spirits rose at this encouragement.

A passing cloud temporarily blocked the sun. I shivered, noticing for the first time that the weather was changing. This morning's occasional puffy white billows had given way to more serious appearing August afternoon cloud piles that often heralded thundershowers. I quickened my step, not wanting to be caught unprotected if the sky opened up!

The path snaked through a copse of second-growth alder, emerging after a few feet into a grassy meadow. Here it split again, one branch heading more or less straight up to the hill's crest, the other taking a more circuitous but less steep route on the diagonal. I rested a few moments while deciding which path most likely led to Annie's cabin (if it still existed). In the end, I went straight up the hill.

Now I am standing atop Quaker Hill. A scattering of raindrops gently cools my face as I gaze at the greater view. I identify our little farm, largely tumbled down and gone to seed. I watch a car trundle along Quilcene Road and turn left onto Hickey. It slows down as it passes the overgrown driveway as if expecting one of "Just Call Me Jack's" grubby children to leap out into the road. I see where Abby lived. The old outhouse is gone—the spot where it stood now proudly sports a red barn surrounded by animal pens, and someone still keeps horses at the Broomer's place, although they are not Clydesdales.

Clinton Road wound downhill past Park View Elementary School and to the west, what was left of Smith's Dairy stood in ruin. Even the city bus stop was clearly visible. All the significant places of those childhood years lay strewn about like the cardboard houses on the sickbed quilts of my youth.

I am seven, and once again confined to bed with a double hit of croup and bladder infection, too sick to risk the cold winter walk to school, but not quite sick enough for pulled shades and long, sticky, sweaty naps. I sit propped up against the guest room headboard by all the pillows Mama can scrounge from the rest of the house. One of my Gramma B.'s patchwork quilts lies like a landscape over my legs. This quilt is done in random triangles, oblongs, and squares of cotton— blues and greens and browns—my raised knees make hills and valleys and meadows. I have stuffed a small throw pillow under the bedding—it serves as a mountain, guarding my imaginary kingdom from the sea troll that lives under the island of my bed. Danny has helped me make cardboard houses and barns and Robbie has lent me his collection of metal and stamped plastic barnyard animals—pigs and cows, sheep, chickens, and geese—all oversized and not in proportion to one another. Some of Danny's vast soldier collection serve as make- do farmers with rifles instead of pitchforks. All I lack is a horse to take me over the hills and through the valleys—a horse strong enough to bear me in battle against the sea troll. I walk my fingers up and down the farms and towns, talking to my subjects, driving the livestock out to pasture, and then back to the safety of their little cardboard barns. I try to sit as quietly as possible, not moving my legs until cramp drives me to rearrange the countryside like the violent upheaval of an earthquake.

As I marvel at the chaos created out of leg cramp Daddy knocks at my partially opened door and pokes his head inside. "What's happening, Little Beaver—can I come in?" he asks as he pushes the door open. I beckon him in with my left hand as my right reaches for a stray pig perilously close to plummeting to its death on the ocean floor of my bedroom rug. The pig falls, and Daddy retrieves it, carefully replacing it on the quilt landscape. He cautiously selects a barren spot on the very edge of my kingdom and sits—an aftershock rumbles through the village adjacent to his left hand. His right holds a shoebox wrapped in brown paper and tied with string. He smiles at my unspoken query. "This is for you, honey."

A shiver of fear freezes me and my stomach lurches. Daddy does not bring me gifts when it is not my birthday or Christmas; we cannot afford them. Does this mean that I am sicker than I thought? Maybe the new magic medicine is not helping my kidneys; perhaps I am going to die young after all.

He sees my hesitation and a look of puzzlement momentarily clouds his handsome face. "Don't you want to take a look at it, Cookie? Mama and I are so happy that the sulfa is working that we thought a celebration was in order." He proffers the package again and touches my face. "Smile, honey! You're getting better every day." My stomach muscles relax, although it still hurts a little to breathe.

I unwrap the box in silence and gaze in amazement at the most beautiful horse I have ever seen. It is made of glossy hard plastic unlike any of the cheap plastic animals on my bed. It *stands eight inches at the withers and is colored like Trigger, Roy Rogers' palomino, golden cream with snow white mane and tail. The saddle, also plastic, tooled and painted to look like real leather, pops off the back, although its bridle is molded onto the horse's face and cannot be removed. A hole through the mouth holds a golden chain to serve as reins. Daddy smiles again and tells me that the horse is not really a toy—it is actually the prototype for an adult collectible figure he bought from a friend at work. I don't understand what he is telling me, and I don't care; it is a wondrous gift and one I will always treasure!*

It sits atop the chest of drawers in my dorm room at college.

Eventually, it took the place of my wonderful Winter Bear who had taken up permanent residence in Montana.

CHAPTER 26
In Which I Learn a Lesson of the Heart

When I was thirteen, we took a summer trip to visit Yellowstone National Park, camping our way across the western states and including a sweep through Harlowton, Montana to visit the Nelsons. As soon as we left home, I began making plans, secretly, of course, to regain custody of my bear. The adults may have forgotten the incident, but the two principles—Mimi and I—had unfinished business to conclude!

When I was six years old, my Uncle Dodo came to visit. We seldom saw Danny's and my biological father's younger brother, as he lived in California and rarely traveled to our rainy corner of the world. He had a smiley, upturned mouth and cheek dimples that gave him an angelic appearance. His eyes always sparkled—especially when I asked to touch those dimples. Mama said they were 'angel's fingerprints,' a sure sign the bearer was blessed. I called them face dents, similar to my own set, but deeper. Mine showed only when I smiled.

Mama called him Will—short for William, his given name. OurFather had his own brother-specific names, most of them not complimentary. They didn't get along, those two. According to Mama, they had a history.

No one knows why my older brother started calling him Uncle Dodo instead of Uncle Will, not even Danny, but the name stuck! He took it with his usual good humor and came bearing gifts. On this Christmas-birthday visit, he presented me with a special present—a unique teddy bear from Germany where he had been deployed in the latter days of WW II. Winter Bear, as I named him, was fully articulated. Around his neck he bore a Red leatherette collar, and when he tilted forward, a wonderful grumbly growl emitted from his belly. Winter Bear was my best friend, always by my side during my many illnesses, until family friends moved in with us for an extended stay. Mr. Nelson worked with Daddy at the shipyard in Bremerton and had been laid off after the war ended. He eventually found work in Montana and when the family moved, my beloved bear went with them.

Mimi Nelson was younger than me, and quite sickly herself. She had taken a liking to Winter Bear and Mama felt she could not deny this toy to her when the family left. Daddy had gone along with them, towing a second trailerful of family property behind our old car, and according to my mama would bring Winter Bear back. In the end, Daddy returned alone. Now, my opportunity for revenge was at hand.

Upon our arrival, I reconnoiter the battleground. Mimi's room is small and sparsely furnished—a single white-metal-frame bed with a patchwork coverlet, a bookcase filled with classics like Black Beauty and Treasure Island, all showing evidence of much use, a chest of drawers and a combination toy chest-window seat covered with throw pillows. There sits the sad countenance of Winter Bear. His mohair, that not worn completely bare, is no longer the creamy white of winter berries, but grey with time and dirty hands. One ear hangs at half-mast and his left eye is missing, replaced with a black button crudely attached with red thread. A cowboy kerchief now adorns his neck instead of the red leatherette collar. He looks smaller than I remember. I stare in dismay at what he has become!

"I s'pose you came for him, huh, Leah?" Mimi had approached so silently I had not heard her enter. I turned, my soul filled with virtue.

Mimi stood before me—small, pale, and terribly frail. Her appearance caught me off guard. Although she had been a skinny little kid, she looked more like the six year old who I had last seen than a young lady of eleven. I hoped the shock didn't show.

"I always knew you would, someday!" She strode past me and gently picked him up, kissed his tattered face, then handed him to me. I was so startled I nearly dropped him. "After all," she continued, "I always knew he belonged to you."

I took my Winter Bear, nodded, and left the room.

During the following days, Mimi and I were cordial with each other, neither mentioning our first-day encounter. I buried Winter Bear deep in my duffle bag under my clothes— just in case Mimi changed her mind. Neither did I mention the matter to Mama, just in case. The muffled sobs coming from Mimi's room at night I chose to ignore. After all, it served her right for all those years I cried.

Our two families spent the next few days exploring the area together, doing a little fishing at the local lake, and getting a tour of the roundhouse serving the Milwaukee Road. Mrs. Nelson worked as a cook at a local sheep ranch and took me along one early morning to help her get out biscuits, eggs, and sausages for the hands. Mimi, who couldn't seem to keep up with our busy schedule, spent the days alone in her room sitting on her bed and reading. Every once in a while, I noticed her glance dejectedly towards the empty window seat. I suppose a week of observing Mimi's obvious infirmity had softened my attitude towards her. Whatever the reason, I needed to talk to Mama.

"What's wrong with Mimi," I inquired as I helped her fold up our laundry fresh from the line. Mama and I had spent the afternoon making sure everyone had clean clothes for the trip home.

"Well, Cookie, you know she's sick, don't you?" Mama hadn't called me that pet name since I started seventh grade. I nodded. "What I suppose you don't know, is that she probably won't live to thirteen, let alone to grow up." I gasped. I didn't like Mimi, but I didn't exactly dislike her, either. Now that our dispute was settled, I had thought we could maybe be friends, someday. Now it seemed we wouldn't have the chance.

"What's wrong with her, Mama?"

"Remember all those sore throats and fevers she had when she stayed with us? They were caused by strep throat—and sometimes, if a kid is very unlucky, strep throat can turn into a disease that damages the heart—it's called rheumatic fever. Unfortunately, Mimi's heart is very impaired. She needs another operation, but the doctors don't think she'll live through it. If she doesn't have the surgery, she'll die within the next couple of years."

"How long have you known this, Mama—why didn't you tell me?"

"I've known about the rheumatic fever for a long time, honey," Mama replied. "She was diagnosed just before the Nelsons left Washington. That's why I couldn't take the bear from her the morning they left. I honestly didn't think you'd care—you held such a grudge against her all these years—why are you asking now?"

I couldn't answer Mama because of the lump in my throat—I just shook my head, instead. I finished folding clothes in silence, then took mine to pack. I had some thinking to do.

When I was alone, I dug down to the bottom of my duffle bag and retrieved Winter Bear. *Now I view his bedraggled state with new eyes. Some dark curtain that has covered them for far too long has dropped away. I see now that the patches and wear are not from abuse, but rather from love. Mimi has worn out Winter Bear with caring and holding. How many nights of tears has that ragged ear heard—how many sick days has the button eye beheld. Close inspection shows how his worn spots are neatly patched with calico—it gives him a rakish look. I remember now that Mimi's room is nearly devoid of toys. She has no need for skates and bikes she can never use, no jump ropes, no baseballs. Just her books and one small bear—and I have taken him away. I think of Annie, and even though we no longer communicate in person or by letter or by our big black telephone at home with its long black snake of a cord, my skeevy little heart opens. In my mind's eye, Annie smiles, and I can hear her say "Leah, thy heart knows what to do. Thee should always follow what it tells thee is right. I am with thee always, little one."*

That night, after even the grownups were asleep, I cuddled Winter Bear close one last time. I no longer begrudged Mimi her nights and days with him. Yes, I had wanted and needed him when I was sick, but at least I was going to grow up! I crept over the camping bags filled with my sleeping family, careful not to wake them.

Mimi's bedroom door was open a crack, the way it was every night, I suppose, so a worried parent could watch the little girl asleep in her bed by the light from the hallway. I watched her now, blankets pulled up to her chin. She breathed so lightly they barely moved. Careful not to disturb her slumber, I placed the grubby little teddy bear on the pillow next to her head. He would be the first thing she saw when she woke. To myself, I finally acknowledged what I should have known for years. Winter Bear didn't belong to me—hadn't for a long time. He belonged to the little girl who had worn him out with loving—and he belonged with her. I said good-bye to them both.

I don't know if Mama ever knew about Mimi and me and the bear during that vacation week in Montana. Maybe she suspected something, but we never discussed it. She said someday I'd understand—I finally did. I would like to think that if she had told me how sick Mimi was on that December morning when Winter Bear and part of my heart drove away that I would have understood then. At any rate, Mimi Nelson passed away in her sleep a few days after her thirteenth birthday. We got the news by telephone one bright spring afternoon. Surprisingly, Mrs. Nelson asked to speak to me. She wanted to know if she could send Winter Bear back. I thought about it for a moment, then told Mrs. Nelson no.

"You just put that old bear with Mimi," I said. "He can keep her company."

And that is what she did.

CHAPTER 27
In Which Danny Learns a Lesson in Humility and Becomes a Hero to his Little Sister

As I sit here atop Annie's hill the memories of all my days and nights in that old farmhouse below slide, one by one, from where I have stored them in that forever place deep inside. Some of them are still too hard to grasp and I save them for another time, but Mama's weeks of trial confined to bed are still vivid in my mind.

Mama was born with a deformed spine that required special surgery when I was six. She spent four weeks in the hospital in Seattle after a surgeon carefully rebuilt it, then came home to several more confined to a special hospital bed Daddy had installed in the parlor. Her windows looked out on the front grass and several rose bushes and, apparently, the special entrance for a creature of the field who took up residence in the basement.

I don't remember when Robbie first spotted the black and white kitty that waddled out from under our house at dusk, or just which one of us mentioned the cat to Mama. I do remember the look of horror that rose on her face as the significance of this bit of intelligence sank in. My brothers and

I were sitting on or leaning against her hospital bed that had been set up in a small bedroom overlooking a patch of scabby grass, ragged flowerbeds, and just-budding bushes that Mama could view through her window. Each evening we gathered here to fill in Mama on the events of our days and listen to the stories she had spent her day 'imaginating'. This particular Friday evening in early spring we had all traipsed in, fresh from out of doors, smelling of wood smoke and newly cut grass, especially pleased that the whole weekend lay ahead with no rain in sight.

"You saw **what**?" gasped our mother. "Describe it for me." She sounded worried. Robbie screwed up his little face and tackled the task of describing the "kitty" to Mama.

"It was black and white, Mama. It had a bushy tail, and it walked funny."

"Kinda waddled, did it?" asked Mama.

"Yeah! Robbie exclaimed, "and when it saw me, it turned around and lifted up its tail. I was gonna pet it, but it ran under the house, right underneath your window!"

"Look, Mommy, Look!" Robbie pointed out the window, gesturing excitedly. "There's the kitty, now!"

Mama glanced out the window and groaned. "Oh, no! Robbie, your black and white kitty is a skunk! Quick, Danny— go get your father. **NOW**!" Daniel shot off the bed as if a bee had stung him.

Daddy was in the kitchen relaxing over a cup of coffee and reading the evening paper. In the background, a barely audible news program, interrupted occasionally by a "Duz for your Laundry" jingle, droned. Mama used Duz, not only for the laundry, but for doing dishes as well. The stuff made everything feel slimy, especially the silverware, and I cringed at the touch, much like the feel of dry dirt on the potatoes we picked after Daddy turned the plants over with a shovel to expose them. Some Duz packages came with dishes inside that Mama collected, white with a golden wheat design.

Danny exploded from Mama's bedroom, galloped through the archway separating our dining room from the kitchen, and skidded to a halt just short of separating Daddy from his chair.

"Whoa, there, Danny. What's the hurry? You know better than to run in the house," admonished Daddy.

"She said to get you awful quick, Daddy. Hurry!"

Daddy dropped his paper and sprang from the chair, in his haste sending it skidding across the kitchen where it fetched up short against the sink cabinet. "Mayleen, what's the problem?" he called as he hurried to her bedside.

Mama laughed. "Nothing serious, honey. Just come take a look at our newest houseguest."

He leaned over Mama and gave her a quick cheek kiss. She signaled toward the window. As his eyes rose from her face, they became transfixed at the sight of something outside her window. "Oh, damn it! Did you see that? We've got a skunk in the yard."

"Hal, don't swear—the children!" Mama shot him a dirty look. "Yes, I saw the skunk," Mama replied. "If it were only in the yard, I wouldn't care, but it seems to have established residence under the house." As if on cue, the skunk disappeared below Mother's window.

"Well," Daddy chuckled, "tomorrow's Saturday. I'll get a couple of the neighbor guys and we'll trap it. It'll only take a few minutes. We'll haul it up the creek and let it go." He smiled, apparently pleased with this solution. Mama seemed a little troubled with his optimistic appraisal of the situation, but Daddy reassured her.

Saturday morning arrived—blue-skied and buttercup fresh. Our old Rhode Island Red rooster crowed the sun up while I fed the hens, gathered eggs, and tended the rabbits. Danny slopped our White Chester sow and tossed hay to the young beeves Daddy was raising for table and sale. I didn't mind doing chores on such a glorious spring morning. In the cold, dark winter, gathering eggs and feeding hens with chilled, blue fingers held no such joy. Then, I hurried back to the warmth and light of the kitchen, often cracking an egg or two in the process. Today I took my time until Danny reminded me of the impending Great Skunk Adventure.

Actually, I was awake most of the night anticipating today's festivities. I hadn't realized such a small, inoffensive-looking animal could cause so much stir among the adults in my life. Intellectually, I knew that the pungent odor that sometimes filled my room at night bringing tears to my eyes came from that cute little animal. Daddy said it was so, and surely **Mama** wouldn't lie. Privately, I still had my doubts! I had drawn assurances from both of my parents that nobody meant the skunk any physical harm, although my bloodthirsty brothers spent breakfast haggling over which of them would have the pelt as a trophy. Daddy was mildly amused—Mama just shook her head from her place in the bedroom.

By 9:00 AM the skunk wranglers were assembled in our driveway. The group consisted of several neighboring farmers, their teen-aged offspring, and Daddy. I had elected to monitor the adventure from Mama's room, acting as her narrator, while my brothers milled about the men, weaving in and out, touching the excitement just enough to feel part of the fun, but sufficiently discrete to avoid detection and ejection by Daddy.

Mama sent me out with a message. With assurances to Mama that he had everything well in hand including my brothers he sent me back.

"How soon are they going to start, Cookie?" Mama sighed, apprehensively.

As if on cue, one of the men produced a cage and quietly placed it at the skunk's last known entrance—directly beneath Mama's bedroom window. He covered the cage, except for its open door, with a tarpaulin. The two teens and Daddy began to crawl under the house from the opening beneath the kitchen porch, intending to fan out and, with luck, gently encourage the skunk towards its exit, now neatly capped by the cage.

Unfortunately, the skunk did not cooperate.

As I narrated excitedly for Mama, events began to unravel with alarming speed! Daddy and his compatriots had crawled under the house on the north side. Between the entrance and exit lay several yards of crawl space, including the foundation and heat conduits for a huge circulating fireplace located in the approximate middle of the house.

This fireplace supplemented our oil heater located in the kitchen and provided fan-forced heat to nearly every room. Once heated, the stones stayed warm for a long time. I suppose the foundation and duct pipes did, as well, for this is where the skunk had taken up residence—above the ground, safe, warm, and dry, directly beneath the fireplace—and this is where the skunk intended to stay.

Our first hint of trouble came shortly after the men disappeared beneath the house. As the three approached the fireplace area, one of the young men came face to tail with his intended prey. We heard strangled shrieks followed immediately by the unmistakable eye-watering gut-wrenching stench of annoyed skunk. Like a shot I deserted my mother's bedside and rocketed through the French doors in the dining room next door, leaving her to choke and gasp as skunk miasma filled her room.

As Daddy and his cohorts fumbled blindly out of the crawlspace, shame forced me back into the house toward my trapped mother. Tears streamed down her face—not just irritation from the powerful skunk musk, but tears of helplessness at her inability to get out of bed. I think she also cried from a mixture of both disbelief and betrayal. I had, after all, deserted my post.

"Mama, are you okay?" I croaked with strangled gasps. "Can I get you something?" My eyes were reduced to watering slits through which I barely saw her motioning toward the tightly closed windows. I opened them wide, sending cool, fresh air sweeping through the room, then rushed to the bathroom for a damp washcloth for her face.

"Leah—where is Daddy and just what is he doing," she gasped. "Go and get him for me, right now!" I knew Mama was upset as she reserved my given name for moments of import. Otherwise, I was just plain Cookie.

I came out of the house into the front yard. No one was

in sight, but I could tell from the commotion that the men were in the driveway by the back porch. Daddy had stripped to his jockey shorts and dunked himself into the rain barrel. He stood in the driveway dripping wet and furious, sputtering and shivering. "Mama needs you, Daddy," I said as I adroitly arranged myself upwind. "She's calling for you."

"OooohmyGod!" he gargled all in one long, throaty gasp. "I forgot her. She can't get out of bed, let alone out of the house. Come on guys, she needs rescuing." Everyone quit milling around while my father, completely alone, naked except for his underwear and dripping water, ran for the house.

Daddy stuck his head out the back door and glared at the group, still standing about in the driveway like sheep. Reluctantly, three men detached themselves from the herd, approached the back door, and disappeared inside. Soon Mama and her bed rested safely on the cement patio near the French doors.

Now Daddy turned his thoughts towards revenge. March days are still short in the northern United States, and Saturday was getting long in the shadow. Soon falling temperatures would drive us all back indoors, whether or not our unwanted guest remained below.

Daddy dismissed all of the neighbors save one—he of the direct hit. The poor lad smelled so bad that his own father refused to allow him into the truck! With a change of clothing, the hunt continued, but now the skunk had run out of time. Working quickly before it could escape, they strengthened the blocking to the opening beneath Mama's window. Then, with firearms and flashlights, they prepared to reclaim our house's nether regions from the paws of the enemy.

Mama was beside herself! Trying to convince two mighty hunters, still reeling from defeat, that crawling about under a house in the dark, armed with .22 rifles was an exceedingly stupid idea proved futile. To compound the problem, Daddy had moved her bed back into the house as the day lengthened and the stench cleared. My brothers and I, realizing the full import of those rifles, were sure stray bullets would kill our mother if the shooting got wild. It had not yet occurred to us that Daddy might also be in danger. Robbie's chin began to wobble as tears slid silently down his grubby cheeks. Mama wasn't too keen on being upstairs, herself.

"What're you worried about," Daddy shouted—"Don't you trust me?"

"No," replied Mama. "I don't trust either of you. Daniel, take Leah and Robin out of this house and stay out until I tell you to come back in!" Knowing when our mother meant business (and cowards that we were) we left.

This time Daddy stomped toward the crawl space, closely followed by his smelly friend. We watched as they disappeared like silent, slightly scruffy great white hunters down Alice's rabbit hole.

No one says a word. Danny and I desert the still snuffling Robbie and sneak as quietly as possible into the bushes that shield the neatly screened crawl space ventilation slots. Flat on our tummies in the gathering shadows, noses held tightly between thumb and forefinger, we watch in silence. Presently, we see the glow of our father's flashlight and hear soft murmuring from below. Then comes crawling sounds—a muffled cough. Someone whispers something inaudible, then silence. Time freezes—Mama, alone in her room, eyes scrunched tightly and pillow over her head—Danny and I watching, and Robbie, open-mouthed and bug-eyed in the driveway, wait an eternity. Finally, we hear a shout and two quick popping sounds followed by great guffaws of glee. A few moments later, Daddy and his stinky fellow wrangler emerge victoriously from beneath the house, skunk carcass in tow.

Normally the sight of some furry critter's dead body would upset me terribly. I thought of this skunk only that it had distressed my mother and caused her pain. Its death, however regrettable, had been ordained from the first moment it stepped below Mama's window and slipped silently through the small opening into the cellar. I ran inside to let Mama in on the end of the hunt. White lipped she asked through clenched teeth "is it over yet?"

"Yes, Mama, the skunk's dead!"

"Is everybody okay?"

"Yes," I answered solemnly, everyone's okay."

She sighed. "What a relief—thank heaven this day is over and we can put the skunk to rest!"

Daddy buried it in a shallow, unmarked grave behind the barn. Thankfully, neither of my brothers asked for its pelt!

Monday morning dawned bright, clear, and breezy. Just the faintest hint of skunk still crouched in dark corners to remind us of Saturday's adventure, and that appeared likely to crawl quietly away through opened windows. I rose to the sound of humming from the kitchen. I did my chores, quickly cleaned up, ate my own breakfast, and dressed for school. Miss Ruth made sure my hair was neat and tidy before I presented myself to Mama for inspection. After a kiss and a hug, she waved Danny and me off.

My older brother and I share the long walk to school. He is in third grade and attends school all day. I spend mornings in Miss Hostetler's Kindergarten class, then walk home alone through the cool, green woods, arriving in time for lunch with Mama and Robbie, who is too young for school. We usually spend the walk arguing over brother-sister things until neighbor kids join us along the way. I am the only girl in the group, so the boys delight in chasing and teasing me. They are never mean-spirited—just letting me know that, as a girl, I really do not fit into the group.

This morning everyone chattered on about Saturday's adventure, which had reached epic proportions via the party line. We shared our telephone with nine other families, all of whom could (and did) listen in on everyone's conversations.

Mondays were Show and Tell for Miss White's third grade class at Parkwood Elementary School. I wished my class had Show and Tell but contented myself with reciting the relevant facts of Saturday's adventure to my classmates. I remember hoping that we would have at least one interesting weekend for me to share when I was in Third grade.

After snack and nap and story, I walked slowly home through the pallid noontime sun. Today soft, puffy clouds huffed overhead, drifting lazily through the pale blue just-barely-springtime sky.

Robbie napped after lunch and Mama drowsed off, too. Since Miss Ruth seemed to find my thousand questions a burden, she shipped me outside to play in the sandpile or wander the pastures. There I waited impatiently for my brother to appear, eager to hear all about his triumph at Show and Tell!

The afternoon drags on. I sit in the sun with my back braced against a wooden fence post and watch red and black ants scurry and hurry amongst grass blades and along dandelion leaves. Finally, when I have nearly given up hope, my brother slumps out of the woods. His shoulders droop, his head hangs down and his feet drag, trailing little puffs of dried earth and scuffed grass behind him.

"What's up—how'd it go at school? Did you get a chance to tell—"

"*Shut UP!*" my brother barked. I clamped my mouth closed so fast my front teeth neatly clipped my tongue tip. "Why are you mad at me?"

Danny continued his slow trudge towards the house. Noting his dejected stance and sad eyes, I silently fell in behind him. He held his books close to his chest with his right arm— in his left hand he clutched a small, white paper. Sadly, he waved it in my direction. "She sent home a note."

A chill ran down my spine and made the hairs stand up on the back of my neck. Having a note sent home by one's teacher was the most horrible fate to befall any child. Notes meant trouble. We both had friends who had brought home the dreaded note, but neither of us had ever before been the subject of such writing! I followed my brother in stunned silence.

Danny began sobbing silently—his shoulders shook. Occasionally he snuffled, small fists surreptitiously wiping away his tears. His steps dragged, slower and slower, until he stopped. For five seconds he stood silent, then whirled around to face me.

"What'm I gonna do, Leah? I'll get a trip to the woodshed for sure!"

"What's the note say?"

"I don't know—that's the problem. She sealed it up in an envelope and I can't read it without Mom noticing."

"Maybe she's just telling Mama and Daddy how well you're doing in school," I suggested, "or how you did in Show and Tell." I brightened. Perhaps things weren't as dark as we thought.

"Oh, no! Not that!" Daniel gave a little moan. "She didn't believe me."

"What?" I was incredulous!

"She didn't believe there was a skunk. She said I made it all up. She says everyone knows there ain't no skunks around here. Do you s'pose the note's about that?" I shrugged my shoulders. He wiped his face again, sighed deeply, then continued his slow procession toward the house.

"Throw it away," I suggested, but Danny said that was not honest. "Sometimes you have good ideas, Leah, but I gotta take it to Mama." He sniffled into his shirtsleeve.

Mama waits every weekday for three things—me coming home from kindergarten, Daniel coming home from third grade, and Daddy arriving fresh from work and the outside world. These daily events punctuate monotonous hours spent gazing out the same window at the same small, square patch of grass and the same leafless bushes, while listening to Our Gal Sunday and Pepper Young's Family on the radio. Recent signs of spring have added a fresh green haze to the gray lawn and buds have recently appeared on the bushes.

When Danny got home from school every day Miss Ruth

had a snack waiting for him. Today she had laid out warm-from-the-oven chocolate chip cookies and a glass of fresh milk. My brother dropped his books on the table and ignored his cookies. I took advantage of this oversight by quietly removing a cookie from the stack and slipping it into my pocket.

"Don't you want your cookies and milk?" Miss Ruth looked puzzled. A day when my brother passed up a snack was highly unusual!

"I'm not hungry." He sighed deeply. Miss Ruth frowned. I removed another cookie from the plate.

"Danny, come on in here," Mama called from her bed. "I want to know about your day, honey. You were late and I was worried."

Daniel closed his eyes and gulped. His body seemed to shrink before my eyes. The housekeeper eyeballed him quizzically. "Danny, is something wrong?" she asked. He nodded his head ever so slightly. "Well, you'd best tell your mother about it. She wants you now."

My brother slowly trudged towards Mama's room like a condemned man to his gallows. I cautiously followed. "Stay away," he hissed. "Don't you dare listen." Usually, I would heed Danny's warnings, but this was a red letter (or should I say white note) day. I simply **had** to know what Mama would say about this message from his teacher. Forewarned is forearmed, and one never knew when some teacher might misunderstand circumstances and send a note home with me!

Daniel stopped at Mama's bedroom door, hesitated, then gathered his courage and stepped into the room. "Hi, Mom. How're you feeling?"

Mama smiled. "I'm better, today, sweetie. How was school?"

Danny hesitated perceptively before he answered. "Fine. Great." I gave him a poke in the ribs. "Stop that," he hissed under his breath. "I'll take care of you, later!"

"What was that?" asked Mama.

"Oh, nothing, Mom. It's just—uh, that is, the tee—tee..."

"Danny, what's the matter?" Mama took in his scrunched up posture and pale, whey-colored face in one glance. "Did something happen at school today? Come here, honey, and let me hold you."

Danny couldn't move. He gave a little sob. Mama held out her arms to him, then caught sight of me at the doorway. "Do you know anything about this, Cookie?"

I couldn't answer. This problem belonged solely to my brother.

Danny took two steps and fell against Mama's bed and into her arms. Burying his head in her covers he mumbled something inaudible.

"Honey, I couldn't hear you. Look at me, will you? Let me help!"

He raised up the note, now limp and grubby from tears and hands, and laid it on the pillow. Mama picked it up.

"What's this?"

"A note from my teacher."

"Well, I can see that you're very unhappy about this, Danny. What on earth happened?"

"I don't know why she sent it, Mama. Really, I don't. I didn't do anything wrong. Please believe me!"

"Well," said Mama, "Let's take a look."

Gingerly she peeled the envelope open and extracted Miss White's note. Holding it carefully with her fingertips, as if she expected it to explode in her hand, she opened it and read. Her eyebrows rose in identical ellipses; her mouth worked itself—first into a little bow, then into a grimace, and finally, into open-mouthed shock.

"What is this?" Our mother's voice began in a whisper and ended in some strangled sound that eludes me still. I was truly frightened for my brother, whose eyes had that startled quality one sees in a head-lighted deer. He didn't even flinch.

"What in the **HELL** does this woman *mean* calling **MY SON a LIAR!**"

In my six years, I had never heard my mother either raise her voice or utter profanity. In truth, I thought we were struck dead or were asleep and this was a horrible nightmare. Mama's face bore a striking resemblance to last summer's beefsteak tomatoes. If she could have risen from her bed, she would have levitated.

"Wait until your father gets home!"

Now, those were words to put the fear of God into any child's soul. I cringed. Daniel slumped to the floor, disappearing so abruptly from Mama's view that she gasped.

"Are you okay, honey? Come up here beside me."

Daniel rose and climbed onto Mama's bed. She folded him in her arms while he cried. "Do you know what Miss White's note said, honey?"

"No, but I promise you I didn't do anything wrong. I swear to you, Mommy. I didn't tell Miss White any lies. What did she say I did? Why are you mad at me? Please, please don't tell Daddy—I'll get the woodshed, for sure!"

"Oh, Danny," our mother crooned, "I'm not angry with you!" She brushed his hair from his forehead and kissed him gently in the warm, pale spot between his eyes and his hairline. "I'm sorry that I shouted. It's just that she made me so angry I could spit! Imagine! A teacher and she doesn't know that these hills and valleys are *filled* with skunks. Daddy and I will write her a note and clear up everything." My brother sighed deeply and snuggled closer to Mama. "I was so scared. Do you still love me?"

"Of course, sweetie." She gave him another kiss. "Nothing you ever do can stop me from loving you. Now, hop down and go get your milk and cookies. I'll take care of Miss White."

Daniel's face brightened. He smiled and slid off the bed. As he passed me at the doorway, he gave me a quick poke. "I saw you kipe that cookie. Give it back!"

I had forgotten the cookie in my hand. Shrugging my shoulders, I cut my losses and passed it along before blowing a kiss to Mama. Then, patting the cookie safely hidden in my pocket, I retired to my bedroom.

Tuesday morning dawned with a low-hanging sky that intermittently spit and drooled. Mist rose from pasture grass, covering the surface with its own private cloud. We walked to school with legs hidden to the knees in cotton wool. Daniel's mood had much improved. Mama had written a note to Miss White which the Housekeeper had pinned firmly to his sweater. When we caught up with two of his buddies, I could see I was in for trouble! They alternately chased and teased me the rest of the way to school.

I got out of school at 11:30 am with the sun shining weakly in a pale wash sky. Nothing in woods or pasture invited me to stop along the way. After eating lunch, I settled down on the rug beside my mother's bed and read to myself until I heard my older brother come in. He stomped through the back door, slammed his books onto the table, and stormed into Mama's room.

"Mom, you know what she did? Just guess what she did!"

"Calm down, Danny. Who are you talking about?"

"Miss White. You can't guess what she did!"

"Probably not," Mother murmured, "but nothing would surprise me."

"She read your note in front of the whole class, that's what she did. And then, she told everyone that you made a mistake!"

"What do you mean, 'made a mistake,' Danny?" Mother's mouth looked pinched and her eyes were squinty. "Just what **DID** she say."

"Well, you prob'ly should read it for yourself. She wrote another note. Here it is."

Mother took the new missive from his hand and unfolded it with great deliberation. Slowly, she read the note aloud.

"To Danny's Parents,

I realize that you honestly believe that you have helped your son by writing a note that appears to substantiate his wild story of a skunk under your house. You are not, however, teaching him skills in truthfulness and honesty, nor are you grounding him firmly within reality. Please discourage his participation in future outbursts of imagination.

Thank you.

Imogene White, *Teacher, Grade Three."*

"Well!" For once, Mama appeared at a loss for words. After what seemed an interminable silence, she continued. "Well. Go change your clothes, sweetie, I'll think of something. Hmm, maybe I should invite her out for tea and light the fireplace!"

Then she sent me to fetch the housekeeper. When I checked back later, she was closeted in her room, door shut, with the telephone. I could see its long cord snaking under the door and wondered with whom she was talking.

As I fed the chickens before supper, hints of skunk essence drifted about, reminding me that its carcass lay, barely covered by earth, not twenty feet away. Daniel muttered to himself as he fed the calves and pitched down hay for the cows. He had been in a dark mood all afternoon. Usually, he delighted in teasing me during chore time, often locking me in the chicken coop or trapping me in with the pigs or cows.

Daddy and Mama spent the evening playing two-handed pinochle and devising some strategy for dealing with Miss White. Daniel kept to himself until bedtime, then muttered under his breath for the longest time, keeping me awake.

My brothers and I shared a bedroom—twin beds for Danny and me and a crib for Robert. My deepest desire was to possess a room of my own someday—a room with frilly curtains and bedspread and places for my two dolls, Patsy and Judy, to sit out in safety. But that seemed far in the future. For now, I sat up and whispered, "Danny, Danny! Can you hear me?"

"Of course, and so can Mom and Dad if you don't quiet down."

"What are you muttering about?"

"Whadda ya think! I'm tryin' to figure out some way to prove to Miss White that Daddy really shot a skunk under the house. Why won't she believe any of us?"

"Too bad," I whispered, "that she can't smell it for herself. Too bad she can't see it! Maybe you could..."

My brother grew oddly quiet, then sucked his breath

through his teeth, making a whistling sound. After what seemed a lifetime, he exhaled with satisfaction and dropped off to sleep. Light from the bedroom door (slightly ajar for Robbie) showed my brother's peaceful, smiling face.

In the morning Danny did his chores quickly, then disappeared behind the barn. For a change, I didn't try to follow. I think I knew what he was doing and didn't want to ruin his plans. After a few minutes, he reappeared dragging something in a gunnysack.

"Don't you dare tell Mom and Dad, you hear me?" He tossed me a fierce scowl, hefted the sack over his shoulder, and hurried up the drive, where he hid it behind a bush. As he brushed past me the air became redolent with an acrid skunk scent. I noticed how carefully Danny washed up at the shed before we went into breakfast. I thought he still smelled, but it must have been my imagination. No one else seemed to notice.

"Now Danny," Daddy said, "Your mother and I have written another note to Miss White. We want you to take it to her this morning."

My brother took the note and put it in his pocket. "Sure, Daddy. I'll give it to her."

"We think this note should help fix things up for you. Don't worry, son—everything will be okay."

"Oh, I'm not worried, Daddy."

Daddy remarked that Danny surely seemed like himself again.

We all finished breakfast in silence.

Danny and I kissed Mama good-bye, waved to Daddy, then started down the pasture path towards the woods. At the bush, he stopped only long enough to grab his neatly stowed sack. He grinned broadly, winking at me. "Well, Miss White's gonna get the message today, for sure—and I don't mean no note from my mom and dad!"

For all my life Danny had spent most of his time teasing me and reminding me that I was, after all, a girl, and the bane of his existence. I loved him, nonetheless. In the pinch, he always stood up for me—even to OurFather. If one little suggestion from me could help him out I would never mention it. He was my hero, but even heroes need someone to cover their backs.

My big brother Daniel whistled all the way to school.

CHAPTER 28
In Which I Discover that Studying Ants Can Teach a Lesson for Life

As I sit here on Quaker Hill my early childhood stretches out below me in panorama; an ant climbs lazily up my left shoe and onto my white sock, pausing for a moment to wander in circles before continuing onto my leg. I flick it off and watch it scramble blindly, searching for its pheromone trail back to the nest. As I watch, I recall a late summer afternoon before we left the farm and my own trail up this hill to Annie's cabin.

Long summer days pass slowly between the last day of school and the beginning of the new school year (and a new grade) that traditionally reconvened the Tuesday after Labor Day. Every afternoon when Danny and his friends shouted and laughed through the woods and Robbie snuggled next to Mama as they both napped, I lay prone on the summer grass watching two colonies of ants whose hills stood about twenty feet apart in our upper pasture.

The hills, each a good three feet high, stuck up out of the summer grasses not yet turned to standing hay by hot sun and lack of water. Our milk cow gave them little notice other than switching her tail in annoyance if she wandered too close and the ant warriors happened to run up her legs.

I didn't worry about the ants. To them I was just another hill, lying nearly motionless in my jeans and striped T-shirt. My feet were bare—a family joke, according to Danny. Everyone knew my shoes could be found under the kitchen table where I deposited them as soon as I arrived home from wherever we had been requiring their wearing. Today, my shoes sat unused beneath my twin bed next to Robbie's crib in the room I shared with both of my brothers. Mama was certain I would die from lockjaw or some other horrid malady caused by puncture wounds to my bare feet, although I had so far survived eight shoe-less years with not more injury than the occasional stubbed toe.

Something tickled my ankle and I absently brushed at the offending scout. He (she, it) climbed up the slope of my thumb. I brought the offender to eye level and watched as it dithered frantically up and down searching for a scent trail to follow back to safety and hill before I scooped it up on my other thumbnail (as little as was left by my nibbling teeth) and deposited the frantic insect at the base of the nearest nest. It slipped quickly into line, following equally blind siblings back into the dark interior of home and hearth.

Rolling over, I reached under my back to remove the small stick tucked inside a mat of dried grasses accumulated over years of grazing teeth and trampling hooves. Above me, the clouds rolled lazily through the hazy blue hot late-summer sky. Folding my arms behind my head, I rested it on my hands and closed my eyes, letting the hot sun bathe my face. My closed lids glowed orange with bright red channels running rivers of life-blood across the surface. I ran my tongue over my teeth, absently picking out a stray caraway seed left behind from my lunchtime peanut butter sandwich on dark rye. My ears picked out birdsong, insect chirps, the low munching sounds of our dairy cow grazing close by. In the distance Cutter creek chuckled, happily washing over stones as it flowed lazily through the meadow and into the wood snuggled at the bottom of the hill. I was at peace.

But, back to the ants! Rolling again to my tummy I rested my chin on crossed forearms and examined the two hills separated by nearly ten feet of pasture. The northernmost hill, approximately two feet high, held mostly red ants, each nearly an inch in length. They scurried in and out carrying bits of straw and grass and chopped up insect bodies. A few struggled man(ant)fully to drag a nearly whole blackberry close enough to the hill so that it could be dismantled and taken inside for storage.

I rotated my head to observe the southern hill, composed of black ants, the same general size as the red ones. They also foraged near and far procuring food for their hill, nearly identical to the one holding the red ants.

Last summer the two anthills had had a battle. Danny and I watched as the red group raided the black anthill and carried off little black ant eggs, transporting them hastily to their own hill and disappearing inside. A few days later, the black ants attacked the red hill, appearing with what, I thought, were those purloined children. Apparently, I was mistaken, as a few weeks later we observed some red ants living in harmony within the black hill community, and black ants doing the same within the red ant colony.

Now, this summer, both ant cities (I thought of them as

places where ants lived together as husbands and wives, raised children, and obeyed the laws of the hill) had residents who were half black and half red. These bi-color denizens had appeared this spring when the hills stirred to life after a long and very cold winter. At first, I had searched for a new anthill to account for these colorful denizens but gave up after I noticed two groups of ants fighting over a dead mouse. One group had our native red ants, plus a few bi-colored members, the other had black ants plus bi-colored members identical to those on the red ant side. This puzzled me until a conversation with Daddy helped clarify the matter.

At first, I approached Mama, who snorted that if I had enough time to scrutinize ant hills, I had too much of it on my hands and could help her weed the carrots. After an hour spent trying to decide what green thing was an emerging carrot and what constituted a weed, she released me to my ant studies. I thought she heaved a sigh of relief as I hopped over the garden row, not unlike a rabbit fleeing Farmer McGregor, taking care not to step where I ought not.

After dinner, I tackled Daddy as he sat on the porch in the twilight smoking his pipe. I loved to snuggle next to him and often shared a few moments of quiet time while he 'unwound' after a day's work in the Shipyard followed by milking, feeding, and other farming duties waiting for his return.

Daddy pulled on his pipe—he made a slickery sound, not quite a puff, when he smoked. He put his arm around me, pulling me close, and gave me a quick kiss, rubbing his whiskery face on my cheek. He smelled of Prince Albert tobacco and pot roast and Mama's garlic carrots. There was also a faint touch of Grampa's moonshine. I felt warm and loved, sitting next to him on the back stoop watching the dark creep up from the pasture and listening to the little night things come awake.

"Daddy," I inquired hesitantly, "do you know anything about ants?" I knew Daddy was a machinist who made parts for the big guns on the ships in the Navy Yard where he worked. That didn't include insects and things like that, but he was smart and knew volumes about the animals on our farm.

"Well, Cookie, I don't know a lot, but if you have questions, I will try to answer them for you. What is it, honey?" Daddy put his elbows on his knees, cradling his chin in his hands. His pipe, clenched between strong, white teeth (except for the gold inlay on one front incisor), emitted blue puffs that rose in lazy circles. I absently swished my finger through them, disturbing the symmetry if the swirling smoke. It curled around my wrist, then rose straight up until a stray breeze caught it and dissipated the misty blue haze. Daddy smiled and puffed out a new cloud.

"Do you remember when we watched the ant hills have their war last year? And they stole each other's little babies? Then some of the red ants lived with the black ants, and some black ants lived with the red ones. Now, some of the ants in each hill are half black and half red. They look exactly alike, but when they meet up, they fight. How come, Daddy?"

Daddy sighed deeply, took a mouthful of smoke, and held it a long time before he puffed out several perfect little circles that expanded as they rose into the night. "That's a tough one, baby. I do remember learning that ants have poor eyesight in general and depend a lot on scent. Ants that belong to the same hill smell alike, so even if they can't identify each other by sight, they know if someone is from another hill by their smell."

I nodded my head. I had seen how the ants followed single file to and from the hill to food and back again, sometimes bumping each other off to the side when they met head to head. "So, the ants don't know that this year they have little ants that look different?"

"I think that's probably true, Cookie. Those stolen eggs hatched out in the new hills, so they smelled like everyone else. Probably one of those new babies grew up to father ants that are now multicolored. Sort of like the black baby rabbits a few years back."

I thought about my chubby, lovable white Easter bunny Daisy Dreamer and what she had done to her own babies and shuddered. Maybe the ants had it right—it wasn't color that counted, but where you are born—although that didn't seem quite the answer, either. I pointed that out to Daddy who chuckled and ruffled my hair. "Go to bed, Cookie. When you grow up you will understand that people and ants are as different as apples and oranges."

I got up and went inside to the light and the smell of pot roast and garlic carrots and the sound of the Lone Ranger on the radio, reserving to myself the idea that people and ants were not all that different.

After my talk with Daddy, I take time to examine in detail how the two hills interact. For the most part, they live in peaceful coexistence, unless they both claim the same dead grasshopper or other food source. Then, they are willing to fight to the death and often did. That is understandable, as each hill is autonomous. I almost understand why they raid each other and bear away eggs as booty. The eggs add new workers to their societies without a burden on their queens to lay them, while stolen eggs reduce the number of new ants in the other hill. That they, themselves, are plundered, is irrelevant. Both hills give off an odor, not unlike the vinegar that Mama uses in the kitchen—a sharp, acrid odor that to my nose smells the same from both hills. To the ants, however, it smells of home, the tiny nuances that separate them as distinctive as house numbers.

I think about my teacher and her horror at Terry with his warm chocolate eyes and his soft chocolate skin kissing me on the cheek. Terry smells of interesting things—different houses and soap and new foods that he brings to school in his lunch bag and sometimes shares with me on the playground when the teachers are not looking. His hair curls tight against his skull, and feels bumpy, like the wool on our lambs—and smells earthy—unlike the bland, slightly soapy smell of my straight blond bob. He smells different, but not bad. Even after two years, the teachers still look at our friendship with funny, grownup eyes and small head shakes. Abby is white, like me, and often smells like pee and dirty clothing but no one cares if she touches my hair or sits next to me at the playground table.

Mama says there is time enough for thinking about that kind of stuff when I am grown up and really know what goes on in the world. I think to myself, she does not know that I was born grown up. My grandmother knows it—that is why I give her the creeps.

I thought I might talk with Annie about the ants, but the time was never right. Eventually, the two hills became homogenous, each having an equal distribution of red, black, and bi-colored ants. To my eye, I saw no difference—but, as Daddy explained, the scent won out. I had a long time to think about this before I made my way into the world—long enough to reach my own conclusions about ants and people and the color of skin. Besides, I know what Annie would have told me. She had in so many ways. "It is not the color of your skin that matters; it is the color of your heart. Think on this, Leah. God made us all. No two of us look alike." *Except for identical twins, I think to myself as my mind's eye sees my two sets of cousins—one pair boys, the other girls. Only small things let me tell them apart, and even then, sometimes I make a mistake!*

In the distance, I hear thunder rumbling behind the sullen clouds piled high above me. I shiver as I stare at those idyllic appearing woods. Deep inside the tip of a memory—something hidden and unacknowledged for who knows how long, but now ready to spring full blown into my consciousness, rises to the surface and explodes.

CHAPTER 29
In Which I Make the Acquaintance of Hamlet and Learn the Dangers of Naming One's Food

I sit on the hilltop with my back against the stump of one of the old trees that has blown down during some winter storm and open my lunch bag. I retrieve the now warm can of cola and pull the tab. The liquid splurts out in bubbly warm foam. I tilt my head back and close my eyes to the warm late summer sun remembering...

That last spring on our Bremerton farm was glorious! Our three apple trees sported fancy blossoms snuggled between growing leaves. Pussy Willows presented their furry, grey-white pellets down by the creek and both the peach and plum trees blossomed in pink and white. Hens clucked in broody fashion and pecked at my hands as I attempted to retrieve their bounty of eggs twice a day. I loved the way they chuckled as they snuggled carefully in the nesting boxes, so as not to crack any potential children. A few brooders managed to slip past Daddy's sharp eyes and took to hiding outside their fenced area in an attempt to incubate a nest of babies. I asked Daddy why he didn't let some of the lady chickens do that, then we wouldn't have to buy new chicks from the co-op. He said that since we didn't have a rooster, the eggs would never hatch. It made sense, I told myself. Even chickens need moms *and* dads!

Spring is a time of renewal and birth on most farms—especially those family farms where all young things take their place in the ebb and flow of life. Our Chester White sow was so hugely pregnant that she had trouble waddling to and from the trough of slop specially prepared by Daddy and delivered twice a day by Danny. I was not allowed this particular job as Daddy felt it should fall to the eldest son, notwithstanding that he was a good deal larger than I was, and the sow was huge. Robbie was banned from the hog pen, permanently. Daddy said he hadn't the sense God gave a goose, so needed to grow up a bit before he tackled anything larger than a hen.

She had no name, other than 'The Sow'. Usually good-natured, she became ferocious at farrowing time, protecting her piglets at all costs. Her generous abdomen bore a double row of engorged teats and writhed and roiled with near to escaping piglets. I was mesmerized! I dreamed at night of being present when she gave birth—watching little babies walk (I had no concept) out of their mother's belly.

I vaguely remembered Mama's tummy filled with Robbie. She had occasionally let me feel the baby move, in order, I now suspect, of instilling maternal/sisterly instincts. No need, as I had them from the instant I realized Mama was growing another human being. My only desire was that 'it' would be a 'she.' I was older now, if not necessarily wiser in the details of birth, but still fascinated.

As the sow's time drew near, her belly quieted. She lay in

the shade of the old barn, making soft grunting noises, arising only to drink or devour slop generously provided by either Daddy or Danny. At night, Daddy gently herded her into a pen inside the barn, lined with straw and fenced off from the cows.

Unfortunately, I missed the blessed event(s). When Danny and I dashed to the barn in the light morning mist we were greeted by grunts and squeals and happy slurp-ings from twelve little piglets, each vying for or retaining possession of a teat. Unfortunately, there were more piglets than food dispensers, and the thirteenth and smallest (Daddy called it the runt) lay quietly behind its mother, with an obviously misshapen front leg!

I reached carefully behind the sow, who squirmed into the straw in an attempt to accommodate her offspring's morning meal and gently lifted the injured baby. Carefully wrapping him (or her) in a feed sack, I sat back and waited for Danny to bring help in the form of our daddy.

When Daddy arrived, he knelt down beside me and examined the injured limb, cursing under his breath in Czech when he saw the protruding limb. "You can fix him, Daddy, can't you?" I inquired, piercing him with my blue eyes.

Daddy appeared to consider (briefly) the results of eliminating the problem piglet offspring but took into account the impact on his impressionable little daughter. "I will take care of it," I earnestly offered. He sighed, mussed my hair, and indicated I should follow him up to the house, taking care not to jostle my precious bundle.

Behind me I heard Danny whisper, "Wow, Leah. I thought for sure he was gonna knock it in the head. That's sorta what he said to Mama at the house!"

Mama's eyebrows rose quizzically as we trooped into the mudroom. She screwed her mouth to the side and gave Daddy 'the look'. He raised his hands and hunched his shoulders. "Cookie says she'll take care of it if I can fix the leg. What am I gonna do?" Mama laughed and indicated we should all go into the kitchen.

The table was covered with old towels and one section was reserved for a bottle of alcohol, scissors, various bandaging materials, and ointments. Daddy's leather cutters, curved needles, and fine fishing leader simmered in a pan on the stove. Now Daddy's eyebrows rose. Before he could say a word, Mama laughed and told him she just knew he wouldn't be able to resist his daughter's entreaty

"What's that mean," inquired Danny to nobody in particular.

Mama motioned me to lay the little wounded piglet on the table as I crooned softly to it that everything would be okay. My mama and my daddy would make it well.

Robbie had wandered in with wide eyes and an "o" mouth. Mama pointed towards him and told me to take him into the playroom, away from the surgical preparations. "Danny, you can help me here."

Danny beetled his brows and grimaced. "Gaw, mom. Whydja want me to help. Leah's the one that wants to save it. I was lookin' forward to seein' how Daddy was gonna get rid of it."

Mama gave him her sternest look. "Okay, young man, then **you** take your brother into the playroom and keep him occupied. Leah can be the scrub nurse."

I was delighted. Mama trusted me to help.

"You get into the bathroom, young lady, and scrub your hands clean! Use the Life Buoy soap and the nail brush." I got!

While I provided hands for the things that Daddy asked for, Mama held the piglet down. With care and as quickly as possible, Daddy cleaned the wound, then he and Mama straightened the little leg and Daddy stitched the tear in the flesh. After he dressed it with iodine and applied a gauze pad, he splinted it with carefully whittled wood pieces tied in place with more gauze. The little pig made hardly a noise while we worked. Mama said it was in shock and hoped it would recover. When we were finished, Daddy made a padded bed out of a cardboard box and Mama placed our little patient inside. The box went behind the oil stove in a quiet, warm spot.

"Now, we wait," whispered Mama. "If he (and yes, Leah, it's a little boy pig) lives, I will feed him some formula later."

I sat with my legs crossed Indian style beside his little box and willed him to live, my hand gently caressing his head covered with short white bristles. His ears twitched a couple of times, and I thought he stopped breathing, but at last he opened one little blue eye, looked up at me, and stole my heart.

Presently Mama came by and knelt down beside me. "I think he's awake, Mama. He opened his eye and looked at me. Can I name him, please?"

"Are you sure it's a good idea to do that, Cookie? He still might not live."

"I want him to have a name. And if he doesn't live, I can bury him and put the name on his little cross."

Mama sighed. "How can I argue with such logic. What do you think is a good name for the little guy?"

"How about Hamlet," I replied. I had thought about a name for the past hour, and it seemed appropriate to me.

"Hamlet?" Mama laughed. "Oh, baby. Someday you may see the irony in that choice. But Hamlet it is. Bring him out of the box and we'll feed him a little milk."

Hamlet thrived! Pigs are extremely intelligent, Danny, Robbie, and I learned. He knew his name and answered to it. We taught him to stand on his hind legs and beg for bits of food. Mama trained him to use a box of sand in the mudroom to relieve himself, and to ask at the kitchen door to be let out. Eventually, he grew big enough to have his own pen down by the barn, although he never joined his mother. And when Daddy took his brothers and sisters to auction six months later, Hamlet stayed at home. I had been a trifle anxious about the auction, but now I was relieved. Obviously, Daddy meant him for me.

He was smart, this pig friend of mine, smarter than our dog and a whole lot smarter than any cow I had ever known. He could shake hands, sit on his haunches and beg for food, but his brilliance was in words, and he knew a lot of them. He would bring me a ball, a sock, herd the chickens if I directed him. And he was affectionate. Daddy had neutered him, so he didn't develop the usually savage boar temperament. For all his size at six months, he was gentle with me.

But all good things must come to an end, as OurGrand-mother used to say. I didn't agree with her, but kept my mouth shut when she made this pronouncement. Besides, in the present case, it would do me no good to complain.

The morning of Hamlet's demise dawned bright and clear—not a cloud in the sky! It was a Saturday morning, and

Daddy told me to sleep late—he and Danny would attend to the chores. I had been sick with yet another bladder/kidney infection and hadn't been down to the barn for several days. Danny brought Hamlet up for a visit on Friday afternoon. He cavorted outside my sickroom window, standing on his hind feet and waving to me. God, what a glorious pig! When the movie Babe came out several years ago, I thought about my Hamlet.

However, on this Saturday morning, I had fallen back to sleep and was jolted from a dream by the sound of a truck rumbling down the driveway and past my bedroom window. I jumped to my window just in time to see it pass on its way down to the barn. My eyes bugged in horror at the sign on its white side. It read "Fred's Humane Kill Service" in large black letters.

From the general direction of the barn, I heard the frightened squeals of a pig—and in my heart, I knew it was not the sow who would soon be giving birth to another litter. Those soul-wrenching cries came from another pig—*my* pig—Hamlet.

Frantically I scrambled into my blue jeans and T-shirt, grabbed shoes and socks, and ran for the kitchen. Mama grabbed me by the shirt neck as I attempted to jig past her. "Whoa, sister. Where do you think you are going? Back into that bedroom!"

I slid sideways, fell to my hip, then continued towards the mudroom door, the wail that had started in my bedroom now rising to a crescendo as I wrenched myself away from my mother. Regaining my feet, I beat her to the back door and was out onto the driveway, shoes still in my hand.

Down at the barn images come into view. I trip and fall to my knees, dropping my shoes in the process and skinning my palms bloody. Hamlet hangs upside down, suspended by his hind legs from a tripod, his squeals climb in volume and his blue eyes are wide with terror. Daddy stands beside him, steadying the tripod with both hands as a strange man (Fred? Humane Killer) squats at Hamlet's head, an odd pistol in his hand. I rise to my knees as he places it behind Hamlets ear and I hear myself scream no, no, no. Daddy looks up from his task and sees me kneeling in the dirt. He makes a moue with his mouth and shakes his head at me. "Do it, Fred," I hear him say and the pistol pops and Hamlet jerks. His whole body convulses then hangs slack.

Before Daddy could move, I was on my feet and turned back towards the house. My shoes lay forgotten, but I felt no pain from the gravel and dirt clods as I bolted up the drive. Mama tried to catch me as I drew level with the back door but I heard Daddy yell from below to just let me go. *"Did she see it, did she see it,"* Mama *screams as I pass and Daddy confirms with addition of a few choice words in Czech. I make the rise and turn right as the driveway met Hickey road, running as hard as my wobbly legs, stiff and weak from days in my sickbed, can take me.* My breath caught in my throat and I had to stop for a moment. A few gulps of air and I continued on, no thought of my destination but the need to be far away from Daddy's betrayal.

I do not stop again until I am halfway up Annie's hill. I turn back when I hear the sound of footsteps behind me. It is Danny. He halts at the foot of the hill. Is he following me? I stare hard at him and detect what looks like a glint of a tear in his eye. He nods, motioning me up the hill, then turns towards home wiping his eyes on his shirt sleeve. I hurry upward, not stopping until I reach the top and look down at Annie's cabin, hidden in its little hollow. She sits on her small porch and looks up at my approach. Her arms go out to me and I fly the last few feet down the hill.

Annie rose from the stoop and I fell sobbing into her arms. She folded me close to her bosom, smelling of sharp lavender and harsh lye soap and chamomile and cinnamon buns. "What has brought thee here in this manner, Leah?" Annie asked as she carried me into her kitchen and sat me on the table. Before I could answer she took stock of my palms and the soles of my feet and tut-tutted with her tongue. "No need to answer now. Let me tend thy cuts."

I gulped back my sobs and snuffled into my fist, wiping the resulting residue on my cuff. Annie gently took my arm away and cleaned my face with her apron, soft from drying on the line and smelling of bleach and wind. "I saw the truck go by this morning, little one. You saw it, as well." She made it a statement. I nodded my head in response.

She turned from me and shuffled about in her neat little kitchen, putting a kettle of water to heat on the back of the black cook stove and returning with clean cloths, a basin of warm water, and soap. We didn't speak as she cleaned my hands, applying ointment of her own making to soothe them. The cuts on my bare feet were deeper and filled with small pieces of gravel and dirt. She worked quickly, humming a hymn under her breath as she picked out some particularly deep debris. "These will heal, Leah," she murmured as she finished the job and patted my left knee, "and leave few scars.

Now let us talk of thy heart."

The kettle began a thrumming as the water rose to a boil. Annie produced a pot, rustled about for herbs, and prepared us cups of tea. She set out some shortbread—my favorite—and a small pitcher of top milk, then helped me to a seat at the table. When we had both had sips from our cups, she took my hands in hers—gently, so as not to irritate my still smarting palms.

"Leah," she began quietly, "what thee saw this morning is part of the cycle of life our Father puts into our keeping." She paused, as if weighing the effect her words might have on me. She did not ask how much I had seen, and the thought that she might made me more than a little queasy.

"He was my friend," I answered quietly, feeling the heat of tears.

"And he will fill the bellies of thy family in the winter to come."

"He was my friend, not my dinner, Annie."

"I know. Dear child, I know. It was not the ending thy heart wished for him. But blame not thy father and thy mother. Thy father has seen thy face, I wager, and thy mother held the little one close and suckled him with milk prepared by her own hand. It is the way of life. God has placed us thus. Thee has fed and nurtured thy piglet and now he will return that to you. Weep not for him, Leah—his life was longer than that of his littermates. As he grew, he gave you joy as you gave him time. Our Father has told us in the Good Word—as ye give, so shall you receive. This is reciprocity, dear child."

I sipped my warm tea and nibbled at the shortbread, deep in thought. It was true that Hamlet had had a few good months. He brought joy to me and had taught me to appreciate an intellect different than my own, but one with its own joy of life. I thought of his brothers and sisters long cooked and served for meals. "It's not fair, Annie. He deserved to be my friend for a long time."

"Life is not fair, Leah. Life just is. What portion thee is given is not for thee to puzzle. It is what God has granted thee. What thee makes of it, is thine alone."

I left the little cabin wearing a pair of hand-knitted stockings a few sizes too large, but they kept my feet out of the dirt. Danny was sitting on a stump at the bottom of the hill looking a little forlorn, his elbows on his knees and his chin in his hands. He turned his head when he heard me bumping down the path behind him.

"Oh, ya finally got here. I waited."

That was obvious, I thought to myself, but it was nice that my big brother cared enough to sit alone all afternoon. I knew he was fond of Hamlet, even though he teased me about being in love with a pig. I supposed he had a little thinking to do, himself. He rose from the log and took my hand in his, taking care not to scuff the now hardening scabs. "Let's go home. Mom's prob'ly worried about'cha."

My big brother Danny—my tormenter, my savior, and the closest person in the universe to me. Not even Mama and Daddy (OurFather, in this case) would ever be closer genetically than this hazel-eyed dark-haired boy a few years older than me. I wouldn't know about genes for many more years, but deep inside I knew this as truth. The day his soul went home to the universe my world was a less safe place.

Daddy had nothing to say when we arrived at the

mudroom. Mama exclaimed over my feet and palms, blessing Annie for taking care of my injuries. I had missed the kerfuffle over Hamlet's head—a story that still makes the rounds at family gatherings. It seems Daddy had arrived at the kitchen with the head on a large wooden square, expecting Mama to relish boiling it down for traditional Bohemian headcheese. She screamed at the sight, announcing that it would be like cooking one of her own children. According to family apocrypha, Daddy stomped off in a Bohemian huff and called our Great Aunt Mary to come and prepare the head—which she did.

I thought long that night after Danny and I were bundled off to bed. Annie's words, plus a little chat from Daddy and a crying spell with Mama gave me much food for thought. In the end, I acknowledged the argument that no matter how friendly, hogs are food. Hamlet was part of the chain of life, existing a step down from humans who are at the top, but still lower than the force that keeps the universe in balance. It didn't seem right to eat a friend, but if the tables had been turned, Hamlet would probably have eaten me. Pigs are omnivorous.

"Lesson learned," I told Danny a few nights later as we lay awake listening to Inner Sanctum through the bedroom wall.

"What lesson is that?" he whispered back.

"Never name your food."

My brother laughed, loud enough for Daddy to tell us to quiet down before we woke Robbie. "You gotta way with words," my brother acknowledged, "You gotta way with words."

It was many years before I ate bacon, although I

succumbed to Mama's crispy pork chops the first time they appeared on my dinner plate. After all, I was just a little girl— even if one with a slightly aching heart

CHAPTER 30
In Which Jerome Teaches an Unsolicited Lesson on Relations Between the Sexes

In winter, we always took the long way to school down the blacktop road. Although cutting through the woods shortened the distance to about half, rain, fog, and gloom made for an unpleasant and usually soggy experience. 'We' included our closest neighbor's ten year old daughter Sarah (sister of my heartthrob Pete and his wonder horse Midnight) and a few of Danny's little buddies we collected along the way.

On this jewel of a springtime day when the sky was as blue as a robin's egg and the air smelled of sweet fresh turned earth and bright green growing shoots, the boys had run off playing some male rite of passage game to occupy them on the homeward trek leaving Sarah and me to carry on alone. We tagged along with the boys through the Park View low income housing that separated the elementary school from the path skewing upward into the cool interior of the woods, putting up with their pranks and jokes until we passed Jerome Whitcomb's house—a little white clapboard cottage surrounded by a white picket fence, nestled against the hill adjacent to the woods.

Technically, Jerome's house was not part of Park View. He lived there with his father, who worked hard to take care of him. Jerome was sixteen and no longer attended school. When it became apparent that he would never progress beyond third grade, his father took him out.

Sometimes Jerome mowed lawns for pocket change but usually spent his days whittling on a broomstick with his jackknife. Danny knew Jerome from his last year at Park View Elementary and there was bad blood between them. Danny didn't help the situation as he and his friends called Jerome names—their favorites being 'retard' and 'idiot boy'. Mama said Jerome was just a little simple and gave Danny an afternoon confined to his bedroom for failing in charity towards someone not as intellectually endowed as himself. Sarah and I thought he was simple alright—simply nasty! A few weeks before as the two of us walked by alone, he ran out from behind the garage and dropped his pants as he leered at us. I told Mama who sent Daddy down to talk to Mr. Whitcomb. Sarah's father called the police over the incident and Mama admonished us to avoid going past the Whitcomb house, but it was the shortest path to the woods, and sometimes we ignored her.

Jerome was conspicuously absent from the white picket-fenced yard when we passed, so we felt safe when Danny and his friends took the long path toward the creek. The woods were cool and dark after the bright springtime sunshine and it took a few moments for our eyes to adjust to the filtered light drifting softly through the firs and cedar trees and gently budding alders and vine maples. Everything glowed in shades of green and brown and the soft underfoot of needles and shed bark dampened our footsteps. Overhead, squirrels and birds chipped and twittered in the trees; in the distance, the boys hooted and called out in whatever competition occupied their pre-adolescent minds.

A few yards along the path Sarah and I separated, having previously decided on a game of hide and seek as we meandered homeward in the lengthening afternoon shadows. She hid first and I quickly found her squatting behind a rotting mother log, giving herself away, as usual, by brushing at the insects swarming up from the disturbed moss. We laughed as I helped her pick a few stray gnats from her bangs. She collected up her school work, moved to a less insect intensive area, and hid her eyes to count as I crept as silently as possible up the trail and took cover behind a huge fir tree. I could hear Sarah counting out loud; slow at first, then speeding up as she passed twenty of her fifty. When she reached thirty-two the counting abruptly stopped.

"Darn it," I thought to myself, "she's cheatin'." I held my breath, not willing to give myself away so easily if she weren't going to play fair but realized quickly that I didn't hear the sound of her laughter running ahead of her footsteps. In fact, the woods were ominously quiet—no birds or squirrels quarreled overhead, no sound of the boys, and although the sun still shone in slanted golden rays through the treetops, I was suddenly apprehensive and cold to the bone when I heard something that sent a chill shuddering down my spine. A guttural voice, quite near, muttered; "What you doin' here alone, Sarah girl! I seen you an' that other little white-hair girl go by my house. Where's she at?"

I freeze in place behind my tree, its broad trunk hiding me from anyone directly down the trail. The voice mumbles again. "Ain'tcha gonna say sumpin'?" Sarah makes no sound as Jerome (and I know deep in my gut that the voice belongs to Jerome even before he says); "You 'n that li'l white hair girl went an' got me in trouble with my ol' man!" I can feel my body shrink as fear tightens every muscle; adrenaline gushes through me—my heart flutters like a hummingbird, beating helplessly against the base of my throat. I hear rustling sounds and grunting, the resonance of a slap, sharp, incised, on the motionless air, and the sudden intake of someone's (Jerome's? Sarah's?) breath. My mind skitters around in my head like a terrified mouse trapped in a shoebox, its shrieks of fear so loud I am certain that Jerome will hear. Then Sarah says in a low and sort of trembly voice; "What makes you think I'm alone?"

The little mouse scream becomes a roar and bolts from my head to my mouth; I clamp both my hands tight over my lips, trapping it before the sound can pass and give me away. No, no, no, Sarah—I jabber silently—my insides and legs go to jelly, and I slide down my tree trunk support, not even feeling the splinters in my palms and knees; and Jerome tells Sarah to shut up. Sarah does not shut up—she raises her voice and tells him someone has run for help—Leah went to get my mom, she says, and I hear another sound, more like a thud than a slap, and Sarah moans!

Maybe I can make a run for it, I tell my spaghetti legs. Sarah wants me to get away—she is a big girl, I rationalize—after all, she is ten years old and in grade five. I am only eight, just a little kid—what can I do except go for help. I rise to my knees, willing life back into my legs. And then I hear a sound—the bzzz of an angry bee, I tell myself, but in my heart, I know *that is not a bee—it is a zipper, and the fluttering hummingbird heart in my throat freezes. **He** is doing something bad to Sarah. I don't know exactly what; my mind does not want to be old enough to know what Jerome is about to do to Sarah, but my frozen little nub of a heart knows enough, and if I run for help (run away, run away, you coward) Jerome will have enough time to do **that thing** to Sarah—hurt her and maybe more. I cannot leave Sarah alone!*

And that is when my legs explode like springs wound near to breaking, and I erupt from behind my tree, screaming at the top of my lungs--running not towards home and safety, but directly down the path to where Jerome, his jeans and underwear tangled around his ankles, grunts on top of Sarah like some nasty rabbit husband, his hand groping for the little pink panties visible under her hiked up skirt. I hurl myself onto his back, beating his head with my fists. He rolls off poor, crumpled Sarah and tries to rise, but the combination of hobbled legs and thrashing whirlwind panics him and he starts to cry, sitting there on his fat, white rump. I snatch at his face like a berserk animal, peeling off four neat curls of flesh. Rivulets of blood compete with his tears as he crawls back down the trail towards Park View, hiking up his clothing on the way.

One night shortly after Jerome attacked Sarah, I heard Mama and Daddy talking about it as I lay in bed. They were whispering in the living room and Daddy was obviously upset about something. I heard Daddy grumble in Czech, and Mama tsk tsked him.

"I don't understand just letting him get away with it, Mayleen. So what if he's mentally challenged, isn't that what they called him? And three weeks in detention isn't likely to change him."

"We can't do anything about it, honey," I heard Mama whisper. "If Sarah's parents don't want to press charges, we just have to let it go and protect our girl."

Mama and Daddy continue their conversation in voices too low for me to hear so I rise quietly and put my head up against the bedroom door. Danny joins me on the floor and puts his arm around my shoulders. He whispers in my ear that he will not let "that little creep get near me," then helps me rise and tucks me into my bed.

A siren in the far distance broke my reverie—a siren like the one on the sheriff's car that took Sarah and me to identify Jerome that day so long ago. He limped out of his father's house like a beaten cur dog, according to Daddy, nursing a lump on his head and still bleeding from the scratches inflicted by my stubby little fingernails. It was a long time before Sarah and I walked the forest path past the Whitcomb house, and though we looked, we never saw Jerome again. It was even longer before the nightmares that made sleeping a risky thing sniveled away into my subconscious. I had buried the memory of that day in the woods until it exploded full-blown into my mind today.

I am not yet ready to risk looking downslope towards Annie's old cabin. Instead, I gaze skyward, watch the dark cloud pass to the east taking its random raindrops with it, and see the sun playing hide and seek behind lighter-colored advancing clouds. Below me a rainbow dances upward, arising in the creek that meanders through the fields and terminates in one of the remaining stands of trees.

Beside that creek, I first caught sight of a little old lady and gave birth to Hatchet Annie. In those trees, my brothers and I played hide and seek, cowboys and Indians, and Peter Pan.

I sat down on a nearby stump after sweeping off a few ants and a splodge of bird droppings with a tuft of long grass pulled from a nearby clump, as my mind traveled back.

For two weeks after 'the incident', as they called it, Mama and Daddy had barely let me out of their sight, all the time pretending that 'it' had never happened. Daddy drove me to school every day and Danny was obliged, on pain of death, to deliver me unsullied to Mama's anxious hands immediately after. I felt smothered. Consequently, when Annie came down with an invitation to tea on the second Saturday, I begged Mama to let me go. After extracting a promise from Annie that she would convey me home before supper, they acquiesced.

Daddy walked me up the hill on Saturday morning, gripping my hand as if he half expected a pack of Jeromes to hurtle from behind some hummock and snatch me. We walked in silence up the driveway, Daddy sucking softly on his favorite pipe. As we turned west on Hickey Road Pete rode by on Midnight, greeted Daddy with a wave, and winked at me. I watched enviously as his legs gripped Midnight's bare sides while he encouraged her into a trot. His back, straight as an arrow, rose and fell with the black mare's clipped gait and I could hear him whistling tunelessly to himself. I wished he would return to Daddy and me and whisk me up behind him. I would wrap my arms around his slim waist and hold on tight to keep myself from sliding around on the mare's silky hide and we would ride away forever, but he didn't, and I struggled to keep pace with Daddy's long stride.

"Daddy," I enquired softly, "can I ask you something?"

"What's on your mind, Little Beaver?" I wished he would stop calling me that silly name. My front teeth had grown in straight, but were too big for my mouth, at the moment, so I guess the comparison was appropriate—just infuriating!

"What happened in the woods with Jerome and Sarah. I tried to talk to Mama, but she just cries." Daddy sucked in sharply on his pipe and stopped dead in his tracks. He turned to face me, cupped my chin in his left hand, held his pipe in his right, and peered straight into my eyes, a look of sadness in his own.

"That shouldn't have happened to Sarah, Leah. And you shouldn't have had to watch. I should have stopped Jerome after the first time. What he did was wrong, but I can't be the one to explain it to you, do you understand? It would be for the best if you just forgot that it happened. Can you do that, honey?" I nodded, but I **didn't** understand—maybe someday I would, but I desperately needed someone to talk to now, and all the grownups in my life were failing me.

He gave me a hug and took my hand again. We continued, not speaking, to the top of Annie's hill, where he let me go on alone, although he stood at the top until Annie gave him the okay.

And now I sit where he stood that day, not so long ago. I wonder what he thinks as he watches his little girl running down the hill. Does he know that her innocence is shattered— that part of her childhood is forever gone? Does he know, (and does my mother know) that their silence inflicts hurt far worse than anything Jerome Whitcomb did because she thinks it was her fault; or does he hope that answers lie with the old woman waving from the cornstalks below.

I did not know that this quiet, late-springtime Saturday would be the last time I saw Annie Marsh. If I had, perhaps I would have opened up to her, but the thought of seeing disappointment on her face was too much for me. I was afraid that even her listening heart could not forgive my transgression. Because of me, Jerome was punished, and because of that punishment my friend was put in danger. That my courageous act had saved Sarah from a far worse fate I would not realize for many years; and so, Annie and I spent those last few hours chattering of nothing in particular, all the while my unasked (and unanswered) questions festered inside of me.

I never spoke of the incident again, even when Mama gathered up her courage and broached the subject a few weeks later. A couple of times Sarah brought the subject up but then, as little kids do, we put it behind us and went on with life. I finally banished them, forcing them into some dark crevice until this August afternoon atop Annie's hill, looking down on those same green woods. I should have felt relieved at the remembering, but something still didn't feel right. I shook my shoulders and breathed deeply, then shut my eyes and allowed myself to slowly settle into an almost trance-like peace.

I find myself once again in the woods below our lower pasture, searching in the warm spring sunshine for trilliums for Mama.

CHAPTER 31
In Which I Remember
What I Chose to Forget

Shortly after Sarah and I had our last encounter with Jerome, I began having nightmares—horrid dreams that involved Jerome chasing me through a swamp, knife in hand. I woke screaming, every night, waking Mama and Daddy and disrupting the whole household, according to Danny. Something about the dreams disturbed me—something I couldn't quite remember—something so horrible that I didn't **want** to remember—until this moment.

I see it now, this thing in my dream that scares me—and it is my fault. Daddy has told me to avoid Jerome. He has admonished me to stay away from his house and from the area of our woods that is close to Parkview and I wander off on this bright late spring day and pay no attention to where I am. Behind me a twig snaps and startles me from my project of picking trilliums for my mama. I look behind me and see nothing but a happy red squirrel swishing its bushy tail and leaping up to a tree branch above my head. He (or she) scolds me for disturbing his/her peace and disappears behind the trunk. I laugh, my voice tinkling in the bright sunshine.

I laughed. The hushed woods sucked up my laughter and replaced it with the sudden bustle of something large moving through the brush, freezing me to the spot where I crouched beside a grouping of green, spear-shaped trillium leaves. The 'whatever' thrashing behind me pounced before I could move.

Someone (thing) grabs my shoulders and pushes me down with my face pressed into the mossy dirt beside a large log. I feel hot breath, stinky with the rancid smell of tooth decay and garlic and lunchmeat on my neck and hot, sticky hands holding me down. Spittle hits my ear, and I hear a voice say that he (it is a 'he') has been waiting for me. He wants to hurt me and he wants to hurt Sarah.

It is Jerome.

Jerome flips me over on the soft moss, sneering into my wide eyes. One hand and an arm push down hard across my shoulders, his lower body pins my legs to the ground. His other hand clamps across my mouth. I cannot breathe. He speaks again.

"I been waitin' to get you alone and pay you back for callin' the cops on me. Too bad that little black-haired girly ain't here. Then I could do this to **BOTH** of ya." He squirmed up further on my body and let go of my shoulders long enough to snatch a wad of cloth from his pocket, release the hand over my mouth, and stick the cloth in deep between my teeth. Then he turned me over again and began pulling at Danny's cast-off bib overalls I wore with a blue and white striped T-shirt. They were cut off to long shorts length and now my knees were cut and bleeding from Jerome's weight grinding them into the twigs and rocks beneath the moss.

"Hold still, you," he hissed into my ear. "You're just gonna hurt yourself if you fight me." His hand snaked up my pant leg and winkled under the elastic of my panties. I bucked like a calf, trying to dislodge him from my back, but he just pressed harder between my shoulders.

He is hurting me, oh, he is hurting me and his fingers are pressing into my private parts and his nails are scratching the soft inner lining and now he is pulling his fingers out and I can hear a sucking sound and now he is putting them back, up inside me and it hurts, it hurts, it hurts! I am screaming in my head and screaming into the horrid cloth stuffed into my mouth. And his fingers are hard inside me, now, pushing, pushing.

Suddenly he withdrew his hand and flipped me onto my back again. His eyes riveted onto the buckles holding up my overalls and he tussled to open them one-handed. He got one free and pulled hard, eventually forcing the un-hooked strap over my arm. With some little trouble, he yanked them below my knees and began prying my legs apart. He stared, hard, at my opened legs, then put two fingers into his mouth, withdrew them, and, smiling, forced them once more into my vagina.

My head screams oh mommy, mommy, mommy and the pain is so great that I forget to fight and then he pulls his fingers free and puts his dirty mouth with its dirty breath right down where he hurt me and pushes his dirty tongue inside me. I went limp with pain and horror and then, he just pulled away and stood up.

"It ain't fun if you don't fight me, ya know. Why ain't you fightin' me no more?" He got a funny look on his face, then lowered himself to my head and whispered into my ear that I better not tell or he would come to my house and kill me.

That is okay I tell myself because I do not want to live anymore and I am hurting and what he did to me is dirty and now I am dirty, too. So, it is okay if he comes and kills me in the night. I will be in heaven with Johnny and Jesus and He will make the hurting go away.

And then he stood up. "And I will kill your mother, too."

His eyes squinch up in an evil smirk and I believe with my whole heart that Jerome tells the truth. He will kill Mama if I tell anyone.

And besides, this is my fault.

He left me lying there in the moss and rocks beside the log, bib overalls askew and half-off, rag in my mouth and all. "It ain't rape, ya know, 'cuz I didn't put my thing inside a ya. My old man says it ain't rape if you don't do that," and, turning his back, he strode into the woods and disappeared.

I sat up slowly and removed the dirty rag (hanky full of nasty Jerome snot) and hurled it as far away as I could throw, then examined myself as best I could. My panties were torn down the side and hung from my right leg, trapped there by the overalls. When I stood up blood trickled down my inner thigh.

All around the birds sing and the squirrels' chatter. Do they not know my world is shattered? I tell myself that no one must ever find out what Jerome has done to me—especially my mama and my daddy. They will know it is my fault.

They told me to stay away from Jerome. This was my punishment, what he did to me, and no one must **ever** know.

I am stunned! Can this memory be the truth? Surely not. How can I have explained the blood and the cuts and the scratches—the torn underwear. *But inside, in the tight little corner of myself that had held the secret for so long, I know the truth. And I remember the lie I tell Mama about falling from a log, and how she holds me close and cleans me up, never once dreaming that her little girl has been so terribly violated.*

Everything is clear now—my nightmares explained.

I sat there, on that hillside in the hot summer sun, stunned by my mind's revelation. *I am twenty, not eight, and I feel the weight of Kurt's ring—third finger, left hand—in place of the little metal ring from the Cracker Jacks box, a token of my friendship with Abby. She had the yellow heart and wore it on a chain around her neck, out of sight of her older brother who takes all things bright and beautiful away from her. (Her innocence, I think to myself, something he shared with her father).*

I am here on this hill specifically to remember that which I have forgotten.

I cannot marry Kurt if I do not know myself.

I twisted the small diamond and gold band around my finger, remembering how I felt the night that Kurt dropped to one knee and asked me to join him in a life's journey. We were so much alike, he and I, and so different. Neither of us fit within our families, but we had found a fit with each other. If ever I needed Anne Marsh and her listening heart, it was now.

Inside me, that crumpled little Leah, so hurt and deserted, tried desperately to hide again. At the last moment, I enfolded her in my arms and drew her back into my being. If Annie were not here, I was. Little Leah fit perfectly into that small, black hole at the center of my soul.

"It is alright," I soothe her. *"It is not your fault. You did nothing wrong."*

"Will Mama forgive me?" that tiny girl inside me hiccups. *"Will Mama still love me?"* I hear Annie's voice inside me saying yes, yes, Mama still loves you. *And more to the point, Leah still loves you. We are one, and there is nothing to forgive.*

Sitting atop Anne's hill on that hot August afternoon, I, at last, began the long road to healing. I adjusted my glasses to bring the scene below into proper focus.

CHAPTER 32
In Which I Find Annie
and Receive a Treasure

Now I saw the reason for that last branching in the path—it led directly to the cabin, bypassing the steep climb to where I stood and the additional steep descent to the apparently occupied cabin. From the west, a two-rut dirt road clung protectively against the hill, terminating in a small lean-to behind the cabin. An old automobile, beat up and rusty with age, occupied the lean-to. The cabin door stood open and smoke rose from the chimney.

Below me lay a garden with neat rows of late lettuces and carrots clearly visible. I spotted potato hills crawling with vines, and squashes and pumpkins interspersed with cornrows. Someone moved through the green stalks, selecting and harvesting ears—someone slightly built and wearing a skirt! My heart beat wildly. With no thought to decorum, I bolted down the path, forgetting for the moment I was a college sophomore and an engaged lady.

Halfway to the cabin I stopped. I could see the corn picker now, a fresh faced young woman with brilliant blue eyes. She gazed at me with curiosity, smiled, then stooped to place her corn in a wicker basket. When she was finished, she wiped her hands on her apron and turned to face me.

"Something I can do for you?"

"Where's Annie?" I demanded.

"I am Anne," she answered quietly. "How can I help you?"

I paused to collect myself. In a less demanding voice, I continued. "I was looking for someone who used to live here— Annie was her name, Anne Marsh. Do you know her?"

The young woman's eyes filled with sadness. "Anne Marsh was my great grandmother. She passed away about two years ago and left this old place to me. Did you know her?"

I buried my face in my hands, stunned by the news, nearly slumping to my knees. I thought I had prepared myself for this possibility—after all, Annie had married grandchildren when I was young—but the very idea of her mortality still came as a blow. Deep down that small child inside had clung desperately to the hope that Annie still lived. Now I might never know the truth about my memories. Without Annie to validate them, I might always doubt myself.

"A long time ago," I choked out. "I knew her when I was a kid. Annie meant the world to me—she taught me so much—I owed her—" My voice failed me.

"I know how you feel. She had that same effect on me. In fact, she always told me I reminded her of a little lady she once knew. Her eyes held a special look when she talked about that other little girl." The present Anne laughed. "I was pure-D jealous of that kid when I was young! Later, I just wanted to meet her. She must have been some girl, to mean so much to my Gran—and, in a way, that made me special, too."

I took a good look at young Anne. She was lovely, about

my own age, with new penny copper hair and that same special quality of gentleness and peace that Annie had had. Except that she spoke quite normal English, even her voice was the same.

"Are you a Friend?"

"Oh, no!" Her laughter tinkled like bells. "My mother gave that up when she married. I'm just an ordinary Presbyterian; although I'm sure Gran influenced me whenever she could."

I didn't see anything ordinary about Anne. She was quite remarkable, and I knew I liked her. She took my hand to help me up.

"Would you like to look around the old place? I imagine it's changed a great deal since you were last here, but most of it should be familiar. Come! I'll put on the kettle for tea."

I pick up her basket of fresh corn and follow her down from the garden. The corn, warm from the sun, has an earthy, slightly musky aroma. Corn is best when cooked to Annie's recipe—put water in large pot, set it to the fire. Go quickly to the field and pick your corn. Hurry back. As water rises to the boil, strip the ears and drop them into the pot. Cook quickly, drain, enjoy with butter (home churned is best!) How I laughed when she told me the secret of perfect corn. I do not laugh now; I just do not buy corn from the market.

"Sorry, the place is such a mess! I've been busy with a sick calf all morning." She must have seen concern in my eyes as she continued; "Oh, don't worry that you're keeping me from something. I'm glad for the distraction. The calf is doing well and I needed a break. When I looked up and saw you on the upper trail, I knew Gran had sent you."

Her words startled me. She must have seen my

expression, as she laughed. "Gosh, don't take me literally. That's just an expression of mine—when serendipity happens, I always give Gran credit, sort of like she's still taking care of me. You see, I came to live with her when my parents died in an auto accident. I was a pretty unhappy ten-year-old, I can tell you! I gave my grandparents fits until Gran took me in hand. She always said she'd gentled me, just like a wild foal. God, how I loved her!"

As she tells her story, I can see Annie's face. She is peering at me over Anne's shoulder, smile crinkling up the corners of her eyes. I can hear her voice in Anne's words. I think to myself that I know how Anne feels—I love Annie, too!

"Enough about me. I'm rattling on and you haven't had a chance to get in a word with a wedge and sledge." She stepped aside at the cottage door and motioned for me to go inside. "After you! Sorry, I didn't catch your name."

"Sorry myself. I don't think I said. I'm Leah."

I step through the doorway into the dimly lit cabin. Basically, it is still Annie's single room—upgraded somewhat, but recognizable. Although the pump still stands outside the door, I see taps over the sink. One drips gently into a half-filled bowl. Annie's wood cook stove has survived, although the place now sports electric lighting. Anne bends over the stove, expertly lighting a fire. She replaces the solid burner over the flame and sets the tea kettle to boil.

"If you need to freshen up, the bathroom's behind that door." She gestured toward the far wall. "Grandpa insisted on indoor plumbing when Gran took me here to live. He said he could endure a lot, but everyone needed an inside toilet on a nasty winter night. Gran put up a fuss, but eventually gave in.

Sure beats the old outhouse!"

Most of the furniture remains, but Annie's huge old handmade bedstead has been replaced by twin beds, set quite close together. I recognize Annie's wonderful family quilts on one of the beds. The other is spread with a newer quilt—log cabin pattern. Its colors are vaguely familiar to me.

Annie's special rocking chair still sits at the hearth, but her sewing basket is gone. In its place, a console radio, its top overflowing with unread newspapers, plays soft music. I hope Annie had the opportunity to enjoy it.

"Do you like tea? I just assumed you did. Gran used to scold that I always took for granted that other people automatically like what I like." She smiled, offering up two jars for my inspection. "Black or chamomile?"

"Either one's fine with me, but I really can't stay." Outside the sky grew suddenly dark and thunder rumbled overhead. Raindrops splattered on the roof and dripped down the window panes.

Anne laughed. "Looks like you don't have a choice, right now. Please, Leah, at least stay until the showers pass. We can talk about Gran." She selected the chamomile mixture and spooned dried flower heads and buds into Annie's old teapot.

Annie and I are out collecting herbs and blossoms for her "cossets". Annie shows me the little yellow chamomile flowers growing low among pasture grasses and forget-me-nots. "Thee must pick them when they are ripe, like these," she explains. I help her gather them and lay them out to dry. When they are "just right", Annie keeps them in jars on the little shelf over her wood stove. "They will stay nice and dry all winter," Annie tells me. "And we will have tea until spring!"

I heard the teakettle whistle. Anne deftly lifted it from the stove and poured boiling water over the chamomile. The water made a roiling noise as it hit the dried herbs. She capped the pot and covered it with a Terrycloth towel. "That should brew up in no time! Now, if only I had baked this morning, we'd have cookies or cake with our tea. Gran is shaking her head at me!" Her habit of referring to Annie in the present tense was disconcerting. I could almost imagine the old lady scolding gently, her eyes smiling to soften the words.

"Do you mind if I look at the quilts?"

"Not at all. Most of them are very old, but Gran finished that log cabin pattern just before she passed away. When I came to live here, those pieces sat in a basket on the hearth. I used to ask why she didn't finish it, and she'd just smile. Finally, the basket disappeared and I forgot about it." Anne leaned down and smoothed the quilt affectionately. "Then, out of the blue, she hauled these pieces out and started working as if she had to finish as soon as possible." She sighed deeply. "I guess she did, at that."

I remembered most of these quilts. Annie had used them to teach me patterns and stitches. A few new ones were intermixed with my old favorites. None held a candle to her double wedding ring—Annie's marriage quilt. "Stitched with love, little girl, every stitch a prayer for happiness and healthy children." She had started the quilt on her fourteenth birthday, she told me and finished it before she turned fifteen. She carefully placed it in her betrothal chest, a gift from her future husband, and turned her hand to sewing bed linens. Now the quilt was missing, and in its place lay the wedding ring quilt Annie had been piecing for her granddaughter's wedding all those years ago.

I especially remembered the log cabin quilt Annie had saved for her last. These were the blocks I so carefully selected and cut, sitting beside Annie in front of the hearth. I could see the squares stitched by my sweating hands as I strove to emulate Annie's neat, tiny, even stitches. She had incorporated all my work into the quilt's center, lovingly building around my small contribution.

Annie is standing at the quilting frame. She is patiently explaining to me how to stretch the backing fabric, the quilt batten, and the front coverlet together on the frame. I help her square the layers, then baste long bias stitches to hold the pieces in place so they will not shift as she stencils on the quilting pattern, itself. These secondary patterns are not delineated with color, as is the coverlet. She outlines them with thread using incredibly tiny stitches to hold all the layers together and provide a quilt's loft, or puffiness. These patterns can be unique to each person, she says, and are often very intricate.

This was not Annie's usual quilting pattern. I noticed a pronounced difference in the style used at the quilt's center— a difference that somehow blended into her old, familiar pattern as the stitches traveled towards the perimeter. I knelt close to it, letting my fingers run along the stitches until I was quite certain. My name was stitched onto the center of that log cabin quilt. Annie had quite deliberately incorporated LEAH into her quilting pattern!

"Tea's ready. Why don't you sit there in Gran's rocking chair and I'll stir up the fire in the hearth—a little glow is so cheery with tea, don't you think?"

I curled up in the old, familiar rocker. Anne handed me a cup of wonderful smelling pale yellow chamomile tea, then passed a plate of gingersnaps.

"I scrounged these up; Gran's recipe, of course, but not as fresh as I'd like." She took one for herself and sat down on the hearth with her back to the fire. "I suppose they're passable." She nibbled at her cookie. "Now, it's your turn. Do you live around here?"

I gave her an abbreviated version of the Hatchet Annie story, filling in details when she asked. "How delicious! How absolutely perfect. Who could imagine anyone'd think my Gran looked like an axe murderer. Oh, how she must have laughed." Anne clapped her hands. "That sounds like something I'd think up. Gran always told me I had a wild imagination. Oh, Leah! Do say you live close by. We'll be wonderful friends!"

She frowned with disappointment as I explained my current living arrangements but brightened when she heard about my impending marriage. "After the wedding," I enthused, "we'll be living right here in town."

We sipped our tea and exchanged stories beside the fire while August belched lightning and thunder and spurts of pounding rain, waiting for this batch of afternoon weather to pass and leave the air clean and refreshing. We both felt Annie's presence so strongly that at one point I yielded the rocker and joined Anne on the hearth, leaving the rocking chair free for our friend. I hope she enjoyed the conversation as much as we did.

Anne and I discovered we were the same age. She had attended Park View Elementary, finishing fourth grade in the same class as Abby Bailey. Anne befriended her in much the same way I had, although Abby didn't teach her about tar chewing. We compared notes on Mr. Anders. He had terrified Anne with his apple knife until her Gran explained that he probably felt unneeded. After that, Anne often took apples and oranges especially for him to cut up.

Abby left school in eighth grade, according to Anne, to marry and tussle her own brood of babies. I silently shook my head at Abby's fate, having thought of her often over the years. I always hoped she had escaped her poverty and created a new life for herself.

I shared stories of my brothers and our struggles. Anne said she envied me and my family, as she had none but her Gran and would have loved a brother or sister.

When the teapot yielded not one more drop and we had scoured the cookie plate clean, I noticed the time. "Good Lord, Anne! It's 6:00 p.m. I've kept you talking all afternoon! Let me help you clean up, then I have to get out of here and catch the bus!" Anne opened the door to a newly cleared sky, brilliantly blue and scrubbed clean of thunderheads. We took deep breaths of exhilarating after-lightning air, luxuriating in its slightly pungent ozone cleanness. Birds took the opportunity to squabble over worms and insects driven above ground by the rapidly draining rainwater.

Now it is time for me to go. I debate whether to tell Anne about her quilt's significance. Her Gran and my Annie had loved us both, of that I am certain. At least she had not forgotten me. For now, I will keep my discovery a secret. Maybe after I savor it for a while, I will tell Anne. For now, the secret is between Annie and me.

"I hate to see you go. Will you come back soon?" Anne stood at the back door, leaning casually against the old pump, a much younger version of Annie, with red hair instead of white. She had folded her arms across her chest and crossed her left leg over the right at the ankle.

"I'll be back," I called over my shoulder. "You can count on it."

I took the lower path—the newer, less steep route down toward Hickey Road. I'd gone perhaps thirty yards when I heard someone running behind me.

"Leah, wait up. Stop!" Anne skidded to a halt as I turned, bumped into me with both arms, laughing and breathless. "I just remembered something—something I gotta ask you. Oh, girl! Give me a chance to catch my breath!" We stood, facing each other, while her breathing slowed.

"There's something my Gran said while she was finishing that last quilt. Something she said, and something I forgot to do. After you left, it occurred to me I hadn't asked. Tell me, are you Cookie? Did she used to call you Cookie?"

I nodded, tears filling my eyes. I couldn't speak—that damned lump in my throat prevented it.

"Then come on back to the cabin. I have something for you and don't worry about catching the bus. I can drive you to town when we're finished."

We walked, arm in arm, back to Annie's place. Inside, I stood behind the old rocking chair, my hands resting on its high, curved back. My thumb gently stroked wood polished to a smooth patina by hundreds of hands. Anne talked as she searched beneath one twin bed.

"When Gran completed this quilt," she patted the subject

coverlet as she pulled out an object, "she said something odd. I didn't get it, at first. But now, it makes sense." Anne rose up on her knees and faced me.

"When she put in the last stitch and took it off the frame, she turned to me and said, 'Now she will come.' I asked her who was coming, and she really spooked me. She got this funny, faraway look in her eye and said that I'd know who to ask when the time was right."

Anne stood up. In her hands, she held a familiar looking object. "Later, Gran gave this to me. She said someday Cookie would come for it—Cookie would come home for her basket. I thought she was just getting old, you know. She hadn't been very well. When she passed away a few days later, I just plain forgot about it!"

Now I could see what she held out. My sewing basket—the one Annie had found for me when she helped me make the sampler—the same basket that sat side by side with her larger basket on the hearth.

Annie is holding out my basket. She looks the same as when I last saw her. She wears the same long black skirt and white apron, sturdy brown shoes peeking out beneath its hem. Her hair, soft and wispy and white as goose down is braided at the nape of her neck and wrapped round and round her crown. I see where she has fastened it with hairpins.

She approaches, holding the basket out to me like an offering. My mind tells me that this is only Anne. I am having a waking dream.

I ignore my mind—I am too busy listening with my heart.

Annie speaks, although her mouth does not move. She wears her own, beautiful smile, all the while whispering in my ear. *"This is for thee. I have kept it for thee all the years, knowing someday thy heart would lead thee home. Take it, child of my heart." I lift the basket from her fragile arms. (She seems so much smaller to me, now). "Open thy basket, Leah. Open it and see what thy past has called thee to."*

Carefully I place the basket in its proper place on the hearth. Gently I lift its lid and set it safely aside. Inside my basket rests something folded between sheets of tissue. My hands tremble as I lift the tissue-wrapped package. The tissue is brittle, so I unwrap with care, tenderly revealing its treasure. I cannot believe what lay hidden for so long! Annie's quilt—her marriage quilt! This cannot be true. I gasp!

"Well, will you look at that! Grandma wondered where that old heirloom had got to! She was mad as spit when Gran told her she'd pass it on to someone worth her salt, and not just because of blood. Look, she left you a note!"

I bury my face in the quilt. It smells of Annie's sachet. I picture her quite clearly, smiling as she selects colored fabrics, intent as she lays them out and cuts the quilting pieces, rocking and humming to herself as she pieces them before some other open hearth. She is young and full of hope, recently betrothed, as am I. Her hair is long and shiny, the color of a newly minted copper penny. She wears it loose, flowing down her back almost to her waist. A lock falls across her face as she concentrates on her work. She absently pushes it aside, slipping it behind her ear. Annie looks up and smiles at me, displaying her quilt pieces, offering them for my inspection. As I reach for them, her image fades.

I don't know how long I stood in silence. Finally, after carefully folding the wedding quilt and smoothing it with love,

I placed it back within my basket.

"Sit down a minute, Leah. You look like you've seen a ghost!" Anne pulled me down into the small rocker and handed me a folded square of yellowed lined paper. After I caught my breath, I looked at the little note.

"Cookie" was written in Annie's neat script.

Finally, with trembling hands, I opened Annie's message from the past. It said, simply;

"For Leah, who was born
with a listening heart—
Never doubt yourself, girl.
Never doubt."

Anne Marsh

I rose from the chair and stepped out onto Anne's (Annie's) porch, carefully wiping the tears from my eyes with my sleeve.

Outside the cabin, the sun peeked from between two of the now slowly separating clouds. A rainbow that terminated in the woods below our old farmhouse suddenly appeared, arching out in vibrant color as if the whole sky were smiling at me. It took my breath away. I stood transfixed by its utter beauty until lark-song broke the silence. The burden I had carried for most of my life dropped from my shoulders. I had remembered.

My childhood is gone, and with it all the pain and heartache and buried grief that Jerome has laid upon me. I will keep it to myself, but now I can start to heal. I remember.

"Do not forget to listen to thyself with thine own heart," Annie whispers. *"Now is the time to begin tomorrow."*

And I step forward.

ABOUT ATMOSPHERE PRESS

Atmosphere Press is an independent, full-service publisher for excellent books in all genres and for all audiences. Learn more about what we do at atmospherepress.com.

We encourage you to check out some of Atmosphere's latest releases, which are available at Amazon.com and via order from your local bookstore:

Twisted Silver Spoons, a novel by Karen M. Wicks

Queen of Crows, a novel by S.L. Wilton

The Summer Festival is Murder, a novel by Jill M. Lyon

The Past We Step Into, stories by Richard Scharine

The Museum of an Extinct Race, a novel by Jonathan Hale Rosen

Swimming with the Angels, a novel by Colin Kersey

Island of Dead Gods, a novel by Verena Mahlow

Cloakers, a novel by Alexandra Lapointe

Twins Daze, a novel by Jerry Petersen

Embargo on Hope, a novel by Justin Doyle

Abaddon Illusion, a novel by Lindsey Bakken

Blackland: A Utopian Novel, by Richard A. Jones

The Jesus Nut, a novel by John Prather

The Embers of Tradition, a novel by Chukwudum Okeke

ABOUT THE AUTHOR

 Lessie Auletti is a writer, poet and advocate for women through P.E.O. and OES. An accomplished artist and Graphics Designer, she grew up in the Pacific NW and is a University of Washington alumna. Lessie's career in journalism began with the *Bremerton Sun* newspaper. She retired as a technical writer/illustrator for General Dynamics, Pomona, CA. Since returning to Washington State, her many readings on the Olympic Peninsula and the greater Seattle area became her memoir, *Holding Up the Sky. Troubled Skies over Quaker Hill* continues that journey. She lives in Sequim, WA with her husband Ron. They have six children.

CPSIA information can be obtained
at www.ICGtesting.com
Printed in the USA
BVHW071436291221
625052BV00020B/1031